The Archaeology of Nostalgia

John Boardman

The Archaeology of Nostalgia

How the Greeks re-created
their mythical past

183 illustrations

Thames & Hudson

for George and Davina Huxley

First published in the United States of America in 2003 by Thames & Hudson Inc., 500 Fifth Avenue, New York, New York 10110

thamesandhudsonusa.com

Library of Congress Catalog Card Number 2002100601

ISBN 0-500-05115-1

Printed and bound in Singapore by C. S. Graphics

Contents

Preface

Neither 'Archaeology' nor 'Nostalgia' is quite the right word for the title of this book, but they both convey the essence of its purpose, to explore the way in which the Greeks visualized and re-created their past, especially the remote past, in images and objects.

In the modern world the past is a commodity of mixed value. It is pointed out to travellers who may have tired of packaged relaxation, while the more focused tours are designed specifically to demonstrate the historical aspects of, for example, the Silk Roads of Asia or the Civil War battlefields of the United States, and they generally offer little more than topography. Relics, both of the remote past and even of contemporary heroes, are assiduously marketed. The educational value of teaching the past may seem to be falling out of favour with Ministries of Education, but at least the physical aspects of the past remain a strong attraction for museum-goers and for amateurs of archaeology, the newest of the academic leisure pursuits, while historians of modern art practise on them various and mainly irrelevant modern perceptions. A personal element, of family or place, lends especial allure, most apparent in researching family trees. The ingenious can feed this interest by exploiting various media, and television can re-create, usually in a very superficial way, what an interested public might need by way of entertaining instruction in their past, or even their future. Physically it can be re-created by both souvenirs and fakes – not always readily distinguishable. Re-creation of the more recent past, especially its wars and politics, is a fruitful field for revision of attitudes and sheer propaganda; so too it was in antiquity. For most people now the remoter past is fun (gladiators, Cleopatra) rather than necessary: for the Greeks it was an essential element in their life, art, religion and aspirations. In this book we look at how they recognized its traces around them, and how their writers, priests and artists supplemented this from their imagination and from what the physical world could offer.

Real objects, whether correctly identified or not (usually not), are therefore involved here, as well as the suggestive configurations of the Greek landscape and its ruins. We can learn something about this subject from artefacts and excavation, but there is at least as much to be gleaned from references in ancient authors, while only in them can we catch some inkling of the reason for the Greeks' obsession with their past, and generally with what we would call their mythical past. This will at the end need discussion with the practices and beliefs of other ancient peoples in mind, to see how far the Greek attitude was unusual or even exceptional. And for the Nostalgia, there is clearly more to this than some sentimental attachment to the past on the part of both the Greeks and us.

The subject has been tackled hitherto mainly with a view to studying the Greek use of 'relics' as objects of worship or with magical powers; or with a mind to the possible political, social and ethnic connotations of identifying or claiming important ancestors, and paying attention to old tombs. Beyond all this lies the simple fact that, by accumulating relics and even creating them, the Greeks were also making the first 'museums', in the sense of them being collections of historical memorabilia rather than works of art.

The museums were in temples, but there was at least as much to be identified as memorials of the past in the Greek countryside, since Greek mythical geography was that of the world they lived in. 'Tell me, Socrates, isn't it somewhere about here that they say Boreas seized Oreithyia?' asks Phaidros in Plato's Dialogue that bears his name. Socrates said that it was farther down the river Ilissos, where there is an altar to Boreas. He refers to the 'scientific' explanation, that the girl was blown to her death off rocks by the north wind (Boreas), but regards 'such theories as no doubt attractive, but as the invention of clever, industrious people' who should then be obliged to explain centaurs, Gorgons and the like. He 'doesn't bother about such things, but accepts the current beliefs about them'.[1] So shall we, but sometimes with an eye to how the stories arose, and with sure knowledge (we hope) that, for instance, the Boreas story was hardly more than a century old, an Athenian device to give a home to the wind god who had providentially scattered the invading Persian fleets early in the fifth century.

We can see from their literature that to the Greeks the past was all-important; it was not for them a foreign country. The majority of representations in their art are of divine or mythical figures and events, and these are also the principal subjects for their literature. The only exceptions to this begin to appear with the sixth century, when writers start to look around the contemporary world, its geography and foreign peoples, and with the fifth century, when they begin to be occupied with 'real' history, as well as what we regard as myth, but which they took for history – so, 'myth-history'. When you can claim a god or hero as ancestor the dividing line between myth and history becomes hazy, and even the rationalists, sophists and philosophers of the classical period were not immune to credulity. Only everyday life can compete as a theme for artists, in early poetry and, with the fourth century, on the stage. In art, depictions of real history or even of contemporary events and portraiture had generally been shunned before the fourth century, and then these were often dealt with only through allusions to a past (Amazons as Persians,

Socrates looking like a satyr) which was readily re-invented or adjusted to suit the context or message – a thoroughly un-historical practice which makes early Greek history and mythography such closely related subjects for study.

The Greeks of the historical period started with some advantages. Their heroic past, what we call the Bronze Age, was apparent to them in some standing though ruined monuments, and in artefacts found in their fields, all of types which were no longer familiar in everyday usage, but the product of a period when Greece was quite heavily populated and its rulers ambitious in their architecture and the arts they fostered. There were many finds too from yet earlier, and even pre-human periods, that were evocative, as they have been for mankind everywhere. The collapse of the Bronze Age civilizations of the Minoans and Mycenaeans and the slow cultural and technological renaissance which took place after around 1000 BC mean that we can treat the subject as if from a new starting point, with a people who had a ready-made past both physically around them and in their story-telling, but no longer as an operational reality, and with most physical links broken in terms of behaviour and crafts, and no ability even to decipher such written documents as they might find. Iron Age Greece became a new society of independent townships, city states, instead of kingdoms embracing wider areas and several centres of occupation; and there was a new attitude to the arts engendered first from within (the new disciplines of the 'Geometric' styles of art) and then from the influence of the near east in the Orientalizing Revolution of the eighth and seventh centuries BC. This was not the case with the older civilizations of the near east and Egypt, where, although there were certainly some dire interruptions in prosperity and life, there was also a certain continuity of style in arts and crafts, and no too drastic new beginnings, as in Greece. They had also a long tradition in writing and recording. A Mesopotamian king excavating an old palace would find written tablets which he could read; a Greek might find inscribed tablets and objects from the Minoan and Mycenaean world, but if he thought any were in Greek he certainly could not read them – and nor could we until fifty years ago, and then only the Mycenaean (Linear B).

We are dealing mainly with the Greek view of what they regarded as their heroic age, when gods and heroes might walk and talk with mortals, even marry them (or more often rape, of either sex), and found families whose progeny might, with some ingenuity, be identified in historical times. It is not altogether wrong to try to equate their heroic age with what archaeology tells us about the Greek Late Bronze Age. For one thing, the concocted genealogies show that they believed their heroic age to precede the archaic and classical periods by about the right number of years. Much of it could be organized into generations of heroes, with some interlocking histories, which implied a heroic time span roughly equivalent to the real time span of the Late Mycenaean Age of Greece, and not aeons before. However, the genealogies were linear and it was always more important to determine ancestry

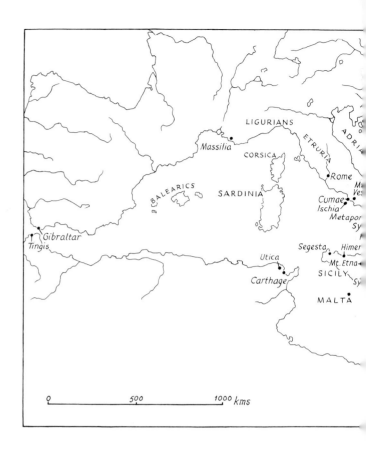

The Mediterranean World (*above*)

The Aegean World (*right*)

The Greeks physically located their divine and myth history in the land of Greece itself, primarily in the Balkan homeland and Aegean world, but extending to all the shores of the Mediterranean and the Black Sea, which they had colonized in the eighth to sixth centuries BC. Farther off, they placed relevant figures and events from the shores of the Atlantic to the Baltic, the Levant, Central Asia, Ethiopia and Upper Egypt.

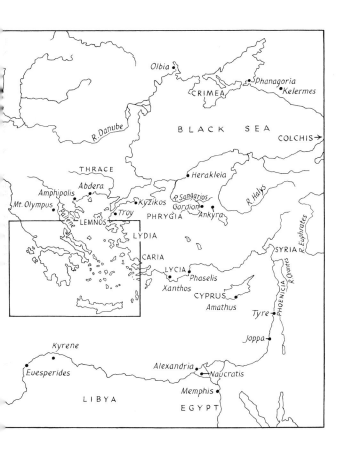

than to make any really plausible links with the genealogies of others. As a result the generations in different 'families' get seriously out of step, and trying to systematize them in a chart, such as no Greek surely ever attempted, appears to place Trojan War heroes over a spread of generations. And a mortal generation of course meant nothing in thinking about the remotest past, when Chaos gave birth to Earth and Darkness, and Gods fought Giants. The principal stories and genealogies were in place in the oral tradition by the eighth century BC, by the time any could get written down by a Hesiod or Homer.[2]

Material details of the heroic age were correctly interpreted by later Greeks, if we discard the supernatural. The many heroic expeditions, within Greece (as against Thebes) and outside Greece (as to Troy), may not be easily equated with what little archaeology can reveal of the military history of the Late Bronze Age, but many are plausible, and much of heroic Greek geography in literature is Bronze Age geography on the ground, both in Greece and Anatolia, even of towns which had declined in importance or even disappeared by the classical period. Somehow the Minoan antecedents, non-Greek, are never properly accommodated, nor is there any obvious recollection of the great volcanic eruption of Thera which seems to have contributed to or caused the collapse of the Minoan world. Instead, for the beginnings, there are some strangulated versions of oriental cosmogonies that never quite embedded themselves into Greek belief about their past, and may well have been introduced after the Bronze Age. There was also the establishment of the Olympian family of gods, most or all of whom were known in the Bronze Age, if never so familial. This involved gods battling Titans, the traditional banished or dispossessed gods, and then Giants, for survival and supremacy. This 'period' is followed by the exploits of the sons and daughters of the gods, especially Herakles, and these are figures of equivocal mortality. Then comes the period of the 'historical' and mortal heroes, of Troy and the like. There are plenty of overlaps, of course, and the poet Hesiod has to interpolate the 'heroic age' of Greek heroes into the oriental succession of the metallic ages of man – gold, silver, brass, iron. Beginnings might then seem to be placed not that far from the time 'the Greeks' first entered their eventual homeland from the north. And with such stories of beginnings goes also the very oriental idea that the gods were suspicious and resentful of Man, who has therefore to be re-invented, more than once, in stories found in the near east and India, probably worldwide. The 'historically' most recent of these in Greece makes the Trojan War the device of the Gods to free themselves of the race of mortal heroes.

This equation of myth and history bears further investigation, but not here, and I offer just a simplified, graphic display of the pseudo-equation [*Fig. 1*]. We might note in passing that, in story, the age of active gods and Giants or Titans is not one for horses and chariots (hallmarks of the Indo-European; possible exceptions are Poseidon and Athena); nor is it in the age of the major national and regional heroes,

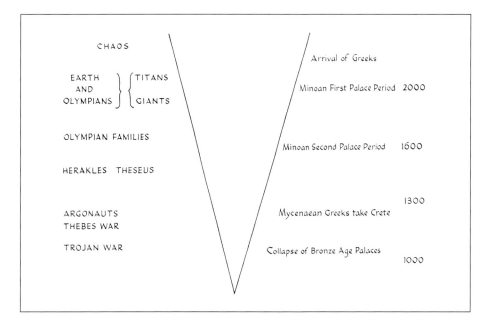

CHAOS

EARTH AND OLYMPIANS } { TITANS / GIANTS

OLYMPIAN FAMILIES

HERAKLES   THESEUS

ARGONAUTS
THEBES WAR

TROJAN WAR

Arrival of Greeks

Minoan First Palace Period   2000

Minoan Second Palace Period   1600

1300

Mycenaean Greeks take Crete

Collapse of Bronze Age Palaces

1000

1. An hypothetical and very approximate equation of early Greek myth and early Greek archaeological history.

sons of gods (Herakles and others); while for the 'historical' heroes of Troy the chariot decidedly is, mainly because Anatolia is chariot country. This colours later conceptions and illustrations of both the heroic and the divine, since gods then appear in chariots (epiphanies) and fight from them.[3] Tangential equations of this sort sometimes clarify, sometimes complicate the issue, and are only of interest in a hypothetical investigation, such as this, not an historical one.

We should also notice that the concept of a very primitive condition for man, our 'cave man', was barely apparent in Greek story until fourth-century scientific philosophy thought more carefully about the matter, and it was best expressed far later, as by Lucretius in the first century BC.[4] The few early admissions of such an unformed period of humanity, rather than an overall degeneration from ages of gold and heroes, did nothing to colour the classical Greek's views of his past, and we shall see that artists were barely moved by it.

In many respects Herodotus was right when he wrote that Hesiod and Homer 'gave the Greeks their gods', Hesiod especially. He was writing in around 700 BC. He busily cobbled together the cosmogonic stories of the Greek and near eastern world, created family trees for everything from Chaos to gods to heroes to monsters, plus much folktale. His work, and that of his followers (sixth-century authors of the *Eoiai* and *Aspis* poems), was a notable achievement of organization, not, of course, all his own work, but the precedents must have been slight and fairly chaotic, and his mission, in Herodotus' terms, was helped by being written down.[5]

He significantly has far less to offer our subject, much of which is based on observation of the physical world, than does Homer, although he supplied material on which others would work.

The place of Homer in all this is not crucial, except for the way he helped inform the Greeks' view of their heroic past and their use of him as a guide to it, especially in matters which concern us here. It is easy to overemphasize the apparently fairy-tale aspects of his poems, especially those of Odysseus' journeys, because stories of Sirens, Kirke, Kalypso and Polyphemos are memorable; but these occupy less than a quarter of the *Odyssey*, while the rest of the poem is a psychological thriller of considerable power. I take Homer to be a seventh-century poet dependent on a long oral tradition about events that may or may not have happened, and with which Hesiod was little concerned, but which were deemed to have happened in years that we designate the Greek Late Bronze Age. His composition was basically oral, but was written down in his lifetime. The Greeks believed him and so can we, for the purposes of this book which is investigating what the Greeks believed rather than historical reality, whatever that might be. After the Bronze Age the tradition that Homer drew upon was a live one, not trammelled with annals and kinglists; that is to say it could be improved, adjusted and added to at will. This makes 'the world of Homer' a mirage dancing over a real enough landscape in which poetic imagination could work as it wished, reflecting new contemporary preoccupations and the *realia* of life, but within which 'Homer' remained broadly respectful of the remoteness of his subject.

This is an odd situation to be investigating, not readily paralleled for its intensity and detail elsewhere in the ancient world, and our sources for it are unusual also: much is to be won from texts since Greek writers were readily impressed by the unusual and were devoted to elucidating their past; much from archaeology, which is rather more difficult to interpret; and lastly, there are ancient pictures. These were very important in Greece. They conveyed information and stories, and could comment on present and past as readily as any text, especially to a mainly illiterate society. So, while the artefacts and practices defined by archaeology or texts will give us much, the illustrations, especially on the pottery of Athens of the sixth to fourth centuries BC, are also a source from which we can judge what their makers and users thought of the appearance of the past which was their major theme.

Some areas of this investigation have been the subject of intense study and speculation in recent years, principally devoted to discussion of the evidence, mainly archaeological, for cult at old tombs and for hero cults, their religious and social significance and origins. This phase of scholarly preoccupation may be expiring, as did the obsession with fertility cults early in the last century; both have been fruitful, if prone to over-interpretation of imperfect evidence. It is no intention of mine to do more than summarize such work where appropriate, not to repeat it, but to focus, not perhaps always exclusively, on the material, archaeological evidence for these and other matters, long neglected by most scholars, and very much guided by what we learn from texts. But it all has something to add to these other studies. It pulls the centre of interest back from social and religious theory to the Greeks themselves, to what they made of the remains of their physical past and how these remains inspired them to re-create it, from motives far more important than simple curiosity.

The material for this book has been collected in a desultory way over very many years, starting from a general interest in Greek dedicatory practices. The way it is presented here will, I hope, instruct the general reader about a subject which he may not have thought to have existed, and for students give a further dimension, much neglected for many years, to their consideration of what ancient Greeks believed, for this is nothing if not a study of the application of ancient Greek imagination to the challenge of re-creating a past to which they so often turned for advice or entertainment. This is not, therefore, a detailed account of the worship of relics, or of the perception and inventions of ancient authors, or of the iconography of myth, although these all find their places. It is parasitical upon studies in many other scholarly disciplines, without pretending to replace or improve any of them but simply to place them in a different and, I hope, revealing context.

Greek myth is in fact a compound, primarily of types of folktale which can be found worldwide, but also of legends that conceal history, of stories that explain things peculiar to Greek life and religion, and of sheer poetic invention. These, often overlapping, categories can be distinguished by modern scholarship but were only observed in antiquity by the few authors who were concerned not to appear over-credulous and who sought rational explanations even for the essentially irrational. So the distinction does not help us much in our enquiry, where we treat the evidence in the terms on which it seems to have been observed in antiquity, where myth is simply a form of myth-history, even where it goes outside the 'legendary' versions of history. By the end of this book the reader may be persuaded that a major source for Greek myth was also the result of the Greeks' imaginative response to the natural world around them and to the artefacts of their predecessors. This is not the main theme here but may be one of the more important messages. This is altogether a subject for which we have, most of the time, to suspend disbelief, and when I write of 'Achilles' spear' I do not always qualify it as 'alleged', or 'so-called', any more than do most of our sources. The rest of the fascinating question of the Greeks' view of their past will long remain a profitable field for scholars of other classical disciplines; I have found it difficult to keep to the material evidence, and I am sure that there is much more in it than I have been able to elicit here. George Huxley kindly read a penultimate draft of this book and offered, from his wide experience of Greek literature, geography and archaeology, many constructive comments, and corrections. I am deeply in his debt, but claim for myself what may be or seem to be remaining errors. My debt to my publisher, Thomas Neurath, and editor, Pat Mucller, is considerable, for their encouragement and advice.

It has proved convenient to assemble the many relevant texts in a single list at the end of this book, with paraphrases rather than translations of their content, and with their own indexes, and to refer to them in the text by their T(estimonia) numbers. Much of the archaeology here is *in mente* rather than *in corpore*. The alleged relics have not themselves survived but their appearance, like the song the Sirens sang, may not be beyond all conjecture, while they, and the ruins and natural phenomena of the Greek landscape, can inspire speculation today as readily as they did in antiquity.[6]

CHAPTER ONE

The Function of the Past in Greece: Our Sources

THE MOST IMPRESSIVE sights in the experience of early man (and early woman) were natural: the landscape, the climate, the other animals – all of which were both a threat and an essential source of sustenance. But they were also unpredictable until man learned to control his environment, both animal and vegetable. Natural phenomena were of course numinous, especially where they might seem to impinge on his ability to sustain life, through climate and the cycle of the seasons. He invented gods to account for them, to provide a focus to which he could appeal for continuing beneficence, or whom he could try to appease when they were threatening; and he invented art to provide images and a form of permanence to what was essential for survival, both the material and the divine, and to communicate a common view of their and of his own necessary functions. Death was a daily and inevitable reality, but what had been killed had to be renewed, sometimes appeased. Dreams revealed another life in which the dead, even the identifiable dead of his family, might reappear. They too could therefore be numinous and require attention.[1] As burial places became more formal and conspicuous they would be permanent reminders of the past, as were the places of worship for gods and any substantial structures created in periods of greater prosperity or population, for rulers or ruled. Travel, for goods, land or sheer survival, broadened the mind. Experience, remembered, reported or recorded, was a resource for survival and progress. Disposing of tens of millennia of the history of early man in this summary way reminds us simply that 'the past' was, and is, ever present, and that recognition of it had, and has, a serious function.

In the settled communities of the great valley civilizations of the Old World the monuments of the past, be they temples, tombs or palaces, were substantial. Oral tradition and eventually writing meant that the record of the past could be preserved, whether or not that was the intention rather than simply, in the oral tradition, a matter of ritual and entertainment, and in the written, an expression of self-esteem and confirmation of authority. Genealogy was important in guaranteeing status and identity. Objects that had served effectively in the past were worth keeping or copying, and might attract the same sort of awe as the remembered prowess of those who used them. Ancestors were always better, bigger and stronger men.

A sense of progress and yearning for betterment also carried with it a certain fear of failure, and often a sense that the past might have been, in its way, golden and worth recapturing; this would have been especially true where the physical remains of a different past – different because created by a different or more affluent and accomplished people – were visible. It is not difficult to understand why the memory of the past was important, and why it might need to be re-created not only in story and literature, but in image and object. We ought to be studying a phenomenon common to all mankind, and in some sense we are; but in the Greeks' recovery, re-creation and use of their past we seem to encounter something more than a little different from that of other peoples. After we have considered the Greeks in the following pages, I shall in the final chapter give some thought to what the rest of antiquity did with its past, to point comparisons and contrasts.

When, in the fifth century BC, Herodotus sought to provide an account of the wars between Greeks and Persians from which the Greek states had but recently emerged, divided but, most of them, still independent, he looked to the remote past for the origins of the conflict. He turned to myth-history and stories of the rape by easterners of Greek queens, and the rape by Greeks of easterners: Io taken by Phoenicians, Europe taken by Greeks, then the eastern witch Medea, and finally Greek Helen taken east to Troy and the revenge wreaked by the Greeks there: none, or very little of it, truly historical. 'The Asiatics, when the Greeks ran off with their women, never troubled themselves about the matter; but the Greeks, for the sake of a single Spartan girl [Helen], collected a vast armament, invaded Asia, and destroyed the kingdom of Priam [Troy]. Henceforth they ever looked on the Greeks as their open enemies'.[2] It was not a very plausible sequence of events and certainly not at all in the minds of the fifth-century Persian invaders of Greece, but a Greek would always look for the reason (*aition*) why things happened, or why they were done the way they were, or why they should be the way they wanted them to be. And they generally sought and found the solution in the creations of their myth-history.

This could be very crudely but effectively exercised to justify theft or invasion, as common a Greek practice with each other as with non-Greeks. It provided them with justification for some odd rituals, whose origins were lost to them since the circumstances of their devising had long passed and been forgotten. It could also be used to exhort, as we can see even in Homer's poems where a hero may be given advice or admonition in the light of the behaviour of his ancestors. This 'lineage boasting' seems an essential part of the self-definition of a hero, and it remains a factor of importance for Greeks through the historic period.[3] In the fifth century the poet Pindar exploited it remorselessly in his *Odes*, which celebrate athletic victories, preying on heroic genealogy and myth to enhance the status of his

2. Voting at Troy. Odysseus and Ajax (right, disconsolate, the loser) watch the voting by Greek heroes for which of them shall receive Achilles' armour. Athena supervises the placing of voting pebbles at either end of a block. On an Athenian red figure vase by the Brygos Painter, about 490 BC. (London, British Museum E69)

patrons and their homes. More sophisticated use of the past is demonstrated by the Attic tragedians, who could, for example, explore the origins of democratic judgements or of the conflict of religion and state, through the story of the trial of Orestes at Athens, where a free but split vote was resolved by the casting vote of the chairman, the goddess Athena (in Aeschylus' play *Eumenides*), or the story of Antigone torn between duty to her brother and to the decree of the king (in Sophocles' *Antigone*).[4] In the former case it involved improving the epic story by introducing an open voting procedure. At about the same time we see that this is also introduced to the story of the decision at Troy as to who should inherit Achilles' armour. The evidence for this is in vase painting [*Fig. 2*],[5] which is revealed as a no less important source for such matters as any text. An epic Trojan occasion had been recruited by art to demonstrate a new democratic principle.

There were also more practical advantages to be won from appeal to the past, and these lie behind much of what will be discussed in this book. An appropriate ancestor can enhance prestige or justify a claim to land or power. Relics may be powerful. Since myth-history, and even history, were fairly flexible in Greek minds, the necessary names and stories could be invented for each case as called for, or traditional stories adjusted to meet the need of the occasion. Where there was some physical record of the past it was open to any convenient interpretation or identification, and could be reinforced by the authority of priestly families (themselves often the inventors) and popularized by various media, written and visual. But the resultant stories were to be taken seriously.

In the circumstances one might have expected the adoption of ancient and heroic names to have played a part in all this, and the fact that it did not requires some explanation, even if only that a human choice of name could not convey the same authority as a 'real' physical relationship to the heroic past. Thus, Peisistratos, the Athenian sixth-century tyrant, was proud of his alleged descent from Neleus and Nestor, legendary kings of Pylos. He bore the name of one of Nestor's sons, but the name was known also in seventh-century Athens. The descendants of Neleus were said to have migrated to Athens, driven out by the descendants of Herakles, and play a part in Athenian and Ionian myth-history. Was all this the invention of Peisistratos and his court? He named none of his sons after a Neleid, but he did name one after a lesser son of Herakles, Thessalos, and he certainly exploited an existing Herakles-Athena-Athens association. He was also said to have collected oracles.[6] It is seldom possible to date the invention of such associations with the past, whatever the reasons for which they were invoked. Greek personal names are often compounds of names of gods or of the extraordinary hero-god Herakles (Apollodoros, Herakleitos, etc.), but not of the other hero names of Greek history. The Athenian roll-call of the classical period is not full of the name of the local hero Theseus; indeed this mortal use of hero-names only began to happen at all often in the second century AD, when Greece was indulging in a very self-conscious invocation of her past, strongly reflected in the work of the guide Pausanias, who is a major source for our subject. It was a very different matter when it came to the naming of places, which can often be seen to depend on myth-historical associations, where they did not themselves inspire them. This suggests that the naming that survived may not have been original, but was the product of a period and attitude of mind in which such links were deemed important.

In many respects the detection and dating of such inventions are easier with the material record, which is our principal concern. The crux is identity, not simply recognition that the Greeks saw about them relics of a past, which might be apparent to any people anywhere and at any time, but that they felt the need and saw the advantage of identifying some of this with specific events or personalities of their myth-history. We shall look at practices elsewhere in another chapter, but men re-create their past at various levels, and it takes a particular disposition to take matters as far as did the ancient Greeks. To anticipate, we can detect with certainty positive identifications and associations of places or things as early as the eighth century BC, and suspect it earlier. Much seems to have to do with establishing the credentials of a state or cult, or even of an individual ruler, but later evidence shows that 'democracies' were no slower to seek authenticity by the same means. We may suspect archaic Greece of the seventh and sixth centuries BC to have been very busy in these respects, though the physical evidence for it is slight. It may be just, however, to see the artists' obsession with demonstrating the past in the decoration of both everyday and religious objects as a sufficient indication of awareness of both their potential and their real contemporary significance.

Our sources for the archaeology of the subject need closer scrutiny. The physical ones, unless inscribed, need to be identified by something more than the incongruity of their context. An object placed in a far later tomb or dedicated in a far later shrine may never have been recognized as belonging to an heroic past, rather than having been a family heirloom or simply a curiosity, and for the most part we are looking for reasons which go beyond simple family possession. When the context of such a misplaced object is in cult it will depend on its nature whether it should be treated as anything other than another unusual treasure, perhaps at the time remarkable only for its foreignness rather than any recognized role in the past of the community. It was from no recognition of antiquity that a Minoan stone 'blossom bowl' was chosen for placing over the head in the 'Bishop's Tomb' in the Byzantine Basilica at Knossos, and pierced for access to the body,[7] but because it was appropriately shaped and exotic. However, where an ancient monument, built or natural, is found to attract the paraphernalia of worship at a later date, we may certainly assume that it was recognized as in some degree a relic or witness to past events, although we need an inscription or our imagination to suggest how it might have been identified.

There appears to have been no deliberate searching for such relics, except in those cases where the bones of heroes are sought out for return to their homes, usually at the prompting of an oracle and for political advantage. This was not the case in Mesopotamia where there is evidence for a positive sense of enquiry for information from monuments recognized as antique, but in that case there was more continuity of tradition than in Greece and old inscriptions could still be read. The Greeks knew that Agamemnon lived at Mycenae and identified buildings and locations there with him and his family, but we have no reason to believe that there, or elsewhere, such associations were sought out by excavation, rather than casually identified or even invented in the light of traditional stories. And at an early date political convenience found even for Agamemnon an alternative home, at Amyklai near Sparta, and some physical justification was concocted (T.305).

But objects were certainly discovered by excavation, usually by chance, and some are recorded in texts; we could never identify them otherwise. Pausanias (T.350) watched men digging beside one of the myth-historical monuments at Olympia and observed that they unearthed any number of fragments of arms, bridles and bits, surely archaic and classical votives of the type found in their hundreds by German excavators a century ago, but not identified as such by Pausanias; nor was curiosity the object of the excavation, rather than laying the foundation for a Roman senator's victory statue.

A Hellenistic epigram records the dedication by a farmer of his rakes, hoe, pickaxe, and earth baskets, since he has given up work having found 'treasure'; we wonder what.[8] Virgil reflects:

Surely a time will come when a farmer on those frontiers
Forcing through earth his curved plough
Shall find old spears eaten away with flaky rust,
Or hit upon helmets as he wields the weight of his mattock
And marvel at the heroic bones he has disinterred.

(*Georgics* 1.493–497; trans. C. Day Lewis)

Dreams and oracles, common stand-bys for Greeks seeking explanations for the unusual, are otherwise invoked to explain how folk were directed to excavate relics, though most were surely found as casually as were the Olympia arms. Even Pausanias had a dream telling him where a bronze urn was to be found; it had been first discovered by an Argive general, also as the result of a dream, and contained tin scrolls revealing the Mysteries of the Great Goddesses (T.328). Rumour can be equally potent but often less reliable. On a walking tour of Boeotia in student days (1949) I was more than once told of a cave in the next village where there was a chariot of bronze; everyone knew about it, but somehow it was always in the *next* village.

A fragment of the True Cross, or a saint's finger, can be any piece of wood, any finger, and many Greek relics were of this type; but many were more sophisticated, probably often real antiquities which we can try to envisage and explain. The act of identification or even of forgery itself implies some common concept of what the past did or should look like. For the most part we have to supply the appearance of the *realia* which are cited from our imagination, and we do this best by envisaging real objects, new or old, recruited for their new identities. But the Greeks also created an iconography for their past, which will occupy two chapters here (Five and Six), exploring the origins of their images for monsters and for the generally divine or heroic, figures or objects. In addition, there is an iconographic source more closely related to relics and other objects identified with the past in the images on Greek coins of the Roman period, which closely reflect the contemporary interests of authors such as Pausanias. A *Numismatic Commentary on Pausanias* published first in the 1880s (by F. W. Imhoof-Blumer and P. Gardner) was ostensibly illustrating 'Lost Masterpieces of Greek Art' but in fact occasionally demonstrated much more.

The other archaeological aspect of the study is topographical, mainly a matter of the identification of natural features (springs, rivers, caves) and of early remains of buildings, with places or structures of alleged heroic association. Of early travellers in Greece Pausanias, and to a lesser degree Strabo, were virtually the only guides whose work has survived for us. The former dwells especially on places identified with the heroic past, and as a result so also have latter-day travellers who have worked hard to identify the tombs and cult places which were mentioned in the texts. They must often have been correct in their identifications, although, to the present day, proof is generally lacking. They knew little about the true date of the structures they were viewing, but then neither did the ancient Greeks in most of their own confident identifications of the heroic. J.G. Frazer's edition of Pausanias, of over a century ago, contains the most comprehensive account of these topographical identifications. Later editors of Pausanias have for the most part been indifferent to the matter, although much has been done by archaeologists in specific areas and sites. This is not the place for re-appraisal of all identifications, plausible or not, and I remark only those where there are substantial remains or where the subject and context are revealing about more general aspects of our study. Frazer was notably uninterested in speculating about the physical character and appearance of relics, except where they seemed to relate to the history of Greek art.

This brings us back to texts, which provide the identifications but seldom do much to help us understand what the relics themselves were, or even what they looked like. So our two major sources of information rarely overlap. We shall often have recourse to the texts of Herodotus, Pausanias, Strabo and others, but what they tell is generally only as good as their sources. These generally have not survived but must sometimes have been the fruit of more rigorous research than is apparent in the compendia which we have. Thus, Strabo, Apollodoros and Pausanias rely extensively on the scholarly activity of Hellenistic writers who are often little more to us than names.

There could be a lingering suspicion that much of the phenomenon of identification and forgery of relics was relatively late, close in date to our prime recorder of such things in the second century AD – Pausanias. This is not true. The archaeological evidence for hero cult and attention to old tombs is enough to demonstrate the antiquity of the general idea, at least as early as the eighth century BC. Our relevant extant texts before Pausanias may be scrappy but they too are revealing and reassuring about the antiquity of the practice, and I review some of them briefly before coming to Pausanias himself.

Homer shows an awareness of heroic tombs, as when he describes the Arcadians as living by the tomb of Aipytos, a monument examined by Pausanias nearly a millennium later (T.393); and the use of an old tomb at Troy as a lookout (T.99).[9] He even speculates on the gods' identification for a tomb at Troy (T.98), which we can probably still locate [*Fig. 3*],[10] and he knows Ilos' tomb (T.514,583,596). Mount Sipylos was close to one of Homer's reputed homes, Smyrna; on it was the rocky feature which was taken for the petrified and weeping Niobe [*Fig. 77*], and this he knows and mentions.[11] It is clear that by his day (mid-seventh century or earlier) heroic tombs and monuments had been freely identified and named.[12]

References in the work of the historian Herodotus, writing in the mid-fifth century BC, include most of the categories we have to consider in this book, as well as observation of historical dedications recording victories, such as the fetters of

3. Sophia Schliemann excavating the tumulus at Troy which is probably the mound Batieia, mentioned by Homer as the tomb of Myrine.

the Spartans at Tegea (T.85), of a type which might have prompted attempts to provide similar heroic relics. I mention some of the relevant passages here (but again later) because they serve to demonstrate how far the Greeks had gone in creating our subject by his day, since he too is dependent on his predecessors' investigation of geography and myth. He recounts the discovery and removal by the Spartans of the bones of the hero Orestes (T.86), politically motivated. At Thebes he notes inscribed dedications by mythical figures (T.91), showing that such relics had already been graced with appropriate archaic inscriptions, in this case forgeries with 'Kadmeian letters', which presumably means early archaic Greek of a style not too readily decipherable by a classical Greek. The dispatch of heroes, presumed to be hero-images (wrongly, I believe), to lend support in battle is recorded especially for Aegina, with Aiakos and his sons sent to help the Thebans (who said they would have preferred men), and to the Greeks at the battle of Salamis (T.93,96). The identity of a tomb at Elaious, opposite Troy, as that of Protesilaos (the first Greek of the expedition to land at Troy), is noted, à propos of treasure from the sanctuary there, perhaps the contents of a prehistoric tomb, taken by the Persians in their invasion of Greece (T.97). And more traditional myth objects, like the flayed hide of poor Marsyas (T.94), are mentioned in passing. Greek lands were already well stocked with relics by the classical period and the exercise of historical imagination on objects and places was well advanced.

The poet Pindar, Herodotus' senior, was preoccupied with myth in the interests of his patrons, and so with relics and observations on the heroic origins of some physical phenomena, such as the volcanic activity in Italy generated by defeated and buried Giants (T.557). He seems to have developed a quite sophisticated view of the past.[13] Later in the fifth century, however, the historian Thucydides managed to tell the early history of Greece without any appeal to divine intervention and wholly in terms of power-struggle. He had the approach of an archaeologist, diagnosing early tombs on Delos as Carian from the type of the burials and the weapons found in them (T.598); and he wisely judged that, if Sparta were deserted with only its temples and ground-plans remaining, later ages would not think it to have been anywhere near as powerful as, in fact, it was, while a ruined Athens would seem to have been far more powerful (T.599). He was, of course, writing at the end of the great conflict in which his Athens had been humbled by Sparta.[14] He took the Trojan War seriously, and speculated on the logistics of the invasion force, but reflected that 'men do not discriminate, and are too ready to receive ancient traditions about their own as well as about other countries', and he had no time for 'the tales of chroniclers who seek to please the ear rather than to speak the truth'.[15] Rationality in such matters was creeping in, and will recur over the centuries, never quite dominant.

In the tragedies of Euripides, Thucydides' contemporary in Athens, the settings were themselves heroic, but allowed their own relics, such as the dress of Amazons, dedicated as spoils by Herakles at Delphi and Mycenae (T.79). How 'real' they were is hard to tell; almost certainly recent products if any were shown, and from its description the woven decoration at Delphi seems not consciously archaizing, but classical – astronomical and orientalizing. The degree to which the Attic tragedians allowed anachronisms in their plays might reveal how much they knew or at least what they believed of life in the age of heroes. They seem to have been very nearly as careful as Homer, although their concern was at least as much to explore contemporary anxieties and problems as those of the heroic age. Homer knew about the obsolete arms of heroes from the oral tradition which must have begun in the waning Bronze Age, if not from surviving artefacts and pictures, and only occasionally does he betray the influence of contemporary (seventh-century) Greek life by assuming that relations with, for instance, the Phoenicians were much the same then as they were in his day, but he manages to avoid any serious allusion to Greece's new age of colonizing. The fifth-century tragedians admit allusions to the use of gold as currency, which is certainly heroic since there were then no gold coins in Athens, but also to silver and to activities which seem to presuppose coinage. Much is of course determined by the need to make their view of the heroic past and its problems accessible to the modern Athenian, and is part of the 'modern dress' in which they presented most of their vision of remote antiquity.[16]

In the fourth century Xenophon noted the odd behaviour of Herakles' armour at Thebes (T.603), vacating his temple to join in the battle of Leuktra, but he was too much a man of the world to take much note of such matters except in passing.

The next major text source is a list of 'remarkable things' compiled in Aristotle's school.[17] Many are myth objects, and a major novelty is the number which lie outside the Greek homeland, prompting speculation about the observation and invention of relics by Greeks overseas.

Colonization in south Italy and Sicily began in the mid-eighth century and continued into the sixth. Greek mythology placed several events in the west, especially Heraklean Labours, and had also sought in the west the eventual homes of some Greek heroes after Troy, notably Diomedes and Aineias. Odysseus' voyages after Troy were westward. Not all of the relics of these need have been inventions of the eighth century and later, although voyages of colonization lent local colour to some stories which need not have survived from the earlier Greek exploration of the west, in the Late Bronze Age. This is when some observations, especially topographical, might have become attached to the tradition. The Aristotelians knew several mythical locations and landmarks in non-Greek Italy, the south of France and Spain, with myth objects not altogether confined to Greek sites. But other natural and man-made features were associated with Greek myth. Of these the most notable are the buildings of Sardinia 'in old Greek style', especially the round buildings (*tholoi*) built by Iolaos, Herakles' companion (T.37). These are the prehistoric *nuraghi* [*Fig. 4*] which went on being built in the island by Sardinians for a millennium, into the third century BC.[18] The Black Sea had attracted colonies only in the later seventh century though it was already the location for Jason's voyage to Colchis (modern Georgia) to seek the Golden Fleece, and his return home which, in some versions, involved the Danube and a 'northern passage' through to the Adriatic and the west. The Aristotelians knew of Argonaut altars and relics on the route (T.38). We do not know how early Greek colonists in the Black Sea located Achilles' race-course opposite the mouth of the River Dniepr in the Ukraine; Herodotus made first mention of it.[19] Achillean associations with the northern Black Sea coast, as on White Island (Leuke), may be yet older, whatever their source, and are recorded in the epic (post-Homeric) cycle; they involve his romantic interest in Helen, and the removal of his body there by Thetis.[20]

These mythical identifications in non-Greek lands show the extent to which the Greeks carried their past with them, and could relocate it as readily as they could themselves. There is more to this than the comfort of identifying familiar stories, religion, and ritual far from home, and many authors, from Herodotus on, were anxious to anchor what they thought they knew of their own past to the sometimes better recorded histories, mythology and religion of other, older cultures. One problem with the myth-tellers is to know whether some details of their stories depend on identified relics or simply record plausible behaviour by their actors. This is especially acute with the prophecies in Lykophron's poem *Alexandra* which include many such details. They are not exactly essential to the narrative, which may be obscure but is basically conventional. The poem, heavily allusive in all its details and requiring long commentaries even in antiquity, was meant to be a record

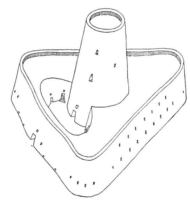

4. A *nuraghe* tower, Sant'Antine near Torralba in Sardinia, and a reconstruction of the whole complex; these were said to have been built by Herakles' companion, Iolaos.

of Kassandra's prophecies about the aftermath to the Trojan War and the fate of its participants. Several of them were involved in alleged Greek foundations, and not only in the west or north but in Syria.

The next important source is more 'real' in that it is an inscription of 99 BC [*Fig. 5*] purporting to list the dedications, from time immemorial, in the Temple of Athena at Lindos on Rhodes (T.605). It includes objects destroyed in a fourth-century fire, and attested by records. Whether these objects were all real may be a matter for discussion (Chapter Four), but the list gives a good indication of what was deemed the satisfactory content of a Local History Museum stocked with relics and memorials to myth-history and history, from arms and armour of the Trojan War and gifts from Herakles, to celebrations of recent victories by the city. It is the fullest list we have for any temple collection. Its nearest rival is one for the

5. The Lindos Chronicle (whole and detail).
A marble inscription detailing the dedications, mythical
and historical, at the Temple of Athena at Lindos on
Rhodes. Written in the second century BC and found built
into the floor of a church on the site. Height 2.37 m.
(Copenhagen, National Museum 7125)

temple of Apollo at Sikyon, given by Ampelius (T.5), a second-century AD (or later?) Roman author, with ten relics, for all of which some link can be found with the city, of variable plausibility.[21] Pausanias, also second-century, mentions just two relics there (T.208), only one of which is in Ampelius, but also says that the temple had burnt down. We cannot date Ampelius closely and it could be that this happened between his writing and Pausanias; or it may be that both relied on other records and Ampelius was unaware of the temple's recent fate.

After Aristotle there is a spate of stray references to swell the testimonia, and a sustained interest in recording *thaumasia*, *mirabilia*, for their own sake, not least under Roman rule, since Roman writers, together with Greek writers of the Roman period, were anxious and ready to assimilate the Greek tradition into the new World Order. The Hellenistic period had been busy with such matters, notably in the great Library of Alexandria where all the texts were to hand. Callimachus' *Aetia* recounted the origins of many Greek beliefs and rituals, but we have his work only in fragments. The search for such causes (*aitia*) was a popular scholarly pursuit of the period, but had occupied poets long before – Euripides is especially ready to explain the rituals that arise from the mythical events that he narrates in his plays. It is an exercise very close to that of identifying physical evidence for the remote past, which is our quest. Sometimes all that is at stake is a name for the founder or builder of a sanctuary, and not necessarily the structure remaining, so not all are taken note of here.

Another preoccupation of Hellenistic poets was the creation of epigrams, many of them dedicatory. These, with similar compositions of earlier writers, were later assembled in the *Greek Anthology*, where it is clear that a high proportion are simply literary exercises and do not relate to real dedicated objects. Without other references in our sources we have therefore to dismiss the trireme mast from the earliest ship, made by Athena, alleged to be at Kyzikos, and the frock that Omphale took off and gave to Herakles when they changed roles.[22] At best they show the sort of relic that was found inspiring.

Strabo, the geographer of the late first century BC, included many relevant observations in the course of his quite detailed description of the world. He may not have travelled quite as much as he claimed, but he used his authorities well, and these included many an account of voyages (*Periplous*) in and beyond the Mediterranean, as well as more ambitious studies of the known world and its history, as by Eratosthenes, whom he rather disdained. Collections of the surviving fragments of the many other Greek geographers simply tantalize.

Strabo did not believe in the authenticity of relics or the truth of outright myth, it seems, but he was an historian too; they were part of the story of the places he describes, and he recognized that they had an educative value. He took the heroes, their deeds and wars, as historical, but not the miraculous elements involved in them. He had great respect for Homer, as the first geographer, but recognized that Homer had added 'myth' for narrative purposes and not because it was true; indeed, much of Strabo's text is devoted to an attempt to reconstruct 'Homeric' geography. He recognized that Homer, and others, were ignorant of more distant places, but well informed about Greek lands, and notably west Anatolia, where the Trojans fought Greeks.[23] Diodorus Siculus, an historian and contemporary of Strabo, reworked myth into more plausible history but without surrendering belief in the figures involved, nor in relics or works associated with them. This is in the tradition of Euhemerus (about 300 BC), who imagined an eastern island (Panchaea) where there was an inscribed golden column which revealed the historicity of gods and heroes, anticipating the goals of various trends in scholarship since our eighteenth century.

Pliny the Elder, who died in the eruption of Vesuvius in AD 79, mentions natural and man-made *mirabilia* rather than relics, but his work reveals the Roman addiction to collecting such things, especially from the Greek world, as a means of demonstrating Rome's greatness.[24] Thus, the general Pompey, in his triumphal procession in Rome, paraded not only eastern rulers, pampered jades, and their court furniture, but the couch of the first Persian king Darius, and himself wore Alexander's cloak.[25] He got the cloak from Mithradates, who had it from the Koans, who were given it by Cleopatra – they said. The Emperor Augustus was an active collector, and by no means alone (T.408,594), though most other Romans concentrated on collecting Greek art, old or recent. Several very late authors make allusions to relics, but may simply be copying their sources, and multiple references to a relic are no guarantee of its survival, or even of its original existence. This brings us to our major source, Pausanias, whose motivation and recording require a moment's attention.

Pausanias was writing in the middle of the second century AD. His object was to present a *Description of Greece* – a *Periegesis* or 'leading around'. The result was not quite like modern guidebooks, however, nor was his manner the rule with all ancient travel writers.[26] Descriptions of landscape or even journeys in the manner of Baedeker or Guide Bleu are almost wholly lacking, and although there is a geographical sequence which could correspond to real travels, one gets the impression rather of a gazetteer arranged in a roughly logical manner from a card index. He was interested in 'things worth looking at' (*theamata*), but his choice was generally dictated by his even greater interest in stories (*logoi*): what was worth talking about as much as what was worth seeing. The physical remains of the remote, even heroic, past and their historical or religious associations were of prime interest. Monuments and buildings which we know to have existed were ignored if no interesting *logos* was available to explain their history or, more often, their myth-historical value. In Greece this embraced a great deal, but not quite everything, and as a 'guide in the hand' for any traveller who did not share his special interests the book would have been infuriating. It was decidedly of more use in the study than in the backpack.[27]

Pausanias remarks many a minor town because it contains some relic or mythical monument, even if only the alleged remains of the house of a hero. To this extent he is perhaps more useful for our subject than for many others, geographical, archaeological or historical. Because much of his writings has survived – ten books for Greece – he has perhaps been overvalued as a source for subjects which were not central to his interests and which he contributes to only peripherally. More than once he indulges in lengthy digests of local history, usually Hellenistic, in case his readers should be less than well informed on the period and place; as often as not this serves simply to introduce names and stories which we then find relevant to the sights he goes on to record. These interludes seem to interrupt the flow of the narrative until one understands their purpose. He accepted that there was a time when the gods walked, talked and feasted with men, but also saw that 'Lovers of the marvellous are too prone to heighten the marvels they hear tell of by adding touches of their own; and thus they debase truth by alloying it with fiction'.[28] A century ago J.G. Frazer's major contributions to traditional classical studies were an edition and translation (which I use) of our Pausanias and an edition and translation of Apollodorus, the mythographer (Loeb edition): understandable, given his other prime interests (*The Golden Bough*), since these remain our major sources for Greece's view of her past.

Some of the following chapters look at classes of physical evidence, whether archaeological or textual in source, which record the Greeks' interpretation or identification of their past – mainly their myth-historical past, although the historical will receive attention where it reflects more generally on their treatment of relics. The textual sources were discussed in 1909/12 by Friedrich Pfister, who was mainly concerned with the cult of relics, but was very thorough. They have been little considered since as a whole except in an article by Leon Lacroix in 1989.[29] My presentation of these sources in the appended Testimonia, in paraphrased translation, is, I hope, adequate for present purposes, and gives references to the original texts for the curious. It is, I think, as complete as it need be, without including many sources which themselves repeat others. There would be no point in rehearsing all items in the different categories of relics listed and perfectly adequately discussed by Pfister, so I deal with them here selectively, and the detail can be gleaned from the indexes to the Testimonia. But Pfister did not concern himself with the archaeology of the subject, even with the possibility of making some sort of guess at the physical appearance of some of the relics and sites he was listing. He made no attempt, naturally enough at the time he was writing, a century ago, to discover what archaeology had to tell of the Greeks' re-use of the past or understanding of its monuments, nor of the Greeks' attempt to re-create it in images as well as in artefacts. These archaeological sources have hitherto received attention piecemeal, usually à propos of hero cult, but one category, the subject of our next chapter, has been profitably treated recently by a folklorist/palaeontologist, and in some detail, and so has been given pride of place.

CHAPTER TWO

Fossilized History: Them Bones

A HIGH PROPORTION of the surface of the earth is formed from the remains of early life, compacted as limestone or other rocks, sometimes revealing their shelly marine past, and ultimately preserving the fossilized remains of vertebrates that preceded man by millions of years. The shells look much as shells do today. Herodotus, seeing them on mountains in Egypt, properly deduced that the sea had once covered the land there (T.87).[1] He need have looked no farther than the shelly limestone from which the Temple of Zeus at Olympia was built for further evidence of a once very watery past in the hills of Greece, one which might lend credence to stories of a Flood. Of this Greece too had its version, with Noah/Deukalion and his wife Pyrrha surviving on ship a mass-destruction of mankind by Zeus, and throwing stones over their shoulders from which a new race of men and women sprang.[2] They were, in the myth, 'the bones of their mother', Earth, and earth was indeed full of many bones. Ammonites are our most familiar fossils, named for the Egyptian god Ammon (Egyptian Amun) who had a ram's head. Rams' horns obey the same mysterious arithmetic of Nature as did the shells of the ammonites, whence the perceived similarity and given name. But they do not look human as did the remains of the vertebrates.[3]

Adrienne Mayor, in her *The First Fossil Hunters* (2000), has surveyed the evidence for the Greeks', and others', interpretation of fossil evidence that came their way. I have but little to add to her account which is thorough and inspiring, a refreshingly new approach to well-worn classical subjects, though it would only be fair to say that several classical scholars have over the years made comparable deductions (for example, G.J. Frazer in *The Golden Bough*), none as comprehensive or well-informed. The intentions of my exploration are slightly different, not least in dwelling on the finds for which we know that identifications were devised.

The skeletons of vertebrates are all constructed according to a single basic pattern although there are obvious differences in size, and especially in proportions, if you compare, say, a sparrow with a human.[4] For the most part leg and arm or wing bones, ribs, shoulder-blades, pelvis, teeth, all look roughly alike, and the discovery of fossilized examples of superhuman size would naturally have been attributed to a race of humanoid giants. Mayor makes the point of comparison graphically in the pair I reproduce here, rearranging a mammoth skeleton to stand upright beside a human [*Fig. 6*].[5] The discovery of such bones in Greece contributed to, and perhaps generated, the view of a primitive age of Giants, children of Earth (Ge), who had to be put down by the Olympian gods (e.g., T.403,498,528,532,545, for the big bones).[6] The same source probably helped attribute, though in a far less emphatic way, more than human stature to the race of heroes. Ajax' knee caps were as big as the disci used by boy athletes (T.158), his skeleton sixteen feet long (T.497), and Pausanias is clear that such bones may be human despite their great size (T.312). The observation may be reflected even in choices of height for some classical sculptures where figures of immortals or heroes may be about a head-height taller than mortals. The explanation for the excessive length of the stadium at Olympia was that it had been paced out by a long-legged Herakles.[7] One of the hero's fingers had been bitten off, it was said, by the Nemean Lion (or a big fish) and buried by him in a mound near Sparta marked by a lion (T.541). There is probably a combination here of a late misinterpretation of a classical lion-topped mound, for whatever purpose, and the discovery of a large bone which was taken for Herakles' finger. His loss was remarked nowhere else in ancient literature or art. Orestes lost a finger too, biting it off (T.404); it was monumentalized.[8] Other hero bones that were moved for various purposes could have been simply from human burials discovered in the right place, though dimensions might get improved in the telling. Orestes' were in a coffin seven cubits long (T.86), and Theseus' were 'gigantic', but found beside weapons, so presumably from a grave (T.530).[9] Lord Curzon was shown the tomb of Noah near Baalbek in Syria, forty yards long, but that of Eve near Jedda measured 173 × 12 yards; 'when Eve fell, with her fell the stature of the race which she originated'.[10]

The reaction to finds of fossil bones is universal. To take just three examples that have come to my notice recently: R. Plot's *The Natural History of Oxfordshire* (1677) records the discovery of what is clearly a megalosaurus thigh, which was at first taken for the remains of an elephant brought to Britain by the Romans, then of a giant. Earlier, and farther north, a mammoth tusk (now in Warwick Castle) and various whale bones displayed in a parish church, a farmhouse, and in places as far away as Lancashire and Bristol, gave body to the story of the 'Dun Cow of Dunsmore'. The beast was an actor in a common folktale of a witch who milked a cow dry. But the poor Dun Cow became 'a monstrous wyld and cruell beast', who had to be slain by Sir Guy of Warwick, a practised slayer of Danish and Saracen giants, dragons and a monster boar, and an interesting mix of history and myth, who has his own relics now in Warwick Castle, and a cave.[11] There are other English giants who owned cattle, no doubt the product of observation of monstrous bones, both the apparently humanoid and tusks; they bring to mind monstrous Greek herdsmen – Geryon, Polyphemos – who might have been similarly conjured. Finally, in St Stephen's Cathedral in Vienna the Giant's Door (*Riesentor*) is named for the mammoth shin which was found during building

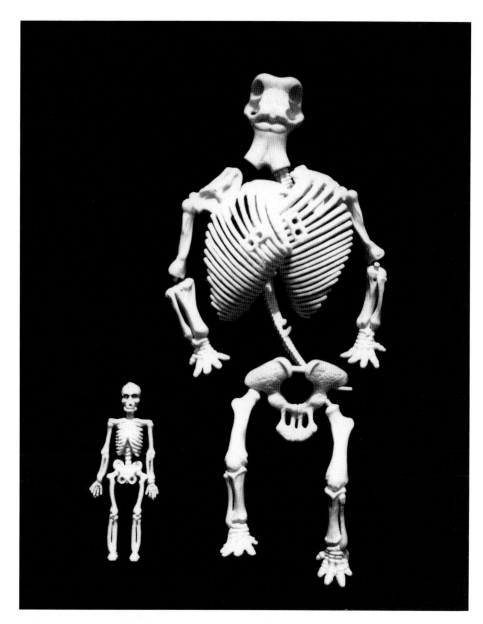

6. A mammoth skeleton set on its hind legs to compare with a human skeleton. Composition created by Adrienne Mayor.

operations in AD 1230, and hung in the door as the remains of a giant drowned in the Great Flood, until properly identified in the 1700s.[12] There are many such stories, worldwide. At a different scale, we find the identification of 'portraits' in rocks which split to reveal fossil patterns and creatures. The phenomenon was observed also in antiquity, generally of an appropriate figure for the countryside – a satyr or Pan (T.56,519). The stories are recorded by Romans but the examples are, naturally enough, in Greece.

I start with a case study which Mayor was the first to observe, not because it is typical – far from it – but because it demonstrates the theme in a novel way, by ancient iconography. On Aegean coasts fossil remains are relatively common and may be observed protruding from a coastline or cliff face. This is true of the coast of the Troad and offshore islands, on the busy routes up to the Black Sea and south to the great Ionian cities. Monsters that ravaged the land of Troy at the time of the Trojan War were held to have emerged from caves on the island of Tenedos, opposite Troy, and ultimately vanished beneath the earth.[13] They are the originals of the serpents that attacked Laocoon and his sons, naturalized in the famous marble group in the Vatican. There were similar stories of the Dardanelles, as at Sigeion, where hero graves of the Trojan War were identified. It seems highly probable that the appearance of seaside fossils gave rise to the story of the amphibious sea-monster (*ketos*) which was said to have ravaged the plain of Troy. The Greeks, characteristically, gave this local legend substance by identifying the creature as one sent by the god Poseidon because Troy's king, Laomedon, had cheated him. To appease the monster, he was told by an oracle to give it his daughter Hesione, who was accordingly staked out for it to consume; but he also offered his divine horses to anyone who could dispose of the beast. This was accomplished by Herakles; but Laomedon cheated him too, so Herakles sacked Troy. The story is mentioned in Homer, and must be much older.

In Greek art a sea monster is generally shown, first, as a big fish with a leonine head and gaping jaws, then according to the classical artist's formula for all such sea monsters, a type which was long-lived enough to serve also as Jonah's whale in art (to these I revert in Chapter Five [*Figs. 117–119*]). However, the very first representation of the Trojan monster is on a Corinthian vase of around 560 BC [*Fig. 7*]. Herakles shoots arrows; Hesione, much daring, throws stones. The monster's head protrudes from the cliff in the form of what Mayor properly recognized as a skull. At the very least this suggests that the artist had some inkling of the origins of the story, which is remarkable enough, or had heard sailors' stories of apparitions along that coast which could be taken as relics of the monster. Mayor identifies the skull as a fossil Miocene giraffe, such as are found on Samos, south of the original monster's home [*Fig. 8*].[14]

We must, however, explore further whatever links there might be between observed fossils, the creation of a myth, and an artist. It is difficult to believe that a Corinthian vase painter, not a conspicuously good one and of a period in which vase painters did not draw from life or models, could have been so well informed. I suspect that his intention was no more than to show an animal skull, which he managed quite recognizably, especially in the way the lower jaw is attached, but relying on little more than general knowledge of what might be appropriate, helped by familiarity with the appearance of the skulls of horses and cattle [*Fig. 9*]. It is no more an accurate drawing of a real skull than are the heads and bodies of the human and animal figures on the same vase accurate images of real creatures, but good conceptual approximations. This is not a period when artists were trained in

7. Herakles and Hesione confront the sea monster at Troy who is to devour her. The monster is shown as a skull protruding from a cave, like fossils found in the area of Troy. On a Corinthian vase of about 560 BC. (Boston, Museum of Fine Arts 63.420)

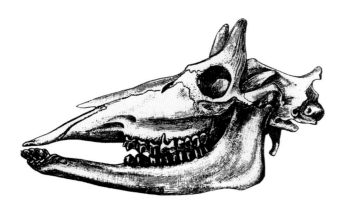

8. Fossil skull of a *Samotherium*, a giraffe of the Miocene period (about 25 million years ago), from Samos.

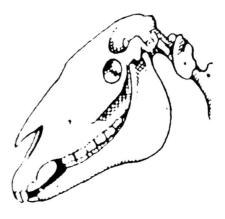

9. The skull of a horse.

the life class or drew still life, and size is irrelevant in such pictures. The upper part of the head is still puzzling: there are on it a black spot, which might be a stone in flight (like the one in the creature's mouth), a smaller spot outlined in red, which might be the eye socket, and a rosette of a dot and four. Is the line stretching up from it an aborted horn? At any rate the artist has made a correct association of a skull with the monster story, based on we know not what; he did his best to express it, and he has given us at last the clue to the origin of the story in its appropriate location. He knew that a skull was a record of the *ketos*, not that it was the origin of the story. So this is a monster and a tale engendered by observation of a physical phenomenon, and not wholly the product of a poet's imagination. I think we shall find many more which may have inspired major episodes and details of Greek myth.

Mayor deals very fully with the finds of fossils in Greece and the Mediterranean in general which were recorded by ancient authors, an activity which she characterizes as an Ancient Bone Rush.[15] It was certainly widespread and long-lived. Our immediate concern is with the Greeks' attempts to identify them with creatures of their past history. It was easy to allow them to be the remains of the Giants who had peopled the land before the age of heroes, and who had to be dealt with by the Olympian gods, as we have seen. The main battle was placed in north Greece at Pallene in Chalkidike, rich in fossil beds and a recorded source of bones identified as of Giants in antiquity (T.498,545). The story played its part also in the later adjusted myth-history created in Athens to allow their hero, Theseus, a degree of giant-slaying. This was located on home ground in Attica, deceptively called Pallene, against Pallas and his sons. Whether it was supported by fossil bones is not said, and the Pallantidai were demoted to being simply dynastic rivals, but Pallene is barely five kilometres from the major fossil site at Pikermi.[16] Buried bones are also implicit in the story that the god Poseidon destroyed his Giant adversary Polybotes by dropping on him a piece of Kos, which became the island of Nisyros (T.579), or that Athena dropped Sicily on Enkelados (T.14), while the last Giant killed by Herakles lies under Mykonos (T.578).

The Giants' birthplaces and burial grounds were naturally identified in areas of volcanic activity and earthquakes – Phlegraiai 'burning fields' – in Pallene, Arcadia, Sicily, and near Cumae in Italy (Pozzuoli).[17] So the bones of Alkyoneus and other Giants are buried under Vesuvius (T.498). The monster Typhon (or Typhoeus), not a canonical Giant, and born of Earth in the Corycian cave in Cilicia, involved Zeus in an extensive pursuit, rousing whole mountains in Thrace, whence one is called Haimos ('bloody'); or rather, a local name was explained by recruiting for it a part in the Typhon story. The monster was eventually chased to Sicily, blitzed by Zeus, and buried. His discomfort accounted for the volcanic areas from Campania to Etna, an identification made by the fifth century BC and recorded by Pindar (T.557):

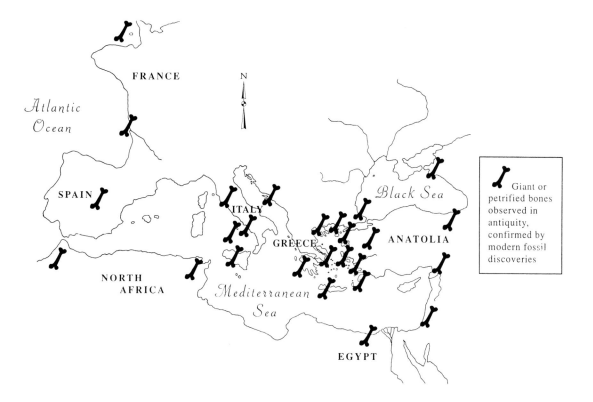

10. Map locating giant and petrified bones reported in ancient sources compared with modern finds of fossil vertebrates. Compiled by Adrienne Mayor, drawn by Michele Mayor Angel.

he who lies in dire Tartaros, enemy of the gods, Typhon of a hundred heads, once nurtured in the Cilician cave. Now the steep cliffs above Cumae and Sicily crush his shaggy chest, and the heavenward pillar of snowy Etna, who keeps her sharp frost all year, holds him down...Such is he who is bound between the dark-leaved peaks and the plain, and his craggy bed wounds his stretched body.

(Pythia 1.15–22)

Alternatively Typhon may be found in the 'burnt up' (*katakaumene*) area of west Anatolia (T.586), the site of a recent (2000) major earthquake, or even in Syria (T.402). The association of volcanoes and earthquakes with buried monsters, Giants or Typhon, who are shifting their limbs, had been made in the earliest Greek literature,[18] and did not wholly depend on the discovery of bones. Phanagoria, in the Taman peninsula east of the Crimea, has its Giant story in a cave (T.580) although it is far from the traditional placing of the battles; but it is a well-known fossil source, and this would have been enough.[19] Here the Giants were said to have been lured into the cave by Aphrodite for Herakles to destroy. The love goddess was not a prominent Giant-fighter and in this case her involvement in the story depended on the false etymology of the epithet under which she was locally worshipped – Apatourios, which (wrongly) implied deceitful. Fossil giants must have been bones of suffciently humanoid form to be acceptable, and they were thought of as human in appearance, though sometimes snake-legged, a feature probably not inspired by fossil finds but by their earthy associations. We look at them in art in Chapter Five. Mayor's Giants Map of the Greek world [*Fig. 10*] corresponds closely with fossil finds and volcanic/earthquake activity.[20]

That the Giants were both born of Earth and buried there readily gave rise to the notion that the earth could be the source of other supernatural beings. Fossil teeth might be taken for seed, and so we find two stories of dragons' teeth which, when sown, gave birth to warriors. One crop has to be fought by Kadmos (T.422), after killing the serpent/dragon which guarded the well of Ares at Thebes.[21] The event was rationalized as early as the fourth century BC as being the hero defeating a King Drako (dragon) who collected elephants' teeth, taken away by his followers who then raised armies against him. That hippopotamus or mammoth teeth lie at the back of the story is quite possible, and several have been found in historical contexts, but this rationalization is typical of a philosophical trend of the period; it had little enough effect on Greek thought and attitudes to such marvels and stories thereafter.[22] The second sowing was by Jason in Colchis, of teeth given him by the witch Medea, on his expedition to secure the Golden Fleece. These grew into warriors whom he set against each other by throwing stones among them, a ruse borrowed for or from the Kadmos story.[23]

The find of a massive shoulder-blade gave rise to a stranger story; it looked a little like ivory, a feature of much old bone, and it was exhibited at Olympia (T.346,517). The story was told of the hero Pelops, important in the history of the site and ancestor of a distinguished but doomed line of heroic kings which included Agamemnon. Pelops came from Anatolia, was butchered and jointed by his father Tantalos to serve in a banquet for the Olympian gods, but then reassembled except for his shoulder-blade which had already been consumed by Demeter (who *eats* shoulder-blades?), and which was replaced by the gods with one of ivory. It was deemed to have been an important enough relic to be shipped to Troy to help the Greeks, then lost at sea on the way home but fished up off Euboea and, once it had been identified by an oracle, returned to Olympia. The essence of this is a fossil, perhaps the shoulder-blade of a whale, probably found on the shore of Euboea, taken to Olympia and put in a hero shrine of Pelops there. When and why the rest of the story was spun around it, we do not know, and in the early fifth century Pindar was already discounting the Pelops casserole, but the odds are that the bone or fossil came first.[24] There is a report of the discovery in Athens of a whale shoulder-blade in a ninth-century BC context, and there is no shortage of fossil finds in other historic contexts in Greece, which shows that they were treasured even if not always attached to a myth.[25] We shall probably never know what they made of them all, but the important thing is that they were kept. More bones 'of Pelops' were stored near by at Olympia in a bronze box (T.358). Was this the remains of a burial in a bronze cauldron (see below) which gave rise to the jointing and cooking story? The size of these other bones is not remarked, nor their relationship to the substitute massive shoulder-blade, but all heroes were big, and Greeks, in such matters, credulous. Another prosthetic, not attested by any relic that we are told about, was Achilles' heel, inadvertently burnt by his mother in this version, and replaced by the centaur Cheiron with a vertebra from the swiftest of the Giants, Damysos, whom he unearthed in Pallene.[26]

Pelops had been jointed and cooked in a cauldron. There are other stories of cooking heroes, but to rejuvenate them or ensure immortality. Medea persuaded the daughters of Pelias to rejuvenate their father and deceived them by demonstrating the operation with a ram; she did the same for Jason, and for his father. It is unlikely, however, that the stories were inspired by fossil finds rather than the discovery of early Greek burials in bronze cooking cauldrons, at a time or place where such a practice was unfamiliar (see Chapter Four).

One other possible fossil story explored by Mayor, and involving the eastern griffins that guarded the gold from the Arimasps, I reserve for Chapter Five, since it concerns Greek iconography at least as much as finds of bones. There is a related story in Pliny about the horns of an Indian ant, the size of a wolf, which were displayed at Erythrai (T.511). This story starts with a modern observation that in Baltistan (the Karakoram area of North West India) marmots burrow into gold-bearing layers of earth, depositing in the spoil scraps of gold. This was confused by the likeness in Sanskrit of the words for powder-gold and an ant, and by the fact that the marmot (*Arctomys Himalayanas*) was called a 'mountain ant' in Persian. The marmots became 'ants', and in Herodotus' story the ants dig up gold in caves, which is then stolen by the Indians with their camels;[27] they are also described as being between the size of a fox and a dog, about right for marmots [*Fig. 11*].[28] Only

11. An Indian marmot, about 80–100 cm long.

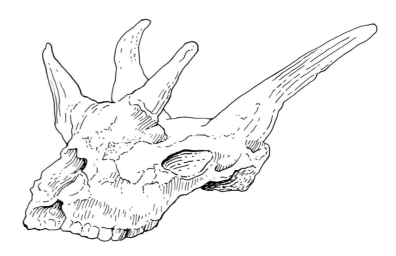

12. The fossil skull of a *Giraffokeryx* from the Siwalik Hills, north India, a 'fossil dragon'. About 50 cm long.

in Pliny's account of the relics at Erythrai do they have horns. The possible analogy with antler pick-axes, a very common tool of early man, has been remarked. It may then have been that a Greek, who was shown the antler-like skulls of the well-known north Indian fossil 'dragons', as [*Fig. 12*], which are recorded by later Greek travellers, decided that these would have been appropriate natural equipment for the gold-digging ants, and he brought specimens home to display at Erythrai.[29] The ants lived long in the pages of would-be travellers such as Sir John Maundevile in the fourteenth century. For him the Pismires (ants) of Taprobane (Ceylon), 'as great as hounds', both dug and purified the gold of which they are then tricked by men.[30]

Not all fossil skeletons needed to be assigned to anthropoid giants. On Chios the bones and skull found after a forest fire were as of a dragon (T.1). On nearby Samos, a rich source for fossils, some of which were found among the votive debris of the sanctuary of Hera and had obviously been dedicated to her,[31] there was a more exotic story. A combination of fossil finds and probable earthquake noises gave rise to the tale of monsters which had split the ground with their bellowing; their bones were displayed (T.2). A little more imagination made them the bones of roaring elephants which had formed part of Dionysos' army when he fought the Amazons who had fled there (T.528). They were even given names, Neïdes or Neädes, probably meaning 'witless' and not related to the gentler Naiads of the Greek countryside. They were a by-word for noisiness.[32]

Non-skeletal fossils could also play a role. Footprints, of heroes and creatures but in stone, were reported and variously identified all over the Greek world. Few if any may have been made by hominids, but large fossil bivalves can leave sinkings like hoofprints, large ammonite rims look like heels, and other natural shallow sinkings in the rock could be recruited when of a suggestive form. Herakles is a common source for them, in Italy and Scythia (T.34,90 – two cubits long). When he is accompanied by Dionysos (T.107) his prints are judged shorter than the god's, which measured 100 feet. This, however, is total fantasy and not based on any fossil find, since Lucian is simply inventing a relic for his *True Story*, a parody of travellers' tales which manages to anticipate Gulliver, Baron Munchhausen and the Divina Commedia in one. Herakles also gave his name to petrified cattle tracks (T.67). Perseus' prints in Egypt are exceptional (T.88).[33]

Finally, in various parts of Greece animal graves are recorded, and some of these may be later interments of fossils of unusual or massive beasts, without closer identification. Any beast involved in fighting heroes was likely to be of unnatural size, and this must have been true of any bones associated with them. The tusks of the Calydonian boar killed by Meleager were three handspans round (T.540), and from no pig. The skeleton of the sea monster faced by Andromeda at Joppa, and taken to Rome, was forty feet long; perhaps of a whale (T.509). An exceptional identification for an animal grave might be Kynossema, Grave of the Dog, on the Thracian Chersonese, which was taken for the grave of the bitch into which Hekabe, wife of King Priam of Troy, had been turned (T.537). Possibly this was the result of an early confusion between the names of Hekabe and of the goddess Hekate, who was at home in the area and kept dogs, but this is an explanation that might have appealed to a Greek rationalist more readily than to a modern scholar.[34]

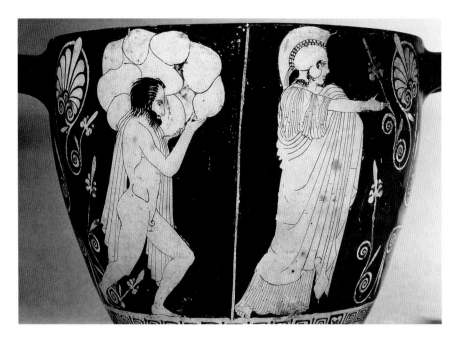

13. Athena directs a giant (labelled *gigas*) bearing a boulder to build the walls of her Acropolis at Athens. On an Athenian red figure vase of about 430 BC by the Penelope Painter. (Paris, Louvre G372)

14. The reverse of the vase [*Fig. 13*]. Two architects with measuring rods and plumbline contemplate Athena's sacred olive tree on the Acropolis at Athens.

CHAPTER THREE

Homes Fit For Heroes

'HOMES FIT FOR HEROES'; the politician's promise of new homes to be built in Great Britain for the returning warriors of the First World War. The Greeks looked to existing monuments for the homes of their heroes, who had lived and fought before History, and especially for their tombs. The shrines built for their worship were generally humble affairs by comparison with what was provided for Olympian gods. The Greeks also had views about the monumental record of the architectural achievements of their ancestors, gods and heroes. However, Greek re-creation of their past may have involved forgery of artefacts but did not go to the length of building substantial 'new' antiquities in stone. I know of no certain example of a structure (more than, perhaps, a trophy) or tomb being deliberately built to be passed off as of heroic antiquity, although several old tombs were given some architectural enhancement appropriate to their new identity, even if no more than an enclosure with apparently venerable trees. In this chapter we look at identifications of standing structures and of tombs, at attitudes to and treatment of old tombs, at the locating of places for worship or commemoration, and of attention paid to other structures not identified, at least in the record that remains. It will be a medley of walls, houses and tombs, of ancestors, heroes and sometimes gods.

On an Athenian vase of around 430 BC the goddess Athena leads a wild-haired, bearded man labelled *gigas* (giant) and his load, a massive boulder [*Fig. 13*].[1] He must be a Pelasgian, not exactly a Giant in terms of Greek myth, but of the earliest race of mortal Greeks, who were all deemed outsize, and his mission here must be to build the walls of Athens' Acropolis under the eye of its tutelary goddess (T.143). Between them stands what is likely to be a measuring rod, such as are held by the two figures on the other side of the vase [*Fig. 14*], one of whom also holds red weighted cords (invisible in the photograph), an architect's device. They are contemplating an apparently leafless tree, probably Athena's sacred olive. They are the modern architects, no doubt, planning how to provide a setting for the major relic on the Acropolis in the new building plan for the sacred hill. When the vase

15. The foundations of the Old Athena Temple of the 6th century BC, visible beside the classical Erechtheion on the Acropolis at Athens.

was painted the Parthenon was already up, and the Erechtheion, to stand beside the olive tree, was already being planned. What may be preparation for the new is being expressed in terms of the construction of the old, and of significant relics of the old.[2]

Other heroic cities had their walls built by the giant Kyklopes, as we shall see. Why Athens should require a different construction team for her walls might be a reflection of Athenian pride in long, indigenous occupation of the city, and the Pelasgians were, in their way, Greeks and involved in the earliest history of Athens. They once lived at the foot of the Acropolis (T.143).[3] But it also happens that the heroic walls of Athens, that is to say those that were built at the end of the Bronze Age, were somewhat later than the first construction of the 'Kyklopean' walls of Mycenae and Tiryns, and so belonged, even in terms of mythology, to a later generation, and one with which Athens claimed a measure of continuity. The massive polygonal walls of the Athenian citadel enclosed its Bronze Age palace, of which there is little if anything left to feed the archaeologist's imagination.[4] In Homer Athena herself flies from Troy to this stout House of Erechtheus,[5] the first king of Athens, to a building which no later Athenian seems to have sought to identify on the Acropolis rock, except possibly in the ruins of the archaic Athena temple, which remained and remain visible between the new classical buildings [*Fig. 15*]. The Pelasgians' walls (they could be called the 'Pelargikon', T.92) had served until the Persian sacks of 480 and 479 BC. When parts were renewed or the

16. Part of the Mycenaean 'Kyklopean' wall of the Acropolis at Athens, south of the Propylaia.

surface area extended to embrace them, some stretches were still to be seen, as they are today [*Fig. 16*]. Athens has a long-visible reminder of her heroic age.[6]

Of the other potentially Kyklopean Mycenaean citadels of Greece the fortified city of Gla in Boeotia seems to have gone unnoticed, lost in a marsh. The most spectacular citadels, then as now, were those in the Peloponnese at Mycenae and Tiryns. Mycenae was as conspicuous as it is today; Euripides called its walls 'heaven-high Kyklopean'.[7] Its Lion Gate was a visible demonstration of a sculptural style long past [*Fig. 17*], and probably more effectively cleared of accumulated earth than it was in the days of the travellers [*Fig. 18*], down to Schliemann and his excavations there.[8] The massive construction of the undressed blocks of the walls is still impressive. The hill town of Mycenae had become the site of a village in the eighth century BC, with a small seventh-century temple then built on the ruins, and a later classical one, while its Mycenaean walls were patched in a style resembling the Mycenaean. The Kyklopes were another early Greek race, either Titans or like the Pelasgians, but best known to us through Homer's picture of the rather unrepresentative Kyklops Polyphemos, the one-eyed countryman giant who was outwitted by Odysseus, though not before some of the latter's companions had been eaten. Homer does not know Kyklopes as builders but by the fifth century they were credited with Mycenae's walls.[9] They were given various identities and skills in antiquity, including sculpture (T.228), and they fit uneasily into any hierarchy.

17. (*left*) The Lion Gate entrance to the citadel of Mycenae, with the excavators Schliemann and Doerpfeld at the left.

18. (*above*) The blocked Lion Gate at Mycenae and the Argive plain beyond, drawn by Baron Stackelberg, as they appeared in about 1830.

19. The Mycenaean citadel of Tiryns; its wall 700 m long.

20. A vaulted tunnel within the walls of Tiryns.

At Mycenae the Lion Gate, which Pausanias remarked, was the obvious access. Its walls, he says, were built by the Kyklopes like those of Tiryns (*Figs. 19,20.* T.218,249,cf.570, and 198 for an altar at Isthmos near Corinth). But there was potentially much more to observe and identify at Mycenae, home of King Agamemnon, leader of the Greeks against Troy. Outside the walls were massive round tombs of finely dressed stone built into the hillside – the *tholos* 'beehive tombs'. Some of these 'underground buildings' were identified by Pausanias as the Treasuries of Atreus, father of Agamemnon, and his children (T.218), presumably because of the riches which local tradition held to have been found in them – as there certainly must have been – and partly because such structures were perhaps unfamiliar as tombs, and the tradition said nothing about finding burials within them [*Fig. 21*]. However, the tombs of Atreus and others, including Agamemnon and, farther off, of his adulterous wife Klytaimnestra and her lover Aigisthos, were also identified. We have no clue from excavation where these were, whether among the beehive tombs or in chamber tombs or elsewhere. One can but wonder whether the story of Agamemnon's murder in his bathroom was a story inspired by the find

21. The interior of the 'Treasury of Atreus' at Mycenae, drawn by E. Dodwell in 1834, when it had been only partially explored.

of a bath-tub (*larnax*) burial, of which there are many of Mycenaean date, and that one of these in a chamber tomb marked his presumed grave. At Nauplion, not far away, there were also chambers and caves made by the Kyklopes, with built 'labyrinths' in them (T.250,570); this sounds like the record of more chamber tombs. All these became perhaps no more than tourist attractions. The round-eyed (whence their name) Kyklopes were, for Homer, idle and unruly monsters who lived in the west where Odysseus met them. Otherwise they were Titans, predecessors of the Giants, with a reputation for artisan skills which they employed for the Olympian gods, making thunderbolts and the like. It is the latter reputation that embraced their wall-building skills, not the rustic Homeric.

The study of the re-use of old tombs, of the evidence for cult practised at old tombs, of the identification of their owners, and of the cult of heroes, has been a popular topic for the last generation of scholars. Carla Antonaccio's book of 1995 gives a very full, reliable and well-balanced account of the archaeological evidence,[10] and there are many articles and books devoted to aspects of the same subject, sometimes a shade repetitive. Before I come to a selection of case histories, a general point needs to be made. Broadly speaking, where there is evidence for later cult at an old grave there is no formal identification by inscription of the recipient as a hero or anyone else, and where we have excavated evidence for an identified hero cult there is generally no grave. This seems a fair observation based on the archaeological record, but we need perhaps to look a little further. Much depends on what is meant by a hero. Where the old grave is not obviously that of a family member of within, or nearly within living memory, it would be reasonable to assume that those who offered cult projected their ancestor back into the heroic age, whether they had a name for him or not. There were, moreover, in Pausanias' day, hundreds of tombs of heroes identified throughout Greece. Where they are described many appear likely to be old tombs, not necessarily as old as the Bronze Age but, for example, archaic or later tumuli edged with stones, which are often remarked by Pausanias, and which had been so identified. Pfister lists at least four hundred hero tombs identified in antiquity.[11] For a few of them there is also mention of a cult. Cult is, after all, a serious necessity of Greek life, and not inevitably or casually to be associated with identifications of the resting places, or homes, of named figures of the heroic past, although there may have been other signals for identification, of an 'historical' (relics) or at least non-cult character. In other words, they qualify as examples of our investigation of the Greek re-creation of their past even if they do not satisfy the criteria for cult required by archaeology. This apparent denial of the archaeological record may be simply because most were identifications made by Greeks after the archaic period, a matter of no little historical interest in itself. Names are important, attaching a famous name to a place or tomb enhances it.[12] But where there is evidence of cult in an excavated cemetery we are often taxed to know whether it is inspired by and relates to a

22. The 'Tomb of Ajax' at Troy with traces of the Hadrianic remains upon it, drawn for Schliemann.

specific burial, or is more generically concerned with the condition of this interface between the worlds of the quick and the dead.

Some further general remarks about identified hero graves are in order.[13] In Anatolia burial in tumuli had been a practice for centuries, not only in the Bronze Age, and the tumuli in the Troad were very readily associated with the heroes slain in the Trojan War. Given the special interest of the area to explorers even earlier than Schliemann, we might expect some archaeological evidence for identification. This has met with limited success, but there was no shortage of travellers ready to visit, identify and write about their re-discovery of Homer.

> Of Dardan tours let Dilettanti tell.
> I leave topography to 'rapid' Gell.

...was Byron's view, who said that Sir William Gell had 'topographised and typographised King Priam's dominions in three days'. Byron took a more relaxed view on his visit: 'The Troad is a fine field for conjecture and Snipe-shooting, and a good sportsman and ingenious scholar may exercise their feet and faculties to great advantage upon the spot...The only vestiges of Troy, or her destroyers, are the barrows supposed to contain the carcases of Achilles, Antilochus, Ajax, &c.' 'Who will persuade me, when I reclined upon a mighty tomb, that it did not contain a hero? – its very magnitude proved this. Men do not labour over the ignoble and petty dead – and why should not the *dead* be *Homer's* dead?'[14]

The original tomb of Ajax was said to have been washed out in antiquity (T.157,158) and his bones reburied by the Roman emperor Hadrian (T.497). The

tumulus for the new burial does seem to have been identified [*Fig. 22*].¹⁵ The tombs of Achilles and Patroklos (T.6,499,582) had also been identified among the tumuli near Yenishehir; these are of late-sixth- or fifth-century date, so the identifications would have been Hellenistic.¹⁶ But we know what the tomb of Achilles was thought to look like at Troy in about 500 BC since it is shown in the scene of the sacrifice of Polyxena on a relief sarcophagus found near by [*Fig. 23*]. It takes the form of a tumulus topped with a sphere, which is how Lydian tumuli of the seventh-sixth century BC are finished.¹⁷ There is also a cut-away view on a fifth-century Athenian cup of an heroic tumulus, deemed to be in Crete, crowned by a pillar [*Fig. 24*].¹⁸ In it the seer Polyidos is preparing to restore to life the young prince Glaukos, son of Minos, having observed how a snake had revived its mate. Glaukos had been found

23. (*above*) Drawing of a relief sarcophagus of about 500 BC found near Çanakkale near Troy. It shows Priam's daughter Polyxena being carried to sacrifice by Neoptolemos, son of Achilles, at his father's tomb, which is shown as a Lydian tumulus.
(Çanakkale Museum)

24. The seer Polyidos kneels, observing a snake which has restored to life its mate. He will do the same for prince Glaukos, who crouches before him. They are in a tumulus, Glaukos' tomb, crowned by a tripod. On an Athenian white ground cup by the Sotades Painter, about 460 BC.
(London, British Museum D5)

25. Two satyrs try to break into a tumulus, crowned by a sphinx. On an Athenian red figure crater by Myson, about 490 BC. (Paris, Louvre CA1947)

drowned in a jar of honey – a circumstance very probably derived from observation of a child burial in a jar, which was common enough in the Bronze Age, and from the association of honey with burials which was also widespread and long-lived. It would be interesting to know why an early fifth-century Athenian vase painter showed two satyrs trying to break into a tumulus [*Fig. 25*]; we cannot be sure whether it was intended to represent an old grave or something more recent.[19]

We have noticed how Homer was aware of landmarks and heroic tombs, earlier than those of the Trojan War, which itself generated many new ones requiring identification both by classical Greeks and by more recent travellers. To start with an 'old' tomb: Batieia (T.98; 'thicket hill') was a simple descriptive name, but Homer knew that 'the gods' called it the tomb of the Amazon Myrine. It can almost certainly be located, was excavated by Mrs Schliemann [*Fig. 3*], and has been the focus for more recent study which reveals it as a Late Bronze Age burial place.[20] Achilles' tomb was later, and Homer describes it as a mound on a headland jutting on to the Hellespont. This is probably Yassi Tepe, and the mound near by (Sivri Tepe) seems to be a Hellenistic reconstruction of a far earlier tomb, prepared for many a pilgrimage [*Fig. 26*].[21] The site by the sea was fortified in the sixth century BC and known as Achilleion, which suggests that the identification had been made already. The tombs of Priam and Hektor are very late identifications, no longer readily located (if they ever were).[22] Julius Caesar was told to step carefully in the long grass lest he tread on Hektor's ghost.[23]

Farther south in Anatolia, on Mount Sipylos, the tomb of Tantalos (T.232,347), an Anatolian king, father of Pelops and Niobe and ancestor of the family that included Agamemnon, was a sixth-century Lydian stone-built tumulus [*Fig. 27*] which is now largely destroyed.[24] The throne of Pelops (T.347) was near by, perhaps identified in the rock-cutting for an altar [*Fig. 28*];[25] such rock-cut seats are a feature of early Anatolia. We shall meet more of Tantalos' family hereabouts in the next chapter [*Fig. 77*].

In Greece tumulus burials continued to be made in the Iron Age, and though they are less common they were conspicuous and their true occupants need not have been long remembered. Most of the hero tombs described in texts are mounds, sometimes remarked as being edged with stones, and such burials readily

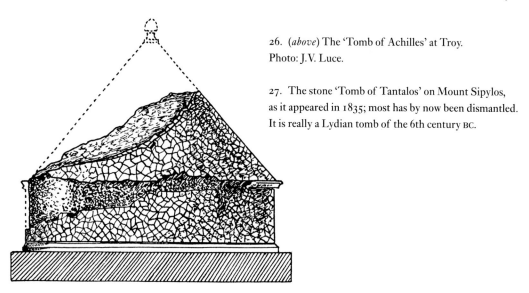

26. (*above*) The 'Tomb of Achilles' at Troy. Photo: J.V. Luce.

27. The stone 'Tomb of Tantalos' on Mount Sipylos, as it appeared in 1835; most has by now been dismantled. It is really a Lydian tomb of the 6th century BC.

28. The 'Throne of Pelops' (?) on Mount Sipylos. Probably a cutting for an altar or monument of the Lydian period.

survived from the Bronze Age or early Iron Age. Statues or stelai remarked standing at or on hero graves must have been supplied after identification and are not original (Testimonia, index); also some appropriate relics, such as an oar (T.597), and often some more elaborate architectural setting (T.360) or cladding (T.192), even a regular mausoleum or *heroon*, especially where cult was accommodated. The statues are generally 'portraits' of the hero; none has ever been found. There was often a grove or some conspicuous trees within a marked-out area (*temenos*). While several of the sites mentioned in texts can be identified, excavation has not shed light on how the graves might have been physically reshaped. The eventual resting place for Theseus' bones already had a Theseion *heroon* in Athens (T.130,282,530). Orestes' bones found a resting place at Sparta, still known in Pausanias' day (T.86,281,285,cf.414), as did those of Tisamenos (T.361).[26]

Not all the sites were standing mounds or even chamber tombs. The Greeks were awake to the possibility of the past being revealed through excavation, though they seem never to have dug purposely with this in mind. Containers (reliquaries) for remains removed from graves are comparatively rare and may often have been simply an original burial urn, or appropriate vases (hydriae) or boxes.[27] Fossils regarded as giant bones all needed new homes. Europe's bones carried in a wreath are exceptional (T.54).

The examples yet to be mentioned range from the sublime to the very ordinary. There were Mycenaean *tholos* tombs in Greece outside the Argolid. One that is often mentioned in this context is the great tomb at Orchomenos in Boeotia [*Fig. 29*]. Pausanias says it was called the Treasury of Minyas (T.470), who was an

29. The 'Treasury of Minyas' at Orchomenos – a Mycenaean *tholos* tomb. A side chamber (left) has an elaborately carved ceiling. The base of a Hellenistic/Roman monument is seen at the centre of the floor.

ancestral Boeotian hero-king, not much associated with myth. The naming of the monument was on the analogy of the Treasuries at Mycenae, so identified for the same reason – the rich burial goods that had been robbed from them and their secure structure. He goes on to mention the tombs of Minyas and of the eighth-century poet Hesiod, but, as at Mycenae, the ex-tomb-Treasuries are to be distinguished from the identified heroic tombs, wherever they may have been. The Orchomenos *tholos* tomb had been excavated by Schliemann. I think the following sketch of its history answers the physical and other evidence. There may be record of the discovery of the tomb in 'Aristotle's' story of the dog who chased a fox into a hole in the ground, where it began to bark in such a resonant way that the folk of Orchomenos dug into it, and reported the find to the authorities (T.36). This is a time-honoured way of discovering caves to the present day, and this one must have been the great *tholos* tomb. The bald reference might suggest that it had not yet been 'identified' in any way with a worthy of the past. Then it became known as the Treasury of Minyas. Its roof was intact.

Orchomenos had been razed by Thebes in 364 BC, but was re-founded under Alexander and became the seat of the new Boeotian League, in place of Thebes. The discovery of the *tholos* may well have been in the fourth century. At the centre of the floor of the vault the remains of a marble monument have been found. This is of Hellenistic date and might well have supported statues of the Macedonian royal family. It is not clear, however, whether this was its original position, or had been moved in during the early Roman period, possibly for imperial cult, since there are signs of it being adjusted at that date. There were associated fragments of statuary, now lost, and a dedication to Zeus Teleios and Hera Teleia found at the door. It is an odd place for any such monument. The simplest explanation is that soon after its discovery the *tholos* was identified as regal and thought a worthy home for yet another tribute to the Macedonians, but was later reworked for other purposes.[28] At an unknown date its roof fell in, leaving a mass of ash, stone and debris from the mainly prehistoric levels which the tomb had cut through, other superincumbent ancient levels, plus remains of any later use of the ruins above the buried floor. So there is no identification of a hero grave here, but of the Treasury of an heroic-age king, re-used as a site for a memorial to king-heroes (if not emperor-deities), and a place numinous enough to justify real divine worship or at least offerings.

Another Mycenaean tholos tomb, at Menidi just north of Athens, has a more typical record repeated, usually in less revealing ways, all over Greece at simpler tombs.[29] It had its *dromos* partly cleared, but, it seems, only to above the level of the top of the original door to the tomb chamber, so that what was left was a long masonry-lined trench in which were placed votive offerings which range from the late eighth century to the early fifth, including pottery of some quality [*Fig. 30*]. There is nothing to indicate the assumed identity of the recipient of the cult, but I cannot imagine that he or she was altogether anonymous, although 'the Hero', like the Unknown Soldier, is a figure acknowledged in many parts of Greece; for example, on a pot inscription found at the old Grave Circle in Mycenae's citadel [*Fig. 31*].[30]

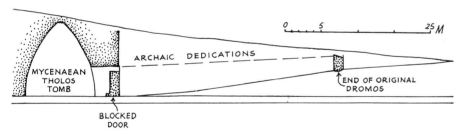

30. The Mycenaean *tholos* tomb at Menidi, north of Athens, showing how the *dromos* approach had been partly cleared and then used for offerings in the archaic period.

31. Classical pottery fragment from over the Mycenaean Grave Circle A at Mycenae. Inscribed (graffito) 'I am for the hero'. (Athens, National Museum)

All this raises a general point, already touched on. Cemeteries are often located in areas which had long been so used, with or without interruption, and the old graves were disturbed. Many a grave epitaph curses those who might move the bones of the dead, but the average Greek, then and now, seems to have taken little notice.[31] The dead were not generally regarded as being dangerous for longer than a short while after burial. At best, earlier interments are put to one side, which was no more than the usual practice for the earlier and remembered burials of a single family or group when space was required for new burials. Amends might be made in the form of offerings, as in the fifth-century disturbance of a Mycenaean burial in the Agora at Athens, where seven small oil vases were offered.[32] Occasionally an old grave is simply re-used, especially if it is of some substance. This has been suspected for more than one *tholos* tomb at Knossos, found to contain burials of the ninth century on, but of masonry that no ninth-century Cretan could have managed. The Tekke *tholos* is the prime example.[33] Publishing its contents I drew attention to a late-ninth-century clay model found at Arkhanes near by, which might easily be interpreted as the discovery of a *tholos* tomb, with the men and their dog (remember the dog at Orchomenos) on the roof, looking in at a chamber occupied by a goddess [*Fig. 32*]. It resembles Cretan 'hut-urns' of earlier years but has been given a narrative dimension by the figures on the roof.[34] There is a possibility that many of the chamber tombs at Knossos are likewise Bronze Age tombs re-used, though this is contested. The evidence is equivocal, and many may be just copies of the Minoan forms, though there was no hesitation about re-using Minoan clay coffins (*larnakes*) removed intact from the old tombs.[35]

Respect for old graves was probably a matter of simple piety and does not imply any heroic or even family identification. If, however, the location and myth associations are strong, there must have been a temptation to make something of them, and this will explain many of those mentioned by Pausanias. These may be quite late identifications, prompted by local curiosity and pride, not religion. The discovery of old tombs would have been an obvious occasion or prompt, but we can see that for many there were other features, natural or man-made, which could have encouraged identification, with or without cult, apart from a growing desire to make interesting local connections. The practice probably accelerated in later years, not without some association with a tourist trade. The modern parallel is the renewed use of ancient names for modern towns in Greece, often perplexingly rendered in demotic spelling and transliteration. It was a trait parallel to that of finding or creating relics, and mainly later than the 'true' hero cults, many of which go back to the eighth century, and which may have had additional civic motivation, to establish rights of possession, boundaries, corporate identity and the like. This is an area much explored in recent scholarship, very speculative, sometimes plausible, and not for further discussion here beyond a few general remarks.[36]

The eighth century (earlier in Crete) saw the beginning of an interest in old tombs and was also the period in which we can begin to perceive more clearly the organization of a Greek city state and its territory. That the two may be related is

32. Clay model from Archanes near Knossos. The door has been removed to show a seated goddess with arms raised within. On the roof, looking into the 'chimney' orifice, two surprised men, with their dog. It may show the discovery of a Bronze Age *tholos* tomb. About 800 BC, height 22 cm. (Heraklion Museum SG 376)

plausible, but we should also remember that this is also a period of expanding population and probably more settled living and farming conditions, a circumstance which would naturally give rise to wider exploration and exploitation of land, in turn leading to the exposure of more old tombs. Attention to the tombs continued through to the Roman period, and there were many opportunities for the interpretation of new discoveries, as at Orchomenos. Whether, in the post-classical period, this meant a new approach to the phenomenon is another matter.[37] In the Hellenistic world there was less call for justifying claims on land or power by appeal to ancestors, than there might have been in the eighth century; on the other hand, in a period when rulers were assimilated to heroes and gods, the identification of heroic ancestry might seem yet more desirable. This is at any rate a period in which Greek thought was taking a far more serious view of both history and of its relationship to 'myth', though usually to the detriment of the latter in terms of positive belief. As soon as the Romans, at first the soldiers, took note of the Greek homeland, there developed a tourist industry which must have done much to encourage the discovery or forgery of worthwhile sights and of anything which reflected on the heroic and classical past which Romans so admired.[38]

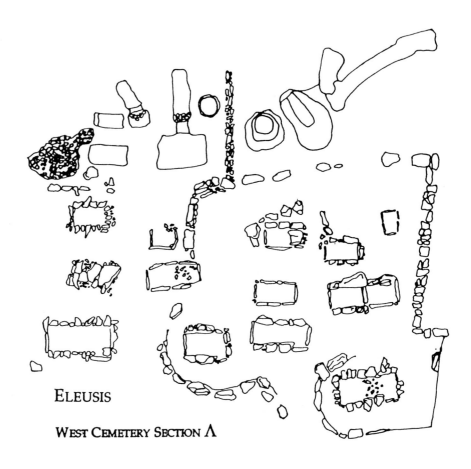

ELEUSIS

WEST CEMETERY SECTION Λ

33. A Bronze Age cemetery at Eleusis where at least seven graves have been enclosed in an eighth-century wall.

We return to finds on the ground, and in the following paragraphs much further reference will be made to Antonaccio's *Ancestors*, though I demur here and there, and also add to the arguments. She gives a very full account of the many instances of attention to, and possible cult at, Bronze Age tombs. I concentrate only on those for which some positive identification can be proved, either by inscription or references in literature. We simply do not know how many remained anonymous in the minds of those who lived near to or even tended them.

In some cemeteries groups of graves were given enclosures in much later periods. They do not differ much from enclosures or plots created for immediate family purposes, even in Athens' classical cemeteries. There was an eighth-century enclosure wall for some prehistoric graves at Eleusis [*Fig. 33*];[39] and at Eleusis Pausanias saw the graves of the heroes who marched against Thebes and whose bodies were rescued for proper burial by the Athenians (T.169). It is easy, perhaps too easy, to think that this enclosure was what he saw. The story was a patent attempt by Athens to abrogate heroic myth from other parts of Greece to Attica,

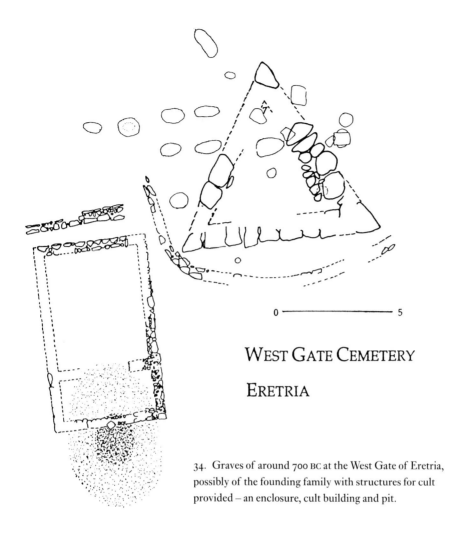

WEST GATE CEMETERY

ERETRIA

34. Graves of around 700 BC at the West Gate of Eretria, possibly of the founding family with structures for cult provided – an enclosure, cult building and pit.

a common practice of the classical period, hardly of the eighth century BC. The original enclosure may have been deemed familial, as it were heroic-ancestral, whatever more specific and grander identification might later have been offered in the interests of Attic prestige. It was possible for others to find burial places elsewhere for the heroes of the Thebes expedition.

A comparable and more easily intelligible circumstance is that of the enclosure of early graves within the West Gate at Eretria [*Fig. 34*],[40] plausibly identified, now as they probably were then, as the graves of founders of the city, who were often said to have been buried at gates or in the marketplaces of the cities they founded. This does not mean that they actually were the graves of a founding family, although at Eretria the assumed identification, made within a century, may well have been correct, since the date is right for a first family in the early (though perhaps not quite earliest) years of the new city, and cult is involved. Elsewhere the tombs and cults of historical, mythical or presumed founders were important in all Greek colonial areas; only the historical might have had some authenticity.[41]

35. A prehistoric tomb on Delos, enclosed in a curved wall (9 m across) with a platform before it. It was regarded as the depository (*theke*) of the Hyperborean Maidens (Opis and Arge) and cult was offered there.

On Delos, the tombs of the Hyperborean Maidens, visitors from the distant north, were identified beside an olive tree in the sanctuary of Artemis, as early as Herodotus; also a depository (*theke*) set behind the sanctuary, presumably for the various offerings they brought with them (T.89). A stone enclosure, Hellenistic or earlier, stands in the right place, and contained part of the *dromos* and tomb chamber of a Bronze Age burial, while a possible place for the tomb marker has also been identified [*Fig. 35*]. The old tomb was unquestionably the one identified as the Hyperboreans' *theke*. The island had been 'purified' of tombs already once before Herodotus' day, but probably only from the known and still 'active' cemeteries, without thorough exploration for any earlier graves. At any rate, the tomb was clearly not identified as such, and so became a singularly sacred relic of Delos' earliest history, since the maidens were deemed to have started their visits from the north at the time of the birth of Apollo and Artemis.[42]

Amazon graves are a rather special case, none of them identifiable on the ground. Homer's gods knew one in the Troad, near their home (T.98), and there was a Samian bloodbath of Amazons killed by Dionysos (T.528). In the latter case they had been chased from Ephesus, which is rich in Amazon lore, but Dionysos has nothing really to do with Amazons, and since the same story mentions his elephants this seems just an extension of his Indian adventures. (We saw what became of the elephants in Chapter Two.) Amazons took part at Troy on the Trojan side, had already been engaged in the east by Herakles, and were generally busy also in western Asia Minor, as at Ephesus. Their invasion of Greece itself, specifically of Attica, was an invention of the early fifth century, echoing the Persian invasion of Attica, and involving the Athenian hero Theseus. This gave them graves in Athens (T.123,536), but it is less easy to explain their tombs in Boeotia (Chaironeia: T.536), Megara (T.174) and in Thessaly (T.536). The Boeotian may be a result of the suggestive river name there – Thermodon – which also occurred in Amazonland; in Thessaly they may have been embraced in the general concept of the north-eastern foreigner, like the Thracians, abetted by the way they could be shown in art.[43] It could be too that tales of them, and their deaths, became associated with recollection of the Persian invasions through northern Greece of 480 and 479 BC, on the analogy of the Athenian Amazonian version of the Persian descent on Marathon in 490 BC. The tomb at Megara was said to be in the shape of a pelta, the crescent shield carried by Amazons and other light infantry. More probably an oddly shaped mound gave rise to the association with an Amazon. In Athens details of the battle with them beside the Acropolis could be pointed out on the ground as well as the place where Theseus made a treaty with them (T.536), while from the scene on the shield made for the statue of Athena which stood in the Parthenon it can be seen that they were thought to have assaulted the Acropolis itself, since they are shown attempting to scale its walls.[44]

I have remarked that old tombs need not have been the only signal for later Greeks to look for heroes to identify or worship, but there had to be something, as well as some religious or civic imperative for encouragement of cult. Hero cults are not in themselves part of the present study, but one or two are worth consideration for their relationship to other cases mentioned.

The excavated shrine of Agamemnon at Mycenae was not at any tomb, but a kilometre away from the citadel and far from the cemetery where heroic Treasuries and graves were identified in Pausanias' day. There may have been a good reason for this, as we shall see in a moment. And at Sparta, the shrine of Menelaos and Helen was built on an old Mycenaean site with palatial remains (Therapne) but not beside or at a grave, although they were later deemed to have been buried there (T.307). The votive offerings begin in the eighth century BC.[45]

The distance of the hero cult of Agamemnon from the cemeteries and citadel of Mycenae has puzzled many, but the explanation may again lie in ancient assessment of a Bronze Age structure, in this case the complex of waterworks and a bridge over the stream Chaos which lay beside it. The sanctuary structures are scrappily preserved and go with offerings naming Agamemnon, of the fourth century and later. But dedications go back to the eighth century, the likely period for both the establishment of the sanctuary and its association with the king. This has been disputed by some, but the votives are in fact compatible, and any change of identity for the recipient is highly improbable.[46] Agamemnon acquired a reputation for 'finding cisterns' (implying some artificial hydraulics) in Greece (T.57), and the unusual water-controlling structures of Bronze Age date by the stream at Mycenae may have been enough to require or suggest the heroic association.[47]

Menelaos' pilot, Phrontis, was drowned offshore at Sounion and buried there. Votives in pits at Sounion have been associated with a cult for him, but can only be accepted with hesitation; and the identification of any of the big archaic kouroi there as Phrontis with even greater reluctance. There are no tombs in the area. The votives are not, however, obviously for the major deities of Sounion, Athena and Poseidon, and among them is a fine votive plaque with a warship, of about 700 BC, on which the steersman is more prominent than the marines [*Fig. 36*].[48]

36. Votive clay plaque found at Sounion showing a warship with marines and a steersman. The corner hole was for hanging it on a sanctuary wall or tree. By the Analatos Painter, about 700 BC. Width 16 cm. (Athens, National Museum 14935)

The tumulus of the tomb of Amphion and Zethos at Thebes was conspicuous, since there were stories about sacred earth being robbed from it (T.439). An Early Helladic tumulus has been associated with the story but there are no signs of early cult attention there.[49]

Poor Pelops' remains, including his mouldering ivory shoulder-blade, replacing the part inadvertently consumed by Demeter and taken to Troy, are variously reported (T.346,358). Pindar (T.503) alludes to his much-visited tomb at Olympia, and there must have been something there to attract attention in his day. Excavation has failed to reveal any obvious Bronze Age tumulus or structure to associate with it, although there is much prehistory in Olympian soil and this has been a happy hunting ground for those bent on proving some sort of cult continuity in the sanctuary.[50]

Hyakinthos at Amyklai had both a good pre-Greek name and a busy Bronze Age site for his sanctuary. There may even have been some continuity of occupation there since the Bronze Age, but this does not necessarily imply continuity of cult or of identity.[51] A cult of Alexandra near by may have been prompted by an alleged tomb of Agamemnon there (T.305). It starts in the eighth century and may have been a matter of the identification of Alexandra with Kassandra, who died with Agamemnon, and at Amyklai in this version.[52] A problem is that the new name for Kassandra may not be pre-Hellenistic (as used by the poet Lykophron), and we would have to postulate a much earlier Spartan Alexandra, later assimilated to the Trojan woman, which seems none too easy. But this was a busy area for identifications with figures of the Trojan War, competing with, and often duplicating, what was identified in the Argolid, and reflecting Spartan bids for the attention of other Greeks in the archaic period.[53]

Before we leave graves the phenomenon of a cenotaph may be noted. They were to be found in historic Greece, for folk lost at sea or far from home,[54] and the idea was projected into the heroic past. Menelaos made a cenotaph for Agamemnon in Egypt – a stone cairn – according to Homer.[55] There was one in Argos for the Unknown Soldiers who fell at Troy or on their way home (T.227); for Myrtilos made by Pelops, who had caused his death (T.353); even for Achilles at Elis, and for Teiresias (T.442) near Thebes, his real grave being where he died (T.466).

The most engaging example of an Homeric site of story and cult is the Cave of the Nymphs in Ithaca to which Odysscus was returned by the Phaeacian ships. It was, Homer says, where he used to worship the Nymphs, and where he now stored the thirteen bronze tripods and other treasure given him by the Phaeacians. Schliemann followed Homer's account of the approach to the island, and found a cave at the right place, near Aetos, even with rock formations that might recall Homer's 'bowls of stone and pitchers of stone' and 'long looms of stone' – stalactites; indeed, even a tiny second entrance, a 'pathway for the immortals'.[56] Others have accepted this identification and more recently John Luce, who has a good eye for Homeric geography as we have seen at Troy, reaffirmed the identification, based on Homer's description of the two headlands and harbour; it is even said that appropriate Nymph dedications have been found there [*Fig. 37*].[57]

37. The entrance to Marmarospilia Cave on Ithaca, probably the Cave of the Nymphs indicated by Homer. Photo: J.V. Luce.

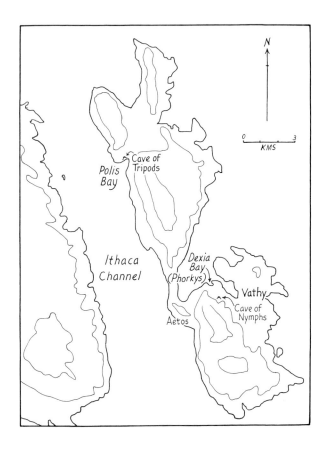

38. Map of Ithaca showing the two Homeric caves. After J.V. Luce.

39. The entrance to the cave at Polis on Ithaca: the Cave of the Tripods [*Fig. 41*], taken in antiquity for those left there by Odysseus.

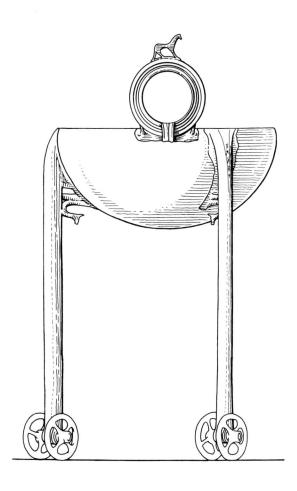

40. Restoration of the clay mask of a woman, dedicated at the Cave of the Tripods on Ithaca. The fragment with her left shoulder and hair locks is inscribed 'a votive for Odysseus', and with what may be part of the name of the donor. Hellenistic. W. of fragment 7 cm. (Ithaca Museum)

41. Drawing of restored bronze tripod from the Cave of the Tripods on Ithaca. H. about 1.20 m.

So far all seems well, and we have Odysseus' Cave of the Nymphs. Schliemann also visited the Polis area in the north west of the island, where there is the main concentration of Mycenaean finds [*Fig. 38*]. He inspected the contents of a recently excavated tomb by the sea shore. It had been covered by an archaic inscription naming Hera and Athena. He also observed that it was by a cave whose collapse, perhaps through earthquake, had brought about the destruction of the tomb.[58] He did not know what was in the cave. Since then it has been excavated, at the water's edge, with its floor partly submerged [*Fig. 39*]. It seems to have been long occupied, with material from the Early Bronze Age on, and much Mycenaean. (The inscription from the grave almost certainly has nothing to do with the cave.) From the excavation there is Hellenistic pottery inscribed with dedications to the Nymphs, and a fragmentary Hellenistic clay mask of a woman inscribed for Odysseus [*Fig. 40*]. From the eighth century there were offerings there of bronze tripod cauldrons, at least thirteen, typical of the period [*Fig. 41*].[59] These must have been more than enough for the locals to make their own identification, and for Hellenistic worshippers to make offerings to the Nymphs and one naming Odysseus. The association of cave, tripods and the naming of Nymphs and Odysseus seems too good not to be true, but we already have the true Cave of the Nymphs, from Homer's own evidence for its location. Tripods are possibly rather grand for eighth-century offerings to Nymphs; I suppose it is not altogether impossible that they had been moved into the cave from some older sanctuary at a late date to enhance the association, but the excavator says there were 'bits of perhaps one hundred Geometric vases' there, so the cave was a busy place in the eighth century.[60] Remember that Odysseus' tripods were not offerings but treasure which he intended to take to his palace, not leave behind.

The complex situation seems to have been ignored by much recent scholarship which is happy to accept the Polis cave as Homer's. One scholar (Irad Malkin) thinks that Odysseus' cult there went back to the ninth or eighth century, with the tripods which echo the story of his arrival,[61] but this would mean that the traditional real cave near Aetos was being ignored. It is perhaps unlikely that a true Odysseus cult could have developed there as early as the eighth century; the cave was simply a staging point in his story, not his home or tomb.

It could be that Homer's indication of the location of the cave derived from tradition, and was never visited by him, but that the Tripods Cave was known to him and provided the colour for his story.[62] There can be no good reason for thinking that Homer's account of the tripods preceded the real dedications in the cave; rather, the latter prompted the details of the story. What is also odd is that Homer's cave seems to have been forgotten or lost by the late first century BC, if we are to believe Strabo who says that the grotto of the Nymphs in Ithaca was no longer known. He assumed it had been lost through 'changes' or through ignorance or lies, but that the cave had once existed, since he trusted Homer as a geographer.[63] There is no way of knowing which real cave had been so identified, but even if the Polis cave is not the one in the tradition which Homer followed in describing Odysseus' home-coming, it was certainly taken for the cave of his story in later times.

At this point, a very special case, not of an old tomb re-used but of a new and apparently heroic burial with unusual furniture, and of a very early date, deserves a note since it might reflect on the antiquity of the practices we are studying. It is the so-called *heroon* at Lefkandi in Euboea. The site had been almost continuously occupied since the Early Bronze Age. There were destructions, abandonment, but none of long duration or obviously involving any radically new population. There is at least the possibility here of a continuous tradition surviving from the Late Bronze 'age of heroes' into the early Iron Age. In the tenth century a nearly fifty-metre long apsidal building was erected, palatial in scale, although whether it was ever lived in is unknown [*Fig. 42*]. Within it were found two shafts, one with the burial of four horses, the other with an inhumation of a woman and a cremation urn for a man [*Fig. 43*] – royalty, we must judge, and their palatial tomb was soon after filled with earth and stones to make a long mound. This is of a period in which the realities of the Late Bronze Age and some aspects of its life were not as distant as they were in Homer's day, yet already we may assume the myth-history

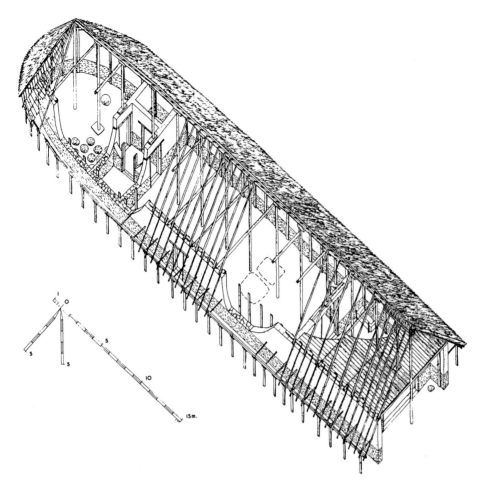

42. Reconstruction by J.J. Coulton of the long building (*heroon*) at Lefkandi in Euboea, 10th century BC. The two burial pits are the dotted rectangles at the centre floor. After the burials the whole building was filled with earth and stones and left as a mound.

which was inspired by that period had been formed in oral, recited traditions, which Homer and others would later relay in writing. Is there anything in these burials which suggests that already some conscious attempt to conjure a heroic past was being made on the part of the Euboeans? The building and its use remain unique for Greece of this period, and for long afterwards, which says something. There is no obvious sign of cult unless the building itself and its treatment should be so understood. The site had already been receiving objects from the Levant and it is clear that the Euboean islanders were the leading mariners of Early Iron Age Greece, especially in their exploration of the eastern shores of the Mediterranean, notably Syria. Their activity was soon to work a revolution in Greek fortunes.

The principal furniture of the Lefkandi royal graves was almost exclusively foreign, and much of it demonstrably far older than the burial. The bronze burial

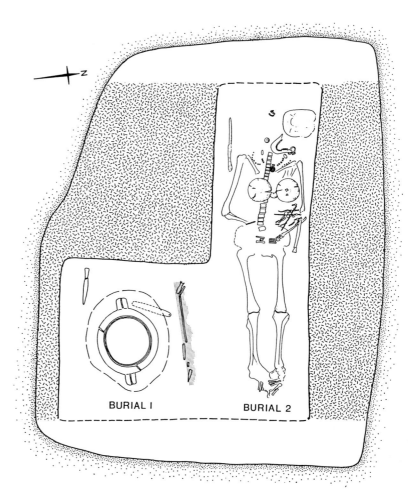

43. The burial pit in the Lefkandi *heroon*.

urn was Late Bronze Age Cypriot [*Fig. 44*], and the lady's jewellery was Mesopotamian of perhaps even a thousand years before [*Fig. 45*].[64] Elsewhere in the Lefkandi cemetery are various objects from Syria, Phoenicia and Egypt, most like the contemporary exotica which we would expect seafarers to bring home. If the much older objects in the *heroon* were heirlooms they could hardly have been in the same family ever since their manufacture or import to Greece, but the arrival from the east of what were already antiques, though not unparalleled,[65] is surprising. Could they, however acquired, have been chosen for their apparent antiquity and links with a remote and indeed foreign past, suiting the dignity of a royalty already deemed to be touched with divinity? Could the buried king, and perhaps his queen, themselves have been immigrants from Cyprus or even farther east, fêted, even heroized, folk who helped forge Euboea's new interest in the east? The horse burial finds its only parallels in Cyprus in the early Iron Age. There had been a tradition in Greece of rulers arriving from the east or Egypt – Danaos,

44. (*above and below*) The burial of a man in the Lefkandi *heroon*. The bronze urn for the ashes has a decorated rim and handles; it had collapsed into itself. Original width of urn 59 cm. (Eretria Museum)

45. The burial of a woman in the Lefkandi *heroon*, dressed with gold jewellery and breast-pieces.

Pelops, Kadmos, Lelex – several of them linked with Euboea.[66] The presence of immigrant or foreign royalty is a long recurrent historical phenomenon; they are generally absorbed into the culture they temporarily control. There are no easy answers, and even more questions than I have asked here.[67]

It was generally Bronze Age graves that attracted cult attention; they were conspicuously different from contemporary burials, for their offerings, sometimes for their construction, and for the absence of the common later practice of cremation.[68] We usually have no means of knowing whether a specific identification was made, where this was more than a matter of making pious amends for disturbing a grave. It is easy, and may often be right, to assume that the old grave was taken to be that of a member of the family of those who owned or farmed the land in later years. If so, this might seem to establish a claim to possession, and it is clear the Greeks were always ready to use their alleged mythical past to bolster claims for status in later times: the hero-graves of one's ancestors might seem as good as title deeds, but cemeteries tend not to be on the best farmland. There is a rare phenomenon of extensive continuity or re-use of Bronze Age graves in Messenia, in years when a people direly oppressed by their Spartan neighbours might have been seeking the reassurance of their more glorious past.[69] This at least reminds us of how physically close the past might have seemed in some parts of Greece.

There has been a tendency in modern scholarship to divorce ancestor worship from hero worship, but this may obscure other truths.[70] In terms of civic identity in the development of the Greek city state the local hero may be no less important than the family, but Greek exploitation of their past was as much a personal as a state concern. For all the collapse of the heroic age at the will of the gods, it was among heroes that ancestors were readily sought, and therefore found. Certainly, accurate knowledge of recent family is unlikely to go back more than about three generations, enough to ensure that, where there was something like a family burial plot, due acknowledgement might be made for immediate predecessors. But that would not have stopped families from claiming, on no grounds at all or at best on a mere similarity in name or from convenience, descent from the age of heroes. A mid-fifth-century Chian could trace his family back fourteen generations, to around 900 BC, and name them plausibly [*Fig. 46*] starting with one Kyprios, who sounds like an immigrant.[71] The Spartan king-lists started with Herakles, son of Zeus.[72]

As so often in understanding antiquity, it is more important to discover what was then believed true of the past, or even of the recent present, than to hope to uncover the generally unattainable truth. Men are motivated by faith and imagination more readily than historical 'facts' of the type we think we can glean from texts and the ground. Our present study has more to do with perception of the past shared, in different ways, by much of mankind, than with particular civic

46. Gravestone of Heropythos of Chios, counting back fourteen generations. About 475–450 BC. (Chios Museum 800)

or cult contrivances. For our purposes it is enough to observe that old graves were a strong stimulus for Greeks of all periods to create associations with their myth-historical past. Where there was no obvious antiquarian value to attach to an older monument a very casual attitude seems to have been normal. Even the heroic Treasuries of Mycenae, lacking the protection of cult, could be abused by later graves or the intrusion of later building, such as the theatre across the entrance of what we call the Tomb of Klytaimnestra.

Finally, we return to houses and other structures, having noted already the House of Erechtheus on Athens' Acropolis, of which there were perhaps no alleged remains to point out. Greek houses generally had stone walls, or brick over stone.

Some had flat, earth roofs, others of thatch, and the better-class were roofed with large clay tiles. They were relatively substantial, and the stone rather than timber element (except in the roof) guaranteed a long life, but also allowed for collapsed houses to serve readily as quarries for new ones. Pausanias records many houses attributed to heroes, which we may assume to be substantial but abandoned properties, mainly of the historic rather than of the prehistoric period (as were the tombs).[73] Interestingly, he mentions one that was still lived in, that of Menelaos at Sparta (T.298), the proprietor no doubt making the most of the reputation of his home: something similar to the status attached to owning a bed that Queen Elizabeth slept in. We do not know who 'owned' other hero houses – private persons or the state. The house of Nestor at Pylos (T.338) had in it a picture of the hero, which indicates some enterprise in authentication for the tourist market. Apart from the houses there are remains of stadia where heroes exercised (T.271, the Dioskouroi), the wedding chambers of heroines (T.430,426,600: Alkmene, Harmonia and Semele, Medea), Bellerophon's camp (T.587), Danae's prison (T.241), Teiresias' observatory for watching bird omens (T.432), Triptolemos' threshing floor (T.166), and the house where Amphiaraos prophesied (T.212).[74] King Minos' Labyrinth, built for him by Daidalos, may have been inspired by no more than the labyrinthine ruins of the Minoan palace at Knossos; the name was applied also by the Greeks to a royal tomb in Egypt.[75] Arthur Evans thought that the foundations of the House of Rhea pointed out at Knossos (T.74) might have been the Greek temple that stood on the ruins of the Minoan Palace but which was out of use by Diodorus' day.[76] Away from Greece, Iolaos was regarded as a notable builder in Sardinia, where he accompanied Herakles, and the early Nuraghic *tholoi* [*Fig. 4*] were attributed to him (T.37). Herakles' fountain (T.265), seen near the 'House of Hippolytos', is figured on Roman period coins of Troizen [*Fig. 47*], but

47. Bronze coin of Troizen, possibly showing the fountain of Herakles with a seated lion upon it, pouring water into a basin. Minted in the reign of Septimius Severus, around AD 200.

48. 'Daskalopetra', the 'teacher's stone' in Chios where Homer was thought to have taught. A flattened area on a rock overlooking the sea, north of Chios town, is edged by the footing for a wall, while at the centre the block ('seat') is a much worn rock-cut model temple of Kybele who appears seated in its door.

it was perhaps the statue of a lion upon it that prompted the identification.[77] In Attica and Boeotia collapsed buildings could readily be identified as shrines destroyed by the Persian invasions of the fifth century BC (T.122,492); they might have been anything. In Chios the identification of the School of Homer (Daskalopetra – the 'teacher's stone') in an archaic rock-cut naiskos of Kybele, set on a prominent rock overlooking the sea north of the main town, is not demonstrably earlier than mediaeval [*Fig. 48*].[78] One might expect more Homeric relics, material or topographical, to have been reported and still identified in the island which most persistently claimed to be his birthplace.

In sanctuaries it is more difficult to associate a name with any special heroic or divine quality attributed to old buildings where some succession, even interrupted (as at the so-called Sacred House at Eleusis), is perceived.[79] Sanctuaries were sometimes founded, in the eighth century (hardly any earlier), on the site of a Bronze Age settlement, which may or may not have contained a once conspicuous cult place. As likely as not it was the obviously heroic antiquity of the site, ruined structures and exotic finds, that attracted attention, rather than any continuity of cult in the same place.[80] The phenomenon is apparent at, for instance, Samos for the Heraion, on Delos for the Temple of Artemis, and at Therapne, Amyklai, Knossos, Mycenae and Pylos.[81] But when, on Delos, the foundations are found to contain Bronze Age material, including fragments of worked ivory, it would be wrong to assume that early objects were deliberately saved, since in this case the pieces are clearly disregarded debris from the earlier occupation in the area.[82] Not that old objects were not sometimes valued *per se*, as we shall see. And it may even be that a site could be re-allocated in the interests of demonstrating an heroic presence. The story of Herakles immolating himself on a pyre seems no earlier than the fifth century. A pyre on Mount Oita, visited since the eighth century BC and probably an open-air ash altar for Zeus, was identified as the funeral pyre of his son Herakles from the fifth century on and attracted appropriate offerings to the hero.[83]

Gods, as opposed to heroes, do not figure much in our narrative. Heroic and familial cults help to emphasize the differences between cities and their relative importance; Olympian cults emphasize common origins and Greekness. Gods have to deal with the greatest threats to mankind and to his moral welfare; heroes are more everyday in their interests. Only Herakles encompassed all the needs of men and gods.

CHAPTER FOUR

Realia et Naturalia

WE LOOK HERE AT the real and reported objects which furnished the Greeks' view of their remote past, the Greek use of natural features, animal and mineral, to the same end, and what constraints there were, geographical and in terms of myth personnel, to this activity.

REALIA

Physical relics of the famous, their swords, pens, guitars, clothes, hold a fascination which goes beyond the simple matter of association or rarity. They evoke periods and places more vividly than words or pictures can, since they were first-hand witnesses. They may also therefore acquire a reputation for a measure of either power or sanctity. They may effect cures or themselves be worshipped as symbols of their owners. Nowadays they can be very expensive. Where the association is with an historical figure they can prove to be the rallying point for a revolution or for worship, and the temptation to counterfeit or multiply them has always been strong. Think of the many fragments of the True Cross, or the distributed body-parts and ashes of the Buddha. When, as in Greece, the relics related to the myth-historical as well as the historical past, there was far more scope within which the imagination could work. All such relics of myth-history must in their way be forgeries, although many may, almost fortuitously, be artefacts of the period to which the lives and deeds of heroes were attributed. For the monsters of the past the fossil record of Greece provided a rich source, though not the only one, as we have seen. For the humanoid there were the many artefacts uncovered by chance in later periods, some even perhaps surviving above ground, and there was the possibility of identifying as heroic any more recent object; or of forging one, which we should not perhaps condemn as being any less honest than the common adjustment by Greek authors and artists of the narratives of their myth-history. Modern rules of evidence do not apply.

The Greeks of the archaic and classical periods had some knowledge of life in their heroic age, the Late Bronze Age. They knew, for instance, that weapons were generally of bronze, even if they deduced this only from Homer's descriptions

(T.283). Otherwise their expectations of heroic equipment did not lead them to look for anything substantially unfamiliar or different from what was in current use. They knew from Homer of boars'-tusk helmets worn at Troy, a true record of Bronze Age armour, but which they did not counterfeit although they might have recognized them in casual finds from Bronze Age sites and graves, or in pictures. And there were Homeric descriptions of exceptional objects like the Cup of Nestor, which some tried to re-create (T.51). The world with which Homer was immediately familiar was that of early archaic Greece, but oral traditions had embedded in his poems descriptions of objects of types no longer being made, and of objects perhaps as baffling to Homer as they were to later Greeks, and often to us. We shall see that in their visual arts also the Greeks made no effort to create the utterly exotic with which to equip their age of heroes (Chapter Six).

The various classes of relics identified can be gathered from the Index of Subjects in the Testimonia assembled at the end of this book. These will form a major source for what is discussed in this chapter because we can be sure that we are dealing with objects to which an identifiable antiquity was attributed, even though we cannot inspect them. We have also, however, to consider a selection of objects from excavation which are clearly out of context and period: not new objects associated with old graves, which might suggest cult and have been considered in Chapter Three, but old objects in later graves, sanctuaries or even houses. In these cases we cannot prove that they are more than heirlooms, though this is in itself of some interest if it suggests some family tradition attached to them; most were probably acquired through accidental discovery or purchase, without any recognition of their antiquity, and therefore irrelevant to the present enquiry. For some objects, however, on the analogy of the stories told about similar ones which were heroically identified, we may reasonably suspect that they were treasured for their associations with an heroic past. Here I also discuss the possible appearance of some of the relics known from texts, and the explanations for objects found, concentrating on the main classes and the more conspicuous examples.

Armament
The Greeks knew that old arms were of bronze although, of course, not all later arms were exclusively of iron (T.283), and Thucydides thought he was able to identify ancient Carian arms in Delian graves (T.598). In Homer corselets are described in modern terms and there is no inkling of knowledge of the strange, if rare, Bronze Age bronze armour, which was so unfamiliar even to archaeologists when first found that a shoulder-piece was identified as a helmet.[1] The old shields were of wood, hide and wicker, and so had not survived, although comparable ones were still in use in Greece in the eighth century until, towards the end, they were replaced by the round hoplite shields which had metal grips and sometimes metal facings. The classical Greek had no idea about the real appearance of the body-covering tower-shields in Homer, which we can now relate to the shields represented in Bronze Age art [*Fig. 139*]. Most shields identified as heroic in later

days were probably archaic ones, which were more elaborately decorated, often with metal blazons. Aristomenes' shield at Lebadeia is described as having a blazon of a spread eagle, a common archaic device, but his status as heroic or historic is debatable (T.327). The two heroic shields dedicated by Herakles at Lindos were covered, one with leather, one with bronze (T.605(5)). Euphorbos' shield at Didyma had an ivory facing (T.76), a feature we recognize only from the royal tomb at Vergina of the fourth century BC, and later. We return to these subjects in Chapter Six where the imaging of heroes and their equipment is considered in more detail.

The slim rapiers of the Bronze Age would have been unfamiliar objects, but there were many to be found in old tombs. Pelops' sword at Olympia had a gold hilt (T.351) and might have been Mycenaean. In Euripides his spear hung in the women's quarters of the palace at Mycenae![2] There were other exotic bronzes which could be taken for weapons, notably axe heads of unfamiliar shapes, including the double axe which had special properties in the Minoan and Mycenaean worlds, not shared by the iron double axe, a wood-cutter's tool, of later days. A number of Bronze Age axes, weapons and tools has been recovered from the archaic period, when they were recognized as holy and worthy of dedication, to judge from the inscriptions upon them [*Figs. 49,50*]; also two Mycenaean rapiers.[3]

49. A Mycenaean bronze double axe, from Pallantion (Arcadia) inscribed in the early 5th cent. BC: 'Thaumis dedicated [me]'. (Athens, National Museum Br. 17439)

50. A Mycenaean chisel, from Boeotia, inscribed for dedication in the 6th cent. BC: 'sacred'. (Athens, National Museum)

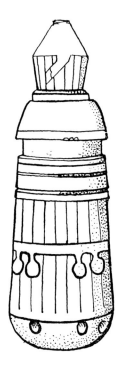

51. A Neolithic greenstone axe (about 2000 BC) with tin inlays, said to have been found at the Temple of Artemis at Ephesus, and probably taken for a divine thunderbolt from heaven. L. 16 cm. (Liverpool Museum 49.18.87)

Stone axe heads are traditionally identified as thunderbolts; there is a fine one from Ephesus, of a type current at Troy centuries before the construction of the temple at Ephesus [*Fig. 51*].[4] 'Men of Ephesus, what man is there who does not know that the city of the Ephesians is temple keeper of the great Artemis, and of the sacred stone that fell from the sky'.[5] A legendary axe in Caria was said to have belonged to an Amazon queen, and became part of the regalia of Lydian kings, which gave rise to a special cult of Zeus at Labraunda (T.527). It was probably a Bronze Age relic.

There were many weapons identified as heroic.[6] The most famous were those of Achilles, but these had been, according to the story, acquired by Odysseus, and they had a later history, said to have been washed ashore from Odysseus' shipwreck at the grave of his rival for them, Ajax (T.157). This was an appropriate if tardy redress for the injustice of Ajax not being awarded them in the first place, after Achilles' death and his rescue of Achilles' body (cf. [*Fig. 2*]). But armour of the time of the Trojan War was kept at Troy, and a set was carried off by Alexander the Great (T.46), who in other ways also tried to adopt the *persona* of Achilles, the most famous warrior hero of the Greeks; indeed he shared his tragic early death, though not in battle. We are led to believe that the arms from Troy were worn or carried before him to India and back, indeed that in India the shield was held over him by

Peukestas as he lay bleeding.[7] I revert to the appearance of the shield in Chapter Six. Achilles' spear at Phaselis had both blade and spike-butt, and so was clearly a developed hoplite spear of classical type (T.283). The healing property of a spear was a feature of the story of the healing of Telephos' wound by the spear of Achilles, which had inflicted it, and may have been extended to other military relics as a form of sympathetic magic.

Herakles' weapons were kept in his temple at Thebes. Their disappearance before the battle of Leuktra in 371 BC was an indication of his assistance to the Thebans on the battlefield (T.603). They were presumably hoplite weapons and not his club and lionskin, which are somewhat less than heroic, nor of apparent value on a classical battlefield. It is tempting to think that the shield was of the Boeotian type (of which there will be more to tell in Chapter Six), which was the device for Theban coins of the day [*Fig. 146*]. We do not know whether the shield of Amphitryon, Herakles' 'mortal' father, was part of the hero's weaponry, but it was said to have served as Herakles' cradle.[8] Since he had a twin brother, they might have been thought well accommodated in a two-lobed Boeotian shield, either side of the central handgrip. The shield of the Messenian Aristomenes was also retrieved from Lebadeia by the Thebans for him to fight his old enemy, the Spartans, in the same battle (T.327,330).[9] The weapons of Herakles that Philoktetes took to Troy and were shown in south Italy were naturally his bow and arrows (T.39).

The story of the Leuktra weapons suggests the explanation of Herodotus' record of the Aiginetans sending their heroes, the Aiakidai, to help the Thebans against Athens (T.93), and again to help the Greeks at Salamis against the Persians (T.96; cf. T.128). This is generally thought to imply that they sent images, but hero-images (apart from Herakles') are virtually unknown and *heroa* normally had no cult statues. Aiakos' tomb on Aegina was simply a low altar, according to Pausanias (T.255). It is far more likely that the Aiginetans sent weapons or other military relics, and the Thebans understandably complained that they would have preferred to have had the men to wield them.

There were many other hero shields on display in Greece, most of them perhaps archaic hoplite shields with bronze blazons, as I have remarked, since classical shields seem not to have been so decorative, but on the whole Greek shield shapes did not change much.[10] Diomedes' shield at Argos became involved in local ritual, carried with the image of Athena in a chariot (T.55), and perhaps related to other shield-prizes there.[11] Pausanias remarks that the Laconian shields dedicated in Athens were smeared with pitch to keep them from rusting,[12] and we may imagine that conservation of metal relics was also a matter for some concern wherever they were housed or displayed. A significant number of heroic military relics was displayed in the Greek west, not all of them from presumed hero refugees such as Diomedes and Aineias, or wanderers like Odysseus.

The practice of erecting trophies on the field of battle, composed of captured arms and armour, and of the dedication of captured weapons to celebrate a victory,

52. Stone pyramid at Hellenikon in the Argolid; a structure of a type apparently later associated with heroic trophies and burials. The detail shows a rendering of the stone at the corner which indicates a date no earlier than the 4th century BC.

lent some colour to the display of heroic weaponry. One heroic trophy/tomb was a stone pyramid with relief shields upon it, located between Argos and Epidauros, celebrating a fight between Proitos and Akrisios in which for the first time generals and soldiers all carried shields (T.248). This makes it more like a hoplite battle than an heroic one, and it was the shields on the monument that presumably suggested the story about the style of fighting. There are various pyramidal monuments in the area. One, of which there is only the base preserved, is probably the one in Pausanias, and another, better preserved, could be related to the common tombs from a sixth-century battle which he mentions [*Fig. 52*].[13] Neither of the extant monuments was in fact a tomb: their purpose is not clear – perhaps guard houses of the fourth century BC or later. The most we can say is that their original date and purpose had been forgotten by Pausanias' day, and other explanations offered of mythical and historical value.[14] Other trophies are a stone pillar with a shield (T.462) for a Theban heroic duel, or are not described (T.284,299).

Maritime

The most famous ship of antiquity was the Argo which sailed to Colchis (modern Georgia on the Black Sea) for the Golden Fleece, manned by the Argonauts led by Jason. The Argo was dedicated by Jason to Poseidon at the Isthmos of Corinth,[15] but no one pretends to have seen it there in later years. However, its parts were well distributed east and west (T.4,5,45,465,520). Odysseus lost his ship more than once and only a sternpost was shown, in Spain (T.550). Ancient wooden ships had a short life, and Theseus' ship at Athens could only be passed off as the one still sent annually to Delos by admitting that its timbers had been regularly renewed (T.504). Hero ships seem to have been thought to be like the classical ones; only the Phaeacian ships had their own stealth guidance systems, invisible and 'using their wisdom to find the goal', without steersmen or rudders.[16] Procopius could not believe the size of Aineias' ship, shown at Rome (T.539), but what was it then?

Ships' prows and rams, regular dedications after sea victories, were to become the major feature of Rome's *rostra*. Anchors were more substantial. The Argonauts discarded their rather flimsy one at Kyzikos, where it was displayed, and went on with a more substantial one (T.520), shown at Colchis where there were Argo anchors of both iron and stone (T.45). More unusual as a relic was the ballast of Diomedes' ships, shown at his landfall in south Italy (T.109), but it would have been from the land of Troy itself. The timber of Kadmos' ship was used for images of Aphrodite at Thebes (T.433). The Spartans could not show the rafts on which their Dorian ancestors (children of Herakles) crossed the Gulf of Corinth at the end of the heroic age, but they carried models of them in the Karneia festival.[17]

Other Military and Related Relics

There were some unusual dedications made in the archaic and classical periods to celebrate victory and these may have prompted identification of comparable heroic relics. Thus, the cables from the Persian bridges at Abydos and over the Hellespont for their invading army were brought back by the Greeks for their temples.[18] The rusty fetters of the Laconian prisoners who worked for the Tegeans were shown in Tegea (T.85,409). The marks of Andromeda's fetters were preserved where she was tethered for the sea monster at Joppa (T.101). In Greek art down to the fourth century she is shown tied to posts, so either the fetters story is a later invention inspired by some feature at the sea side – an old tying-up point, perhaps – or one which was not known to earlier artists in Greece.[19] Diomedes' bronze necklet in Peucetia could have been a piece of native, Italic gear, attributed to the Greek hero who settled in Italy with his companions (T.42).[20]

Bronze Age chariots were distinctly unlike Iron Age ones, which were used only for parade and racing, not fighting – at least in the Greek homeland. The chariot of Pelops was shown at Keleai on the roof of a building (T.213) – it was a major player in the story of his race against Oinomaos to win his daughter Hippodameia. The chariot at Gordion (T.47) might have been of Anatolian type and was remarkable mainly for its fabled knot, severed by Alexander the Great.

Vessels

Various types of metal vessels found in old graves or on sites could have been evocative. Most were probably not of the Bronze Age, and at any time a vessel of precious metal might have been thought more deserving of the melting pot than of veneration. Once Greece had adopted cremation, though not universally, in the early Iron Age, bronze cauldrons could be used for the ashes of the dead. The discovery of a cauldron burial could have given rise to the stories of Medea's exercises of rejuvenation through boiling, of animals or heroes, since 'ashes' regularly include many recognizable bones. Her bronze pot for Pelias was shown at Sikyon (T.5). A storage jar labelled 'Idas' with parts of three skulls in it was found at Messene and associated with that Idas who was, for Homer, the strongest mortal of his day; it could have been a pithos (storage jar) burial of almost any date (T.500).

The bronze tripod cauldrons were probably more promising as relics since many were of an early period, ninth to seventh century BC, and were common dedications in sanctuaries, notably at Olympia [*Fig. 53*].[21] They could readily be re-interpreted and appropriately inscribed. We have seen good examples of the probable re-interpretation of tripods in the cave on Ithaca, where eighth-century dedications

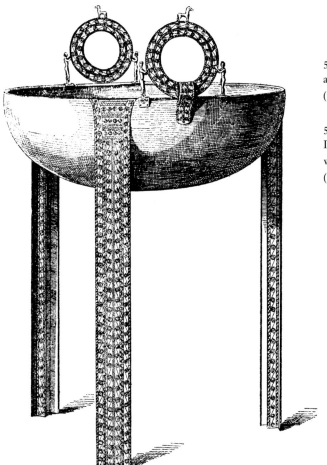

53. Typical bronze tripod dedication at Olympia. 8th cent. BC.
(Olympia Museum, restored drawing)

54. (*right*) Bronze wheeled stand from Larnaka, Cyprus; a model for 'Helen's workbasket'? 12th cent. BC. H. 34 cm.
(Berlin, Staatliche Museen 8947)

[*Fig. 41*] might evoke Odysseus' treasure. In the Apollo temple at Thebes similar tripod cauldrons had been inscribed as heroic offerings (T.91,424) some time after their original anonymous dedication, which was of a period when inscribed dedications were still exceptional; alternatively, they were deliberate forgeries but of early date. Cauldrons and tripods are among the prizes offered by Achilles at the Games for Patroklos at Troy, and the one which Diomedes won was shown at Delphi, inscribed (T.49). Others were royal gifts, as by the Argonauts to a Libyan king, also inscribed (T.70). Among the tripod prizes in the grove of the Muses on Mount Helikon Pausanias saw one (T.462) which had been won by the poet Hesiod (around 700 BC): it was just possibly the real thing.

Helen's golden 'tripod' at Thebes (T.533) had been thrown overboard by its owner and later fished up by Milesians. It was probably deemed to be the wheeled work-basket described by Homer as of silver, with wheels, with its rim finished in gold, the gift to her of an Egyptian noblewoman.[22] There are indeed Greek tripods on wheels, as those from the Ithaca cave [*Fig. 41*], but the object was very probably of a type well known in Syria and Cyprus, brought to Greece and copied in bronze versions [*Fig. 54*]. They were available in eighth-century Crete, and the wheels of one had accompanied a burial at Lefkandi in Euboea in the ninth century.[23] If the Thebes 'tripod' was such a one, this was an inspired work of identification on the part of the finder, but it was not literally a tripod.

55. Bronze coin of Patrai showing a box on a pedestal or altar, probably that deemed to contain spoils from Troy. Minted in the reign of Marcus Aurelius (AD 161–180).

Boxes and chests of various materials could have been common casual finds, often containing valuables, put away and not recovered, or inscribed documents such as religious texts (T.328). Spoils from Troy were in one at Patrai (T.372), which probably appears on Roman-period coins [*Fig. 55*].[24] A bronze vessel at Argos was surmounted by ancient statues of Artemis, Zeus and Athena (T.232). Since the vessel was 'of no great size', the statues were statuettes, and the whole reminds one of the many Praenestine (Italian) cylindrical bronze cistae of the fourth/third centuries BC, with figures on their lids. A very few have three standing figures, Dionysos and satyrs on the famous Ficoroni cista [*Fig. 56*], but gods are no less likely for the position.[25] By the time it was identified or installed and then recorded by Pausanias such a box could well have been an unusual antique. It was held to mark the place of epic oath-giving or, totally implausibly, to contain the bones of Tantalos.

Cups and wine-mixing craters could be evocative, especially of heroic masculinity, though Helen's cup at Lindos was said to be incidentally of the same size as her breast (T.518): there are archaic cups in the shape of a breast [*Fig. 57*] and the relic could have been a metal specimen of the shape.[26] Alkmene's cup at Sparta (T.53) was given to her by her lover, Zeus, who used it at her home in Thebes to decoy her into sleeping with him, pretending it was from her husband Amphitryon, away at war. It was described as a *karchesion*, which is like a footless kantharos, with upright handles. It was an uncommon shape but one which appears often in fifth-century art in the hands of Alkmene's son Herakles [*Fig. 58*],[27] who was the product of the deception. It sounds as though there is a real connection here between the story and a specific shape, by no means common in the classical period. The footless shape is more at home in the Bronze Age [*Fig. 59*] and perhaps the relic at Sparta was one found locally. It may not have given rise to the story, since a special cup was a plausible identifier for any male, but it might have determined for a while what Herakles' favourite cup should look like in art – it was his mother's and of divine origin.[28]

56. The Ficoroni cista. A bronze casket of Praenestine type of the late 4th cent. BC, decorated with scenes of the Argonauts which derive from a classical Greek model, and with cast figures of Dionysos and two satyrs on the lid. Made by Novios Plautios in Rome. H. 74 cm. (Rome, Villa Giulia Museum)

57. An Athenian black figure breast-shaped cup (*mastos*) decorated with eyes and satyrs. About 510 BC. H. 9.5 cm. (London, British Museum B376)

58. Herakles holding his *karchesion* cup. On an Athenian red figure amphora by the Berlin Painter, about 480 BC. (Basel, Antikenmuseum BS456)

59. Mycenaean gold kantharos from Shaft Grave IV at Mycenae. (Athens, National Museum)

60. A relief clay 'Homeric bowl' showing the murder of Agamemnon – all figures named. At the left his adulterous wife Klytemnestra kills the Trojan princess Kassandra; Aigisthos rushes Agamemnon with a sword; above him the artist has stamped again the figure of the dying Kassandra, as if falling on to him, perhaps indicating that she had prophesied what would happen; help comes too late from the right. An episode from the *Nostoi*, poems on the 'Returns [from Troy]'. (Berlin, Staatliche Museen VII.4996, from Thebes)

Odysseus' phiale at Kirkaion (T.554) was presumably Kirke's poisoned cup which he successfully evaded after it had turned his companions into swine [*Fig. 127*]. The most famous cup of myth-history was Nestor's, described in some detail by Homer.[29] A silver version was made by Dionysios of Thrace, in Rhodes, later displayed at Capua as a dedication to Artemis, and inscribed with Homeric verses (T.51). This was not a forgery, and some seem to have alleged that it was even the original, but this is a very rare example of a deliberate attempt to re-create an antiquity. It sounds like an elaborated metal version of the Hellenistic clay 'Homeric bowls', which are heavily inscribed. I show one with a detailed study of the murder of Agamemnon [*Fig. 60*].[30] Modern attempts, in terms compatible with our knowledge of Bronze Age metallurgy, to re-create on paper the appearance of Nestor's cup as described in Homer's lines, which were presumably based on an old tradition and describe intelligible Bronze Age techniques, have not proved very convincing. However, Nestor's cup has the distinction of being evoked in a purely

61. Cup found in a grave on Ischia. It was made in north Ionia and inscribed, probably in Euboea, with two verses. There are pieces of a similar inscribed cup (too incomplete to decipher) at Eretria in Euboea. About 720 BC. (Ischia Museum)

domestic, not heroic or cult context, as early as the later eighth century BC. It is mentioned in verses scratched by a Euboean on an East Greek cup which was taken to Ischia. 'I am the drink-worthy cup of Nestor; whoever drinks from me will straightway be seized by desire of fair-crowned Aphrodite', or words to that effect [*Fig. 61*].[31] Such an evocation of the heroic age for an everyday object says as much about the Greeks' obsession and acquaintance with their heroic heritage as many an heirloom or relic.

We have remarked the ninth-century royal graves at Lefkandi which contained a really antique Cypriot cauldron for the warrior's ashes [*Fig. 44*], while his consort's jewellery [*Fig. 45*] seems to have been an even older acquisition from the east – although when it was acquired cannot be known. Elsewhere in the cemetery was an example of a bronze jug with floral handle of a type made in Egypt and Phoenicia [*Fig. 62*]. There are several other such jugs found in Geometric contexts in Crete, but it has been suggested that all were by then of considerable antiquity, up to five hundred years older than their find-contexts, rather than examples from the

62. Bronze jug with an openwork lotus handle of Egyptian type, from a tomb at Lefkandi in Euboea. 8th cent. BC. H. 8.6 cm. (Eretria Museum)

continuing production of a popular type, so far not certainly represented in their country of origin at this date.[32] One might doubt whether these were in fact all so old, or at least whether they were of a type to be taken by Greeks as obviously heroic, although the utterly foreign was always likely to be so regarded. The concentration in date and place of finds suggests a recent origin.

Inscriptions

Homer was not being anachronistic when he mentioned writing in the heroic age, even though it appears only once, with what was meant to be a fatal letter sent with Bellerophon to the king of Lycia, inscribed on a folding tablet and instructing the recipient to kill the carrier.[33] The letter's form, as described, was like the classical, as it is shown in a vase scene [*Fig. 63*].[34] If any Greeks dug up inscribed objects of Bronze Age date they would have been unable to read them, although some may have noted a generic similarity to the syllabary used in Cyprus for writing Greek. There was a late record of an earthquake uncovering written tablets in a tin box at Knossos in the time of the emperor Nero, which has been understood as an early discovery of Linear B tablets in the cists of the Palace Magazines there – by no means impossible.[35]

The earliest Greek alphabetic inscriptions are of the middle of the eighth century BC and there is no good reason to believe that there were any earlier. In Cyprus, Greek was being written since about 1000 BC in a syllabary which was not exported for use by other Greeks but which continued in use in the island down to the third century BC, beside alphabetic Greek from the sixth century on. The early alphabetic inscriptions might have looked odd to a classical Greek, more used to that regularity in shape and form of letters which was current on stone inscriptions but also even in graffiti. At Thebes the archaic inscriptions added to the re-identified Geometric tripods were wisely diagnosed as being 'Kadmeian' (T.91),

63. Campanian red figure crater by the Manchester Painter. King Iobates reads the letter brought him by Bellerophon (with Pegasos). The woman at the left may be Iobates' daughter; she seems shocked at the contents (instructions to kill the bearer), but Bellerophon will survive and marry her. About 330 BC. (Winterthur Museum 364)

that is to say, somewhat Phoenician in appearance, since one version of Kadmos' story has him an immigrant from Phoenicia who introduced writing.[36] But Herodotus also describes the letters as similar to 'Ionic', which he would have known about, and this is less easily explained since early Ionic scripts are not especially closer to the eastern models than many others, although Herodotus thought so.[37] The Thebans were also able to decipher an inscribed pillar sent to them from Thessaly (T.44).[38] There was something totally exotic about the inscribed bronze tablet found before Alkmene's tomb at Haliartos that baffled even Theban decipherment; it was sent to Egypt to be read (T.523), but we are not told what the translation was, and may suspect here a Bronze Age or foreign script. But some forgeries proved detectable by ancient philologists (T.275).

The deliberate collection of ancient texts might be paralleled by the sixth-century Athenian Peisistratos' alleged collection of oracles, but his literary pretensions are generally implausible, though he took some care to keep on the right side of his and others' gods. The Assyrian Assurbanipal collected old texts, as did, much later, the emperor Constantine Porphyrogenitus, and several Chinese emperors, all on a most ambitious scale.[39] The collectors of the great Hellenistic libraries, as at Alexandria, had other, more scholarly motives. The bronze tablets of the Hyperboreans in Delos contained eschatological lore (T.506). Sarpedon's letter in Lycia, seen by a Roman governor (T.513), might have been anything, and was on paper (*charta*). Other inscribed relics might reveal the date of the forgery or identification, if we could but see them, but we have surviving only the inscribed 'sacred' axe heads and their like [*Figs. 49,50*].

Musical Instruments

These were mostly of perishable material and early examples were unlikely to have survived intact, and at any rate many were of the same general form over centuries, except perhaps the special varieties of lyre. Of the famous musicians Orpheus and Marsyas were the obvious candidates for identification. Marsyas' pipes were shown in Sikyon (T.5,208), and his hide at Kelainai in Asia Minor (T.94) – he was flayed by Apollo for presuming to challenge him in musical ability; moreover, the hide had magical, musical properties (T.3), as did the river in which, in another tale, he drowned (T.118). Orpheus' lyre and singing head also found more than one alleged resting place (T.58,103,111,461), and sometimes with magical properties – nightingales sang more sweetly at his tomb (T.111). Innovators, such as Timotheos (T.291) who increased the stringing of the kithara, and Amphion (T.421) who invented the highest pitched string, were commemorated by a lyre and a place name. The stones that followed Amphion's playing bordered his tomb (T.439): like Orpheus, he could move the inanimate. Alexander the Great was shown Paris' lyre at Troy but said he would have preferred Achilles' (T.529).

Athletic

Athletic prowess for heroes was generally, like most basic Greek sports, in exercises of military value. Throwing lumps of stone was an Homeric sport, and therefore disci are favourite identifications for the hero Argonauts, the scraping from whose oiled bodies after exercise were also found to have discoloured pebbles (T.38; cf. T.600 for their disci). The pebbles were on Elba, an iron-rich island, and may simply have been a cache of slag debris from old workings. The discus of Iphitos, re-founder of the Olympic Games, was inscribed with the Eleian truce (T.348) which established a cease-fire in Greek lands for the period of the Games.

Jewellery, Dress and Regalia

Sceptres were important symbols of power in Homer and, *in corpore*, have been thought indicative of regality in Late Bronze Age Cyprus, which had been much affected by Mycenaean manners. The famous sceptre from Kourion [*Fig. 64*] is short, more like a mace.[40] They were no more than a staff or spear in classical Greek art, and this is why the assembly of hero-kings (one named, Menelaos) on a seventh-century Attic vase proceed in civilian dress, holding spear-sceptres [*Fig. 65*].[41] Agamemnon's sceptre at Chaironeia (T.474) could have been more imposing, since it was said to have been made by the god Hephaistos and so must have been either an elaborate forgery or a notable antiquity; the Chaironeians called it a spear (*doru*), so it was bigger than a Cypriot mace.[42] Hephaistos, the craftsman god, was the alleged maker of several fine relics, but Pausanias thought only the sceptre of Agamemnon to be 'genuine'.

Minoan and Mycenaean jewellery was impressive, and the eastern contacts developed from the ninth century on in Greece brought exotic new forms from Syria, any of which might have seemed venerable beside the generally more restrained products of the classical period, or the obviously classically-Greek inspired ones of the Hellenistic. Jewellery also played a part in myth, so Harmonia's necklace, a divine wedding gift, could be identified, in both Delphi and Cyprus. But this was only after it had played a second role in myth as the necklace with which Eriphyle had been bribed to send her husband Amphiaraos against Thebes (T.18,50,400,476). Eriphyle's dress, also a bribe to send her sons to their death, was shown in Palestine (T.197). These were surely all unlucky relics.

The engraved gems of the Bronze Age were different in shape and style to all later gems in Greece, and, until the mid-sixth century, in the hardness and splendid colours of their material. In latter-day Crete and the Cycladic islands they have been prized by nursing mothers as 'milk-stones'. Many were uncovered in antiquity and they are found in graves or among the votives in archaic and classical

64. Gold enamelled sceptre from Kourion in Cyprus, topped by two falcons. 11th cent. BC. L. 16 cm. (Cyprus Museum J99)

65. Athenian clay stand showing heroes in procession, one named Menela[o]s, holding spear-sceptres. About 660 BC. H. 68 cm. (Berlin, Staatliche Museen A42, from Aigina)

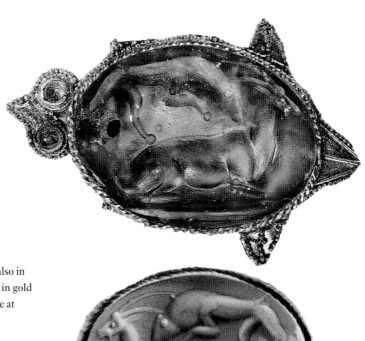

66. A Late Minoan amethyst gem (shown also in impression) with a lion attacking a goat, set in gold in the early 8th cent. BC and found in a grave at Knossos. L. 30 mm. (Heraklion Museum)

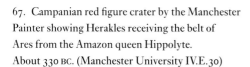

67. Campanian red figure crater by the Manchester Painter showing Herakles receiving the belt of Ares from the Amazon queen Hippolyte. About 330 BC. (Manchester University IV.E.30)

sanctuaries. Some years ago sixty-eight were listed from sites all over Greece and from a north African colony. It would be good to know whether any special properties were assigned to them beyond their beauty.[43] One Minoan seal was recovered and given a fine gold setting in the eighth century BC. It was no doubt worn, and then put in a tomb at Knossos [*Fig. 66*].[44] Oriental seals, especially the cylinders, were no less persistent and have been found all over even the Roman empire, probably as legionaries' amulets or keepsakes.

When Euripides describes the woven scenes on the Amazons' dress dedicated at Delphi by Herakles they are remarkably non-oriental in subject (T.79), when they could have been modelled on eastern types, thought to be becoming increasingly well known in Greece in Euripides' day. His description of Amazon dress shown at the Argive Heraion ('Mycenae') sounds very formal rather than warlike (T.81), including the gold-decked belt worn by Hippolyte, which she is shown handing to Herakles in the art of this period [*Fig. 67*].[45] I revert to the belts in Chapter Six. Imagined appropriateness in form and material may have counted for something in these identifications. Helen's fur slippers reached Italy (T.110), her jewellery elsewhere (T.50,605(11)). Few pieces of male clothing rather than armour are mentioned – Odysseus' cloak, but together with his corselet (T.5).

Furniture

Bronze Age thrones are likely to have been decorated with ivory plaques, and the known Minoan ones are decidedly non-classical in design. Ivory pieces were found in the fill of the Artemision at Delos and have been rather too hopefully adduced as evidence for a whole throne which survived – not impossible with a stout wooden frame but unlikely, and a full set of ivories was not found. Egyptian furniture was especially influential and the myth-historical Daidalos' folding stool shown in Athens (T.141) was probably Egyptian, of a type which was very popular in Greece from the archaic period on. The royal throne of Danaos was shown at Argos (T.222). On Pittheus' tomb were three marble thrones, his own and for two fellow judges (T.258). Hera's couch-bed (*kline*) was at her sanctuary near Argos (T.219), Hippodameia's at Olympia (T.348), and Penelope's loom at Sikyon (T.5).

Bric-à-brac

If Leda's egg from which Helen emerged, which was displayed at Sparta (T.301), was in fact an ostrich's, we might wonder whether it was shown intact, or broken for the birth: a problem which could easily have escaped the attention of the devout, on a par with those who have admired the skull of Cromwell as a little boy. Implements other than military are surprisingly rare given their appearance as attributes for various myth figures (Aristaios, Daidalos, Argos, etc.), but Epeios' carpentry tools with which he made the Trojan Horse were shown near Metapontion in south Italy (T.40).

68. Diomedes escapes from Troy with the Palladion statue, on an Athenian red figure cup by the Diomed Painter. About 400 BC. (Oxford, Ashmolean Museum 1931.39)

69. Impression of a cornelian gemstone showing the Palladion statue on a base. The bull's skull beside it indicates sacrifice. The pose is archaic but the figure has been updated by giving her a triple crested helmet, inspired by Pheidias' Athena Parthenos. H. 20 mm. 4th cent. BC. (Boston, Museum of Fine Arts 23.583)

Statues

The most famous statuary relic of antiquity was the Palladion from Troy, stolen by Odysseus and Diomedes in a story which may involve two Palladia. It appears as a wooden statue of the goddess Athena, legs together, with raised spear. Since no less than three places in Greece claimed to have received it, Argos, Sparta and Athens (T.240), a further excuse for duplication was invented by having Demophon, who brought it to Athens, make a duplicate which was given to Agamemnon.[46] But Italy enters the lists also in the Roman tales of Diomedes bringing it west, giving it to Aineias who took it to Rome, or of Aineias taking it to Rome himself from Troy. There were various cities in Italy claiming to have it (T.560). Almost any seventh/sixth-century wooden statue of Athena would have served, variously dressed, and have seemed venerable by the time identifications were made. This may have been early in the fifth century, when a long series of vase scenes begins showing the theft, sometimes of two Palladia, with the statue type copied for later scenes [*Fig. 68*], and still recognized without the story attached [*Fig. 69*].[47]

70. Silver coin minted by
L. Hostilius Saserna in Rome, 48 BC,
showing an archaic Artemis statue,
frontal, holding a stag by its antlers.

The wooden statue of Artemis brought from the Tauri (Crimea) by Orestes with Iphigeneia multiplied no less readily, at Brauron, Sparta, Argos, Rome and Aricia (T.138,303,542,551), and its history is no little bound up with the establishment of the cult of Artemis at Ephesus, where the image comes to have far more complicated and Anatolian references. Any early Artemis would probably have been represented by a simple 'Daedalic' wooden figure with no more than animal attributes, and sometimes winged.[48] A common group, on vases and no doubt in sculpture, presents her as a huntress-mistress of animals holding a stag by its horns. Massilia (Marseilles) was held to have promulgated the type in the west, including to Rome; soon after Massilia was taken by Rome in 49 BC Lucius Hostilius Saserna minted in Rome coins with a most plausible archaic figure of the goddess [*Fig. 70*].[49] A wooden statue of Artemis at Leukadia was probably archaic, wearing a cylindrical *polos* crown; but the latter was explained as a mortar, placed there by invaders as an insult, instead of her golden crown.[50]

Many other statues are mentioned as extant dedications of heroes in Greek sanctuaries. None are closely described but most are wooden, a few of stone, fewer metal, and several are ascribed to the artist Daidalos. The latter was rather more of an epithet than a man (meaning 'cunningly worked' or 'ornate'), and most of his alleged works of the heroic age had a magic quality, to judge from their descriptions, but there was a tradition that assigned to him also work which, as described, seems likely to be of the later seventh century. This still does not make him a person rather than a recognizable style, evinced by many archaic figures which long survived in Greece and to which his name was readily applied. Apart from whatever later forgeries there may have been, we may be sure that most alleged heroic-age statues were archaic, of the eighth to early sixth century.[51] The habit of attributing visible works to the most sublime of the earliest artists, whether real or not, finds its echo in the enthusiasm of the tourist guides for Romans in

71. The funerary statues of Phrasikleia and of her 'brother' excavated in a pit at Myrrhinous in Attica, after the former had been damaged. The base of her statue had not been buried, and had been found long before the excavation of the pit with the statues. The pair may have been overthrown by some natural disaster, or possibly by Persian invaders. The statues are mid-6th cent. BC. (Athens, National Museum)

72. Statue base for a bronze warrior (missing) from the Acropolis at Athens. The upper inscription of six lines is of the early 5th cent. BC, naming the artists Kritios and Nesiotes and the dedicator; below it is an inscription recording a re-dedication of the 1st cent. AD honouring a Roman official. (Athens, Acropolis Museum)

associating major but anonymous works of the classical period with whole teams of the most famous names of the fifth and fourth centuries BC: the alleged super-competition for the Amazons at Ephesus, and the choice of names for the sculptures of the Mausoleum are probably to be explained thus.[52]

Other revered statues might have been from ancient wrecks, found by fishermen (T.375,485, cf. 367), still a prolific source, but any that fell from heaven taxed the credulity even of Pausanias (T.140). Hera at Samos was like a plank (*sanis*).[53] The appearance of most can be readily guessed, though the three-eyed Zeus at Argos (T.245) challenges the imagination.[54] Relic statues were sometimes hidden from sight (T.141,184), perhaps with good reason.

The removal of statues both as loot, which was the principal motive in Greece, and for their possible powers, a more oriental mode, was a commonplace in antiquity; Pausanias listed some examples from the heroic age to the Romans (T.408), and there are many attested from texts, excavation and inscriptions. Another practice related to that under discussion was that of the careful burial of statues that had been damaged through earthquake, fire, or vandalism by an enemy, or had been replaced. This could happen through both Greek and Roman times and not usually with very old statues. They could be protected by lead or pottery, and it is clear that they were not expected to be recovered [*Fig. 71*]. This seems a mixture of the piety accorded to many discarded votive offerings and of veneration of what was to become an antique, in our terms. Much the same happened to parts of buildings which had suffered from earthquake or war, including whole sculptural pediments, the most notable being the earlier archaic pediments at Aegina.[55]

The re-use of old statues to celebrate later events or people was probably mainly a matter of opportunism, tempered with some respect for antiquity since the old dedicatory inscriptions were not always effaced. For example, the statue of a warrior by Kritios and Nesiotes, famous Early Classical sculptors who had made the Tyrannicides group in Athens, was re-used by the Council and Demos of Athens as an honorific statue for one Lucius Cassius in the first century AD [*Fig. 72*]. Classical tombstones of Thespiae in Boeotia might be re-used for Roman dead.[56] Pausanias noticed that in Athens the names on statues of Miltiades and Themistokles had been altered into those of a Roman and a Thracian; and at the Argive Heraion what passed as a statue of Augustus was said to be really an Orestes.[57]

Men who fell in love with statues may have been in part moved by the fact that they represented divine antiquity: Praxiteles' Aphrodite at Knidos was indecently assaulted, and there is the story of Pygmalion's wish-fulfilment, but with his own work. This takes obsession with the antique rather far; talking statues, of which there were several, were more natural encounters.[58]

NATURALIA

The natural world, live, once-live (fossils), fluid or inert, can work upon the imagination no less than any mysterious artefact, for all that it is the more familiar and may be taken for granted. But any unusual feature invited explanation, promoted by the same imaginative play that identified relics; and all the most obvious features of the natural world had been around for a long time, even trees, and so were ready candidates for identification with the remote past. This is largely the subject of Pfister's ch. 5. He included many instances which do not appear in my lists, since positive record of the identification on the ground in the historic period is lacking, though this was most likely to have been true in many cases, the natural feature itself giving rise to a story. Pausanias clearly had an eye for such natural curiosities.[59]

Virtually all myths were located in sites still occupied or identifiable in the historic period, whether or not any specific relic or locale was pointed out. The whole of Greece was the setting, indeed the whole Mediterranean world settled or travelled by Greeks, not an imaginary Camelot or Discworld, and the pious Greek was well aware that he walked and lived in a physical world which had been shared by heroes, nymphs and gods. The places where they lived or which they visited were as real to him as the Stations of the Cross in Jerusalem are to many of our contemporaries. The Thebes of the Seven was the Thebes of history; even Olympus, the home of the gods, was located, and not a make-believe Valhalla. That it could be climbed without encountering gods was no bar to belief. This fact alone imbued the whole of Greece with a mythical aura. There are few imaginary lands in Greek literature – Homer's Phaeacia is simply an idealized colony, and there is Atlantis, Euhemerus' Panchaea and Lucian's fantasy land in the west.[60] Here I deal only with specific features for which explanations were offered, not the many to which heroic names were attached, for good reason or none.

Natural Features and Landscape

The landscape itself is evocative and a skyline or unusual juxtaposition of rocks and streams would be enough to indicate some measure of divine presence. The actual personification of natural features was commonplace, with or without any mythological event: rivers (Acheloos), springs, and even mountains – Helikon and Kithairon have a personal contest in a poem by Corinna. This is generally not so much a matter for identification with a specific figure or story, as a reason for creating a place of worship. The transcendental setting of Delphi is an obvious example, and at a lower level, virtually any stream, spring or wood on which the livelihood of the community might depend. These were accordingly occupied by an appropriate nymph at the least, if not a god, while less predictable phenomena such as springs might be attributed to the beneficence of a hero. The only problem may be that what we see today is not as it was in antiquity, and this is a field on which the modern imagination may graze no less greedily than did the ancient. It is, at any rate, not quite within our remit of the archaeological reconstruction of the past.[61]

Caves invite heroic activity, usually of a predictable nature.[62] Many in Greece may well have been occupied from early prehistory on and might have contained

73. A Bronze Age tomb on Thasos used by Greeks later as a cave sanctuary of the god Pan.

74. The entrance to the Dictaean Cave at Psychro in Crete, sacred to Zeus. On the right stands
D.G. Hogarth, the excavator, who had to remove the boulders blocking the entrance with dynamite.
(Oxford, Ashmolean Museum)

still some significant or suggestive remains. Animal bones were probably enough to
identify the many caves of Pan. That near Marathon had rocks near by that could
be taken for his goats (T.153). One on Thasos seems to have been a prehistoric and
non-Greek rock-cut tomb [*Fig. 73*],[63] but it was probably not recognised as a tomb,
or perhaps even as an 'antiquity', since in that case Pan would have been a most
unlikely claimant or occupier. Caves are good places for clandestine births and
nursing, and some were still identified -for Antiope at Eleutherai (T.167), the Sibyl
at Erythrai (T.483), Dardanos in Triphylia (T.565), Tityos in Euboea (T.575),
Epaphos in Euboea (T.577), Dionysos at Prasiai (T.316); and for making love
(T.383) – remember Dido. They are homes for the wild, like that of the Nemean
lion (T.215) which was still pointed out, or for tamer beasts (cattle – T.339, or
Pan's); or refuges for prophets – Sibyl (T.33), Trophonios (T.471); studies for poets
– Homer (T.368); cells for the deranged – the daughters of Proitos (T.395). Many
holes, especially where rivers disappear underground, may qualify as entrances to
the underworld or places where Herakles dragged up the hound of Hades,
Kerberos. Rivers rather than caves generally qualify better for this function,
perhaps because of the riverine geography of the Underworld, but Hades himself
carried Persephone down through a cave in Sicily full of flowers (T.29,73, cf. 559),
and otherwise it was generally a matter of identifying an entrance (for Persephone
T.164, for Amphiaraos T.420), or exit (for Kerberos dragged up by Herakles,
T.257,272, for Semele T.257,277) for specific occasions.

The Dictaean Cave at Psychro in Crete [*Fig. 74*] is unusual in being visited by
worshippers with offerings continuously from the end of the Middle Bronze Age

to the seventh century BC. It was excavated over a hundred years ago, with the help of dynamite to remove the massive boulders which had fallen and blocked it.[64] Its original resident deity is unknown but at quite an early date in the Iron Age it must have seemed an appropriate cave for the nurture of young Zeus, though there were other claimants later, and his main cave sanctuary in the island was the Idaean, to the west.[65] The Cretan Zeus was no ordinary Olympian, and late sources even found him a tomb in the island near Knossos.[66] The probable early identification of the Dictaean Cave at Psychro is contrary to the general current of heroic and divine identifications in the rest of Greece which only begin in the eighth century BC, as is much else in the religious archaeology of an island relatively bereft of heroes.

Some unusual rock formations or skylines could readily be equated with mythical events and probably inspired the stories of petrifaction. The Phaeacian ship which had carried Odysseus to Ithaca and was stopped by Poseidon off Corfu is the obvious example (T.507), though none too easy to identify today. John Luce tells me that the Corfiots identify it as the islet Pondikonisi, which 'has what might be imagined to be a bluntish prow' and is conveniently near the main town.[67] A human-shaped rock can be poor Lichas, thrown into the sea by Herakles (T.115), and a cliff on Mount Sipylos in Lydia, the weeping Niobe (T.134). The latter's story of petrification was known to Homer and could even be a subject for vase painters [*Fig. 75*],[68] but it presents a problem of identification on the ground. There was a wholly intelligible and early Hittite rock-cut relief of the seated Anatolian goddess, later recognized as Kybele, on Sipylos [*Fig. 76*], which could easily have been taken for Niobe. But Pausanias (who was a local man and went to look) and others were clear that the real rock Niobe was less convincing close to. A

75. Niobe in a shrine, already half turned to stone (white from the waist down). The agitated man is her father Tantalos. On a Campanian red figure hydria by the Libation Painter. About 330 BC. (Sydney, Nicholson Museum 71.01)

(*Right*)

76. Hittite rock relief of a goddess on Mount Sipylos, probably identified as a Greek/Anatolian goddess.

77. Rock profile on Mount Sipylos, probably the one taken in antiquity for the petrified, sorrowing Niobe.

78. From a panorama of Athens drawn by Baron Stackelberg, published in 1834. The hill Lykabettos is to the left.

very plausible rock feature which looks much like a weeping woman from a distance
has been observed on Sipylos [*Fig. 77*], and this is likely to be the prime candidate,
whatever might have been thought of the Kybele on other occasions.[69]

On a larger scale, the whole of Lykabettos, the highest hill in Athens [*Fig. 78*],
had been carried there by Athena to subdue Hephaistos (T.10), while the regular
shape of Mount Titthion (Nipple) earned it the reputation as the place where
Asklepios was nursed (T.251). And there were various heroic rock-leaps for the
distressed or victims on the coasts of Greece (T.193,194,453, cf. T.114).[70]

79. Cave at Eleusis with, at the centre, a rocky seat which was probably taken for the 'Mirthless Stone' on which Demeter sat mourning the loss of her daughter Persephone.

More humble identifications were of Pan's goats changed to rocks (T.153). Simple stones might be identified as seats. The most trivial is that on which Silenos sat when Dionysos came to Attica (T.137), or Aktaion's lookout where he spied Artemis naked (T.416). More serious are those for Demeter, distraught at the rape by Hades of her daughter Persephone: the Mirthless Stone at Eleusis (T.13) and the *Anaklethra* at Megara (T.182). The former may be identified as the rocky outcrop in a cave at the sanctuary of Eleusis [*Fig. 79*], where a cult drama re-enacting the loss of Persephone and her mother's grief may have taken place.[71] Even the stone on which Apollo laid his lyre while he built the walls of Megara was identified (T.176). It gave forth the sound of a lyre when struck, so hollow stones would always be good candidates for mythical identification. This calls to mind the Memnon at Thebes in Egypt, performing in the heat of the rising sun, which is discussed later in this chapter.

Balanced rocks are a fairly common phenomenon, carried by glaciation or created by erosion; in Greece a pair were set up by Herakles (T.35, cf.548). Palamedes' gaming table at Troy (T.83) recalled one of the more relaxed aspects of the epic war; his dice were at Argos (T.225). If Athens had the Areiopagos stones on which accused and accuser stood (T.145), Sicyon had the pebble vote cast there for Orestes by Athena (T.5). Delphi had the stone that Rhea gave Kronos to swallow in place of baby Zeus (T.488). Stones that hid famous tokens of

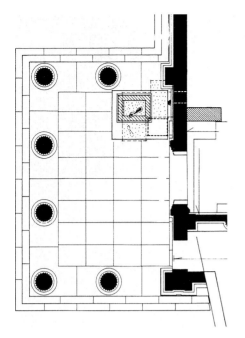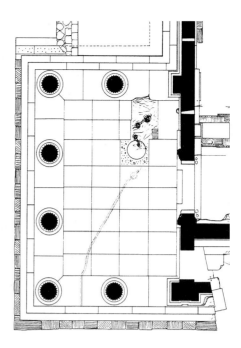

80. The arrangement of the roof (a) and floor (b) in the North Porch of the Erechtheion on the Acropolis at Athens, showing how the clefts in the rock, taken for the marks of Poseidon's trident, were left open to the sky.

recognition, as those of Theseus at Troizen (T.266, *Fig. 169*), naturally invited identification. It is not easy to envisage the circumstances of the stone near Megara said to have been shot through by Persian arrows, but a rocky hill with the stones riddled with natural holes may have been the inspiration (T.189).[72]

Clefts in the Athens Acropolis rock were readily identified as the point where Poseidon's trident struck, recorded by a writer of the third century BC and by Pausanias (T.573,139), beside the pool (*thalassa*) which the god gave the city, and which was as well known to Herodotus as Athena's olive tree (T.95). The markings on the rock beneath the north porch of the Erechtheion seem the obvious identification, and there would have been the pool beside it in the west end of the building, though lost now through the construction of a cistern. However, the marked rock ('three groups of fissures of different sizes and varying depths') was given free access to/from the heavens by the architect of the Erechtheion, who put a hole in the floor over it, which by the end of the fifth century had an altar for Thyechoos (Pourer of Offerings) set beside it, as well as a gap in the ceiling above it [*Fig. 80*].[73] Modern scholars prefer to have this the place where Zeus' bolt fell, either separating the quarrelling Poseidon and Athena, or, at Poseidon's behest, blitzing Erechtheus, though the fifth century had him struck by the trident.[74] 'Thyechoos' tells us nothing, and we know that Poseidon was worshipped in the Erechtheion. I am inclined to think that there was only one such mark – the one we can still see – near the pool which Poseidon gave and Athena's olive tree, all of them recalling their struggle for Attica as shown in the West Pediment of the Parthenon. It may, however, have been open to more than one explanation with time, even possibly an earthquake, since Poseidon was the god of earthquakes. One shook Athens in 422 BC, and may have been the inspiration for a remark of Euripides in his play *Erechtheus* where Athena bids Poseidon turn his trident away from her land and not destroy her city.[75] The architectural setting would suit a divine trident blow as well as any thunderbolt, and the Zeus-Erechtheus story may be late, while the trident mark was noted already in the third century BC and Poseidon as the slayer even earlier.[76] This could be a case of choice of interpretations offered in antiquity for a possibly natural feature which cried out for an identity of some sort.

Meteorites were natural objects for veneration, but are 'fallen from Zeus' (*diopetes*), so associated with the gods and only with the past when they also become identified with a specific deity or occasion. We have met one at Ephesus [*Fig. 51*]. They contribute to the Greek placing and often worship of sacred stones, *baityloi*, especially at entrances – a practice with strong near eastern associations. Rough stones, *argoi lithoi*, attract the same treatment.[77]

The stony Plaine de la Crau (flood plain) at the mouth of the River Rhône just west of Marseilles was explained as the ammunition provided by Zeus for Herakles while he passed through the lands of the hostile Ligurians (T.552). Kassandra's stone tethering-point at Troy yielded milk or blood when rubbed (T.6). One wonders what made the lumps of rock-clay on Parnassos smell like human flesh and be explained as surplus from Prometheus' creation of mankind from clay (T.477). An early traveller, Sir William Gell, wrote that in the area 'is found a species of stone very different from the limestone of the country, and which on rubbing emits an odour'.[78] Anything is possible, but allowance must be made for modern as well as ancient enthusiasm in making identifications.

Areas subject to earthquake or volcanoes have figured already, in Chapter Two, as the resting places of giants. Those in Italy were particularly evocative and could override the fact that in stories most giant battles were originally located in Greece. The Greek colonists must have effected the re-location in the face of such compelling natural evidence for their presence (T.557).[79] The notion could even be extended to explain a volcanic area in Asia Minor (T.586). Related to these are natural marine features such as dangerous whirlpools or rapids leading to rocks, where naturally a Skylla or Charybdis might lurk, or even wrecking agents such as Sirens; the stories follow the observation or experience of the phenomena and then, at some stage, poetic associations with voyagers of myth whose travels were in the real world of the Mediterranean – in these cases, Odysseus. Such monsters can then be somehow accommodated by Greek mythographers, from Hesiod on, in monster genealogies, as a form of authentication, and then have to be figured by artists, as we shall see in the next chapter.

Finally, there are features which may be natural, or man-made. Substantial feats

81. A bronze coin of Corinth, showing the tree where Melikertes was brought ashore by a dolphin, both shown beside it. Minted in the reign of Commodus (AD 180–192).

82. A bronze coin of Tanagra, showing Hermes standing beside the strawberry tree where he was nursed. Minted in the reign of Marcus Aurelius (AD 161–180).

of engineering, or what might seem to be such, are attributed to either the wizards (Daidalos) or the strong (Giants, Herakles). Diodorus describes as the work of Herakles several major projects, damming rivers to make lakes, draining waterlogged valleys (T.63, draining the vale of Tempe, and making Lake Copais in Boeotia; T.65,67, lakes in Italy and Sicily). He made highways through the Alps (T.64), roads and a mole elsewhere (T.65,555). In Greece there were several places where Mycenaean waterworks were apparent, as that at Mycenae which may have been associated with Agamemnon. Since they were 'public works', rather than fortifications more easily attributed to giants, it probably seemed natural to associate them with Herakles, who was more consciously a benefactor of mankind than were most gods and heroes.[80] Major waterworks in Greece belong to periods of imperial rule, Mycenaean or Roman, with a few exceptions in the ambitious age of tyrants, such as Eupalinos' great tunnel on Samos.

Trees and Flowers
The olive, plane and oak, all long-lived, are the trees most popularly associated with the remoter past (Testimonia, index s.v.). They are commonly noted at the site of an heroic tomb and they often signpost the enactment of a notable event; the one near Corinth where Melikertes' body was brought ashore by a dolphin was still to be seen (T.193), and it figures on a Roman-period coin of Corinth, beside Melikertes spread on the dolphin's back [*Fig. 81*].[81] The strawberry tree at Tanagra where Hermes was nursed (T.451) may appear on other late coins beside a statue of

the god [*Fig. 82*].[82] Then there are the trees from which Marsyas was hung to be flayed (T.516), where Io as a cow was tethered (T.515), where the dread Hydra lurked (T.276). Famous trees mentioned in epic were ready candidates for identification, especially in the Trojan plain (T.514,583,596).

Trees and woods are peopled by nymphs, Dryads. Several nymphs turned into trees to escape gods but, naturally, the results could not still be visible – except for some willowy victims of Boreas on Mount Olympos (T.116). A tree gives support and shade for giving birth – the most exotic was the palm on Delos (T.596), to which Leto clung (but also claimed for an olive near Ephesus, T.590),[83] but there is also the willow under which Hera was born, visible on Samos (T.366), the strawberry tree at Tanagra for nursing Hermes (T.451, see above); also for making love – Zeus with Europa at Gortyn (T.512). The olive is important, which is not surprising given its role in the Greek economy. The most famous is Athena's gift on the Acropolis at Athens (T.95), which, when cut down by the Persians, sprouted again, as olives will (T.142). Herakles took a cutting from this or from another of Athena's olive trees in Athens to Olympia to supply the victor wreaths there (T.24,516).[84] Herakles' club was cut from an olive tree and, out of use and planted at Corinth, lived on (T.263). Even dead trees played their part, as that at Aulis mentioned by Homer (T.447), timber from Semele's chamber, dressed in bronze (T.431), and a pillar from the house of Oinomaos given a protective cover at Olympia (T.349). Theocritus conjures a plane tree for Helen at Sparta, with a Doric dedication 'Adore me; I am Helen's tree'.[85] All these were still to be admired by the credulous apart from the many more alluded to in myth.

83. The flower of *Delphinium ajacis*, which was thought to have sprung on Ajax's grave, and carries the IAI markings that give his name and a cry of mourning.

84. The scene on an Etruscan red figure stamnos showing Ajax with drawn sword and a woman beside a plant with his name written on the stem. Early 4th cent. BC. (Paris, Cabinet des Médailles 947, from Vulci)

Of the flowers, the Greek larkspur (*Delphinium ajacis*) acquired on its petals at Ajax' tomb the initials of his name which are also a cry of mourning AI AI (*Fig. 83*, T.156).[86] The Greeks called such plants *hyakinthos*, which Theocritus calls 'lettered' (*grapta*), while Virgil evokes flowers inscribed with the names of kings.[87] The Etruscan artist who drew a plant bearing Ajax' name beside the hero was no botanist [*Fig. 84*].[88] Sophocles has Ajax himself note the correspondence between his name and a cry of grief.[89] The oddest floral tale is of the effect on myrtle leaves at Troizen of Phaidra's distracted pricking of them in her unrequited passion for Hippolytos (T.136,264). This sounds most like some local infestation by bugs.

Watery
Rivers and springs have their nymphs, Naiads, and can be the setting for various mythical events or themselves have been created by heroic or divine figures. In the latter category are several made by the time-honoured process of striking a rock (remember Moses): Poseidon's trident is a natural instrument (on Athens Acropolis, T.139), Pegasos' hoof is more unusual, at several places (T.262 at Troizen, 462 on Helikon, cf. 572); Atalanta's spear (T.315) and Dionysos' thyrsos-wand (T.340) could also serve. Chalkon kicked a spring into action on Kos and this might be identified as one which has served as a major source for the town at various periods (T.595).[90] Others marked where Achilles leapt ashore at Troy (T.78), and where other gods or heroes walked; Achilles had one at Miletus where he was purified (T.48). Agamemnon discovered cisterns (T.57) and we have noted

the proximity of his shrine at Mycenae to Bronze Age waterworks. Danaos and his fifty daughters provided Argos, 'thirsty' in Homer, with her wells (T.568).[91]

Herakles has much to do with fountains and springs (T.265), especially in the west.[92] For his comfort the nymphs made the warm baths for him in Sicily at Himera and Segesta (T.66), and in Greece he made Thermopylai warm himself by casting into the water his body, inflamed by poison (T.601). Midas' famous fountain was still shown in Ankyra (T.125, cf. 604), but no longer dispensing both wine and water to catch Silenos. Tears as a source are more beguiling, as those of Peirene (T.203), of the nymphs mourning dead Marsyas (T.118), or Niobe's for her children, dripping from her rocky face on Mount Sipylos [*Fig. 77*]. The river Marsyas otherwise derived from his blood.[93]

Of mythical events set at springs and fountains several involve bathing heroines and goddesses (T.200 – Helen in warm salty water), and rapes are to be expected (T.410 – Herakles and Auge, cf. T.11), the location being one at which women may be found alone and vulnerable, a quality shared also by any bathing place where a nymph or goddess might be espied naked (T.416 – where Aktaion watched Artemis). Springs and rivers are for washing divine infants also: Zeus (T.331,567), Hermes (T.392). Narkissos' spring and pool (T.464) were his downfall. Springs that resembled breasts naturally sent forth water like milk (T.468).[94]

Smelly or discoloured patches of sea or river could be judged the result of the decay of giants or monsters or the spilling of heroic or monstrous blood (Testimonia index s.v. discoloration). They are probably the result of localized mineral or vegetable contamination and may be poisonous to humans (T.117). Odder are the pebbles discoloured by the oil scraped from the bodies of hero-athletes at exercise (T.38; see above), or Herakles' club in Rome whose smell repelled the dogs (T.544).

Fauna

There were many animals as well as trees into which the less fortunate actors of myth were judged to have been metamorphosed (e.g., T.175 – Tereus into a hoopoe), but there are also special properties attributed to some creatures as a result of their encounters with the heroic past. The cicadas of Rhegion (T.8) and the frogs of Seriphos (T.9) were judged quieter than most because they had once annoyed Herakles' rest. Mute frogs are indeed possible – at least, some may be quiet during the summer months – but one cannot help thinking that the silent frogs of Seriphos were just as likely to be those that normally figured noiselessly on their coins [*Fig. 85*], and that we are being treated to a version of a harmless ancient joke.[95] Like St Patrick with the snakes in Ireland (there is none), divinity could be the cause of the alleged absence of harmful or other creatures from locations sacred to them (T.30,420). The birds into which Diomedes' companions had been turned were said to attack all non-Greeks (T.27); otherwise Diomedes' presence in the west seems to have promoted tame wildlife (T.553). Animal tombs can be locations for oath-taking (T.309,326).

85. Silver coin of Seriphos. The frog device may refer to the legendary 'silent' frogs of the island.

The relics of mythical animals were far more popular, especially of the Calydonian boar whose tusks and hides could be found in more than one place in the Mediterranean world (T.105,397,408,409,540; cf. T.397). Most were probably fossil bones such as we have considered already, and we shall meet more imaginative creations in the next chapter, imaging monsters. Heroes and heroines might have pet-cemeteries for their dogs (T.537). The horn of Amaltheia (T.329) was ivory, inscribed with a dedication by Miltiades; probably an elephant's, not a goat's as it should have been.

For the human animal, it was natural to blame the foreign witch Medea for some personal problems experienced by the women of Lemnos (T.113),[96] but many diseases, especially the mental, were attributed still to the malice of the divine. Hair relics are less common than one might expect and involve the quite exceptional such as Medusa (T.16,411, and her blood, T.80); they are only substantial in the case of the rope of tresses at Erythrai (T.367) by which the sea-bound statue of Herakles was hauled in. Hair offerings were a common ritual gift and some are heroic (T.59,371).

THE LINDOS CHRONICLE (T.605)

Throughout this chapter reference has been made to testimonia from various ancient authorities, and these have included entries in the Lindos Chronicle. This is the fullest account we have of the relics said to be at a single site, and it deserves fuller discussion. It is the most informative, if puzzling, epigraphical document for our subject.

The Temple of Athena Lindia, at Lindos in Rhodes, had attracted offerings, including those that we might judge mythical as well as many historical, that is, associated with historical personages and events; the latter I have also listed in T.605 for their general interest. The temple was burned down in the 340s BC with its contents, but, by the late second century many new and notable 'historical' offerings had accumulated. The loss of the earlier heritage was something that no self-respecting community could easily tolerate, so two men were commissioned to list all known dedications, both those lost and those surviving from more recent times, as well as certain other events (epiphanies of the goddess), so that there should be a record of the importance of the sanctuary both in the years long before its rebuilding, and in its recent past, to attest its, and the city's importance. The list was inscribed in 99 BC and, incomplete, was found in 1909 by Danish archaeologists in a church at the site, where it had been serving as a floor slab, with other major marble inscriptions [*Fig. 5*].

The first list (B: items 1–17) is of the early offerings, mythical and historical; the second (C: items 23–42) is of the later, historical; a third (D) is of epiphanies of the goddess, one occurring before the destruction of the temple (item D.1), others later. The first list includes the expected miscellaneous offerings of founders and heroes, several of them reflecting the role of Lindian heroes at the siege of Troy, or its aftermath, with three others (B.15–17) from plausible historical occasions in the archaic period. It is sometimes assumed that the heroic dedications are simply inventions, lending credibility to the antiquity and importance of the sanctuary. The credibility hardly needed enhancement since there was no doubt about the antiquity of the cult. The temple was said to have been founded by Danaos, or his daughters, and the town had sent a contingent to Troy. Most of the dedications are from heroes or events which play a part in the history of Lindos, as we would expect.[97] Obviously, they are 'inventions', but are they inventions of the classical period (or earlier) and once represented by objects displayed, which had been made or conveniently identified for the occasion? None is an object which could only have been created after the fourth century, and which might have been recruited by a compiler lacking antiquarian knowledge.

Of the 'mythical' offerings most are phialai, a common archaic and classical dedication; there is a lebes with a Phoenician inscription (B.3, from Kadmos, recall the Kadmeian letters of T.91); two shields, one covered with skin, the other with bronze (B.5, from Herakles); various pieces of jewellery, weapons, oars (B.12, from Menelaos' steersman). Any could have been made in the archaic or classical period for their new identity, or could have been an older object (such as the inscribed lebes) which had been re-identified. Of the early 'historical' there is a crater stand (B.16), a statue group (?; B.17) of Herakles and the Lion with Athena (who does not attend the contest much after the classical period), and 'very archaic' plaques (B.15) depicting a phylarch and nine runners shown in an archaic manner, presumably from games. The last is very plausible and not likely to be an invention of the second century. Of the later 'historical' offerings a late archaic wooden cow and calf from Sybaris (C.26) is quite acceptable – we recall the big silvered wooden bull dedicated in archaic Delphi.[98] Phalaris' relief-decorated crater (C.27) sounds less plausible for the mid-sixth century, both for its technique (metal craters of that date do not have major myth scenes on them) and its alleged subjects (Titanomachy – but perhaps simply a Gigantomachy; and Kronos with Rhea); it better fits the fourth to third centuries, together with its alleged association with Daidalos, although the subjects could have been misread by the Chroniclers' source. Deinomenes' acrolith gorgon (wood with stone face; C.28) and the Akragantine acrelephantine Athena (ivory extremities, probably the flesh parts; C.30) are exactly right technically for late archaic Sicily, which specialized in statuary of mixed materials, fine white marble being unobtainable locally. It is by no means likely that a late Hellenistic compiler would have been so knowledgeable about archaic art among the western Greeks.

In the long run it does not much matter when the early dedications were invented, or even whether they ever had any corporeal reality, although this seems highly probable for most if not all. They indicate what seemed appropriate in any period for a sanctuary of such antiquity. The same might easily be true of the gifts of the Persian general Datis in 490 (D.1), whether or not we believe in the epiphany that occasioned them, and of Artaphernes (C.32) and Artaxerxes (C.35); they are plausible Persian gifts, such as are attested elsewhere.

One of the historical gifts, a linen corselet given by Amasis (C.29), was also mentioned by Herodotos who includes other gifts from the Egyptian king, and this gives it pre-destruction respectability. For a majority of the others the Chronicle cites sources from mainly local historians of the third and second centuries BC, which at least shows that the inventions cannot all (or need any) be a product of the compilers of the Chronicle itself. Indeed, Pliny knew the breast-cup of Helen there (T.518) which is not mentioned in the Chronicle at all. Overall the inscription gives an idea of what a respectable and ancient sanctuary might hope to possess and exhibit by way of memorials to its past, mythical and historical.

GEOGRAPHY AND PERSONNEL

The geographical distribution of the places and objects identified with the past which have been considered principally in this chapter reveals little. It was determined in part by the record of myth-history, itself no little determined by what was observed, and in part by the presence of old sites and graves or of suggestive natural features. Our record from archaeology is slight and open to more than one interpretation, and with texts we are rather at the mercy of what Pausanias and others saw and recorded in their surviving works. At any rate it is only a fraction of what must have been identified in antiquity, since I have concentrated on what was alleged to be still visible. Often it was simply a matter of what a state, ruler or priest perceived as expedient for exploitation. I thought to give a map of them, but that would be misleading, given the extremely eccentric nature of the evidence. North Greece offers a sparse record, but perhaps this is not only because it has no place in Pausanias' extant itinerary. Its excavated cemeteries are relatively innocent of indications of even anonymous heroic identities, and it was at any rate on the periphery of the Mycenaean world;[99] for relics of Jason, Achilles and Peleus we have to look in places other than their ancestral homes.

Pausanias hailed from East Greece, probably Lydia, otherwise we would know even less than we do of Anatolian relics and identities, but he mentions much in passing without actually presenting a Guide to the area. Greek colonists were quick to find heroic roots in their new homes, whether for comfort or self-justification, and some natural phenomena almost forced such identifications. No Greek was 'at home' without something of the trappings of his heroic past. Benghazi hardly looks like a Garden of Eden these days, but it was fertile enough in antiquity to justify association with the Garden of the Hesperides and the apples of immortality which Herakles was to seek. The Troad naturally lent itself to identifications of places, trees and tombs, thanks to the epic associations and despite its essentially non-Greek population for much of antiquity. Euboea seems well established in the story, supported by relics, for being on the homeward route from Troy for the Greek heroes (an image and Pelops' shoulder; T.237,346), and where many of the heroes perished thanks to the wrecking skills of the Euboean king Nauplios. There was, however, no security even in well-established traditions, and as early as the sixth century BC it could be held that Agamemnon returned to his death at Amyklai in Laconia, where some placed his tomb, and not Mycenae (T.305).[100] The alternative home was a product of later politics.

Troy and the Trojans present a special problem. We know them through Homer, and it is easy to think of them being as Greek as he makes them appear. Historically, whether there was a Greek expeditionary force there or not, they were not Greek, but they are made to live and worship like Greeks and their divinities are Greek, though with the very best eastern connections (Aphrodite, Apollo, Artemis), and even their foe Athena was worshipped within their walls (the Palladion). So ancient re-creators of the past were bound to treat them as Greeks, much as they did the Amazons who were yet more remote, and who were Trojan allies, as were the non-Greek Lycians of south west Anatolia. We shall see that only with the fifth century did the convenience of assimilating the Trojans to contemporary eastern enemies, the Persians, begin to influence the way they were depicted in Greek art [*Fig. 142*], although they had before been given less threatening eastern dress, as of Scythians. Euripides' Greeks call Trojans barbarians and Phrygians, folk who prostrate themselves to royalty, indulge in incest and witchcraft, but the poet is always sympathetic to their plight.[101]

The Greeks were not slow to recruit also the evidence of foreign countries, beyond their colonies, to support their interest in placing and identifying their past. Herodotus was an enthusiast in this matter and was probably not the first, but there was a continuing exercise by Greeks to assimilate Egyptian monuments and figures, notably their attitude to 'the Egyptian Labyrinth' and various Memnoneia,[102] also to place figures of their myth-history in an Egyptian context, such as 'King' Proteus, a son of Poseidon.[103] There are, however, few examples of physical identification of the Greek heroic past (Perseus' footprint; T.88) beyond the iconographical or cult assimilations which are mainly Hellenistic. Isis' locks shown at Memphis (T.105) might seem a wholly Egyptian phenomenon but her long, loose and curling locks were a feature of Greek representations of the

86. Athenian black figure amphora by Exekias showing Memnon as a Greek warrior flanked by two negro attendants. About 540 BC. (London, British Museum B209)

goddess, adapting her Egyptian coiffure, and so probably inspired by the foreigner.[104]

The case of the Colossus of Memnon at Egyptian Thebes deserves a closer look. Memnon was the son of Eos (Dawn) and Tithonos, ethnically Ethiopian and therefore black, but never thus shown in Greek art, although his attendants are [*Fig. 86*].[105] His associations are otherwise eastern, in Persia, and there is no little confusion of identities. He was the handsomest of the heroes at Troy in the view of Homer's Odysseus,[106] but killed by Achilles. His body was rescued from the field of battle by his mother, and on one vase by his black companions [*Fig. 87*].[107]

87. Memnon's body removed from the battlefield by two negro followers, on an Athenian black figure lekythos from Gela. Early 5th cent. BC. (Gela Museum 41)

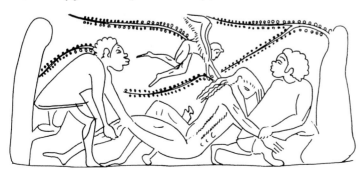

88. Monolith statues of Amenophis III at Egyptian Thebes. The statue at the right was taken for the hero Memnon. Its upper part was thrown down in an earthquake and restored with courses of sculptured masonry in Roman times. H. about 21 m.

89. Memnon [*Fig. 88*] drawn by Frederick Catherwood (about 1830) showing the split base and the courses of restoration of the upper part, lost in an earthquake. (London, British Museum)

90. As [*Fig. 88*] in a painting by David Roberts, showing 'Memnon' and his double facing his mother, the Dawn (Eos). Painted 1838/9. (Huntington Library)

91. A detail of the leg of 'Memnon' [*Fig. 88*] covered with Greek inscriptions made by visitors in the Roman period.

In archaic Greek art the outcome of the duel was predicted by the weighing of their souls or fates before Zeus. Soul-weighing is an Egyptian practice and it may be that Memnon's ancestry inspired the story. For all that, in Homer, the weighing is done only for Achilles and Hektor.[108]

Similarities between Memnon's name and various 'throne names' of Egyptian kings, especially Amenophis III and Sethos I, had prompted identifications, and his name was much attached to the western, cemetery area of Egyptian Thebes, the Memnoneion. Here he was, at an uncertain date, located in one of the grandest of all Egyptian sculptural monuments (T.119,177). Before the funerary temple of Amenophis III (mid-second millennium BC), to the west of the Nile but within range of occasional flooding, stood two seated statues of the king, monolithic, each some twenty-one metres high [*Fig. 88*]. There was an earthquake in 27 BC. When Strabo arrived shortly afterwards he observed that one of them had lost its top, above the seat, but that the ruined statue gave out a noise at sunrise. This was Vocal Memnon, not with the 'rivers of melody' that Lord Tennyson evoked, but what, from various accounts, seems to have been more like a resonant 'ping'. Lord Curzon's description of it (deduced from ancient texts not audition) was 'a clear, somewhat metallic, sound, varying in pitch and intensity – sometimes a shrill, sharp, twanging note, at others a fainter and more ringing vibration'. His account of the whole phenomenon is better than most – he was as good an archaeologist as Viceroy of India.[109] Strabo had wondered whether the noise was faked for tourists, a scepticism shared by others down to recent times. A favourite theory was that the sun's heat produced a flow of air through some orifice, but this would not have produced the alleged sound. Curzon was cautious; sure that it was no fake but the product of the sudden heat of the sun on part of the cracked statue, two surfaces of which were thus rubbed together. He observed that the figure was cleft from the waist to near its base [*Fig. 89*], and remarks the presence and absence of cavities which might either have generated a noise or hidden a priest who was ready to excite the tourists. Similar noises are attested elsewhere in similar circumstances with ruined stone monuments. It was, of course, the broken Memnon crying to his mother, Dawn, in the most grandiose of all Greek identifications of their mythical past [*Fig. 90*]. The statue became a great tourist attraction under the Roman empire, visited by poets (Juvenal), emperors and generals, and its base is covered with nearly ninety approving inscriptions in Greek and Latin [*Fig. 91*]. I quote the translation of one cited by Curzon, written by an imperial officer in appropriate doggerel:

> O sea-born Thetis, know that when
>   His mother's torch is lit
> Memnon awakes and cries aloud,
>   Fired by the warmth of it.
> Beneath the brow of Libyan heights,
>   where Nilus cuts in twain
> The city of the glorious gates,
>   He wakes to life again.
> Yet thine Achilles, who in fight
>   Ne'er slaked his savage joy,
> On the Thessalian plains is mute,
>   Is mute on those of Troy.

The last recorded visit was by the emperor Septimius Severus in about AD 200, and it was no doubt at his behest that the upper half of the statue was restored, with courses of a different stone set on the broken lower half, to take the form in which we see it today. Memnon was repaired, and never cried again.

It was not only the Greek past that Herodotus and others sought to recapture in alien monuments. They proved as adept as the Egyptians in promoting the reputation of the Twelfth-Dynasty king(s) 'Sesostris' (also confused with a Nineteenth-Dynasty 'Sesostris' – Sethos I), by identifying his monuments in the Hittite reliefs of kings and gods in Anatolia. For Egyptians and Greeks he had become close to being a conqueror of the world, more legendary than historical.[110]

To the east, although the Greeks took much from Syria and the Levant, there was little of relevance to our subject. The River Orontes had attracted their attention as early as the eighth century BC, and became a source for stories of giant or monster (Typhon) burials (T.402), while Joppa (Jaffa) was the place where Andromeda was

92. Indian schist relief in the Gandharan style. Drunken Silenos on a mule is fed wine by a woman; another woman follows, holding a jug, a wine crater on the ground; at the right a man of Central Asian aspect greets them. The head-garlands are Indian but the dress Greek, as are all elements of the composition. Probably from the decoration of a stupa. H. 15.5 cm. 1st/2nd cent. AD. (Private Collection)

exposed to the sea monster, and so displayed relics of her ordeal (T.101,509). A hippopotamus tooth found in a Greek-built temple near the Orontes mouth could be an heroic relic.[111] The story of the Flood was essentially an eastern one, but Greeks created their own version, with Deukalion as Noah, and Lucian could even impose it on what must have been an eastern 'relic', a soak-away for the flood waters in a smallish hole beneath a 'temple of Hera' in Syria, where he was promised a great chasm (T.106); the Greek equivalent was shown in Athens beside the Temple of Olympian Zeus (T.132, cf. T.233).

Farther off, the site of Prometheus' daily suffering from Zeus' eagle, which ate his renewable liver, was moved east from the true Caucasus to a Central Asian Caucasus, the Hindu Kush in Afghanistan, and a cave site for it was identified there (T.592). In the fifth century BC it could be thought that Dionysos himself had travelled east from his Lydian home, to as far away as Bactria (north Afghanistan), where, in the Persian period, Greeks certainly lived as exiles or refugees. He then returned to evangelize in Greece.[112] Only with Alexander the Great's journey of conquest to the east, to the very borders of India, did a complex of stories of his illustrious predecessors' expeditions begin to be woven. These involved both the god Dionysos, whose Indian campaign became a popular motif in the Roman period, and Alexander the Great's reputed ancestor, Herakles. Such stories, however, found no response in Indian literature and myth, even after a Greek kingdom was established in Bactria in the third century BC, to be succeeded by Indo-Greek penetration of India itself. The most we find is the identification of a few places which might be associated with the mythical expeditions – notably a

93. A clay figure of Vajrapani attending the Buddha in a shrine at Hadda (near Jalalabad, Afghanistan); his features and pose are those of the Greek Herakles devised by Lysippos in the 4th cent. BC, a thunderbolt replacing the hero's club. 2nd/3rd cent. AD. (*In situ* or destroyed)

town and mountain Nysa, where there was ivy and the vine, and so must have fallen to Dionysos, or the mountain town of Aornos where Alexander consciously sought to succeed where Herakles had failed![113] Lucian says that springs sacred to satyrs, Pan and Silenos, were visited annually by Indians.[114] However, the Dionysiac associations that Greeks brought east had a profound effect on the iconography of many Buddhist monuments in the early centuries AD, from generalized scenes of Bacchic and vinous behaviour to adaptations of scenes of Dionysiac processions [*Fig. 92*];[115] while the iconography of a classical Herakles was borrowed by the Indians to depict Vajrapani, attending the Buddha, and clasping an Indian thunderbolt instead of his club [*Fig. 93*].[116]

The personnel of this story of relics is dominantly drawn from the names associated with epic poetry about the Trojan War and its aftermath, especially, probably, for the later identifications, once Homer had become an accepted authority for early Greek history and even geography. The actors in other stories, such as that of the expeditions against Thebes, also attract some interest and it is the local heroes, preferably those engaged in 'national' epic events, whose relics are sought or manufactured. The ubiquitous Herakles was the most popular other single figure and had a special role in the more recently concocted myth-history of colonial areas, especially in the west. His name had become the epithet for a great range of the familiar and unfamiliar – the Pillars of Herakles at Gibraltar, a poppy, epilepsy, big cups, hot baths, soft beds, magnets.

Other travellers, such as the Argonauts, Odysseus and many another hero of Troy attempting to return home, also play an inspiring role on colonial shores. How far stories of the post-Trojan War wanderings to east and west conceal evidence for some sort of late Mycenaean diaspora of Greeks is a subject for no little historical discussion these days, and to be contrasted, sometimes correlated, with archaeological evidence. The alleged physical evidence which supported such stories and which is our concern is but a small part of the broader picture.

I am not tempted to offer maps of the journeys, locating monsters and mythical kingdoms, largely because it is virtually impossible except for a very few obvious locations such as Troy, Colchis and Ithaca (which has even been questioned, too). The Argonauts are better mapped than many but some ancient authors thought they managed a passage from the Black Sea to the Adriatic which involved more than rivers. Diomedes and Aineias, the Greek and Trojan princes from Troy, are also quite well located – both in the west, and this probably the result of either Late Bronze Age knowledge of the areas (see above) or more recent colonizing. Odysseus is far more of a problem and even antiquity was indecisive about placing many of his adventures. The popularity of some western locations was probably also the result of colonist enthusiasm and not by any means necessarily in the mind of Homer or his sources. A stocky seaman king of Ithaca at the end of the Bronze Age would have known all about the Adriatic coast and probably south Italy, especially if he was a merchant/pirate and as devious in his behaviour as are all merchants (and Odysseus himself) in Homer. Sailors' tales about Ithacesian adventures would readily condense into Odysseus' journey and I have some sympathy with the modern sailor-explorer who places most of them no farther away than the west coast of Greece.[117] The record of the Ithaca caves (Chapter Three) shows how vivid the mythopoeic imagination of the area could be.

We have noticed that relics associated with particular heroes could not only be duplicated but be housed sometimes in places where the connection is slight or obscure; Odysseus can be carried to Spain (T.550). In the same way hero cults may be identified in unexpected places. It is suggested that this conceals early relationships between cities,[118] but the reason might be either far more obscure and non-political, or simply the product of fortuitous and barely relevant speculation. Generally, however, it seems not necessarily to have been the figure or story that was the major inspiration for identifying relics, rather than that rich exploitation by Greek imagination of features of the natural world and of accidentally uncovered artefacts, which, supplemented by ingenuity and forgery, they employed to provide a physical setting for their distant past. And there were, of course, also hundreds of other locations with heroic and divine names which were inspired by, or may themselves have given rise to, such story-telling. Our survey of what was deemed to be physical evidence of the mythical past covers but a fraction of the geography of Greek myth.

CHAPTER FIVE

Imaging the Past: Here be Monsters

MONSTERS BELONG, AND belonged, to the mythical past. No one met or meets griffins or centaurs. Yet the Greek prescriptions for the appearance of monsters are remarkably consistent and plausible, far more so than those of most other ancient peoples. Indeed they anticipate Leonardo's recipe 'How to make an imaginary animal appear natural': 'having its limbs such that each bears some resemblance to that of some one of the other animals'.[1] This is part of the monsters' Greekness but no part of their origins. We find this to be a canny blend of folktale, observation and imagination. Sometimes the text or story, possibly foreign, comes first, sometimes the image, again often foreign, to which a story can be attached. Fossils played their part, and we saw in Chapter Two the probable contribution of one to the creation of a Greek story, Hesione's sea monster, whether or not we have also a Greek artist's accurate portrait of it [*Fig. 7*]. This chapter is essentially about how the Greeks re-created images for the monsters of their heroic myth-history. This will be found to owe more to the imagination and the imaginative use of images taken from the arts of others, than to any literary prescriptions, and very little even to the record of fossils.

We start with a monster carefully investigated by Adrienne Mayor – the griffin. It differs from others considered in this chapter in that it was not assigned only to a mythical past, but also to a quasi-mythical distance from Greek lands. In Greece it was called *gryps*, which means 'hooked' and could be applied to a nose or beak as well as to talons.[2] Greeks heard a tale of griffins in the distant north or east, who guarded gold and were fought by a race of men called Arimaspoi, who were said to be one-eyed though never shown thus in Greek art. It was recounted in a poem by Aristeas, who travelled the Black Sea and returned with a near-mythical reputation as a shaman, and a lot of Scythian lore from the northern steppes. His date is disputed and can probably only be placed securely earlier than the first occurrence of the griffin/gold story in Greek art. The creature's name is Greek but there are similar eastern words meaning the same ('hooked') and it may have been suggested by them.

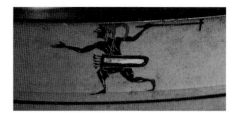

94. Athenian black figure cup showing on one side a griffin, on the other an Arimasp shooting at it. About 550 BC. (Angers, Musée Pincé 1006)

We get no image of the fight in Greek art until the mid-sixth century [*Fig. 94*],[3] where the monster is attacked by a figure in Scythian dress. There is, however, a bronze mirror from Kelermes in south Russia (east of the Crimea), and so nearer the griffins' assumed home, which shows two hairy men fighting a monster which has an eagle's head, with long ears and a forehead knob, and a winged lion's body [*Fig. 95*]. The nakedness of the men allows no ethnic clothing to help identity, but this cannot be doubted. The composition, with the rearing beast, is eastern, and it is possible that eastern groups of a king confronting a griffin monster inspired the image and story, just as a comparable group provided Greeks with an iconography for Herakles and the lion. The creature on the mirror is the typical archaic Greek 'griffin' [*Fig. 96*] and it had appeared long before in Greek art, on its own.[4] Here it is on an object which is Scythian in type but decorated in a manner common to the Greeks of Anatolia, and beside other subjects which look Greek, as well as just one small animal which looks like the Scythian 'Animal Style'. It has been dated to various parts of the sixth century BC, and now, in a recent Russian reassessment of the whole find, back into the seventh century, which is possibly too far, given its other stylistic associations.[5] There are later representations of the fight in Greek art, in some of which the Arimasps are dressed as Persians, not Scythians – a change of dress observed also by Amazons; none alludes to the gold [*Fig. 97*].[6]

95. Bronze mirror from Kelermes (south Russia) of Scythian type. The top segment shows two hairy men (Arimasps) fighting a griffin. The others have various, mainly Greek, orientalizing motifs. W. 17 cm. Early 6th cent. BC. (St Petersburg)

96. (*below*) A griffin drawn on a Samian vase (crater), about 600 BC. (Samos Museum)

97. (*right*) Athenian red figure pelike by the Painter of Munich 2365 showing a griffin attacking Arimasps. H. 28.2 cm. Early 4th cent. BC. (Texas, McCoy Collection)

98. Skeleton of *Proceratops*, from the Gobi desert.

Mayor suggests that the story originated in east Asia with the finds of fossil beasts with a strongly hooked face profile, one of which (*Proceratops*) also has triangular frills at the back of the skull which could have suggested the ears [*Fig. 98*].⁷ Gold may be found in the relevant areas, and it seems possible that some connection between the gold and the fossil creatures may have been made in antiquity, though not in any local story or image that has survived. For the Greeks the distant north and the distant east were much the same thing, especially where Scythians were the intermediaries, and, as we have observed, they represented Arimasps in their art as northerners or easterners, Scythians or Persians.

The problem is not unlike that with the Corinthian vase painter [*Fig. 7*] and the question whether he could have had sources for Trojan palaeontology. The 'griffin' image had a long history in Greece and the near east, whatever its name. Closely comparable monsters appear in Mesopotamian art from the third millennium BC and the succession can easily be traced to later centuries. There is even occasional borrowing of the type in the Greek world – a twelfth-century vase showing two griffins feeding nestlings [*Fig. 99*].⁸ In Mesopotamia there are monsters with eagle heads and lion bodies, often also winged, with the legs of a bird of prey and even a

99. Two griffins feed nestlings on a Late Mycenaean pyxis from Lefkandi, Euboea. 12th cent. BC. (Eretria Museum)

100. Griffin demon on a relief from Carchemish, on the Euphrates, 8th cent. BC.

101. Bronze griffin attachment for a cauldron, from Olympia. About 625 BC. H. 35.5 cm. (Athens, National Museum 6159)

scorpion's tail. There are also humanoid demons with eagle heads and necks. They can have nothing to do with any eastern story of our 'griffins'; they do not fight heroes or guard gold, rather than embody demonic power, but they were influential. Syrian versions of them in the eighth century (usually humanoid demons but also with winged lion bodies) have lions' ears, and curls on their necks ending in a loop or knob above the forehead [*Fig. 100*]. This is the type which is copied in Greece for bronze attachments to cauldrons [*Fig. 101*], an eastern mode but in the east done with the heads of lions or bulls (both also used in this way in Greece), not eagles. We call them 'griffins' because they are the obvious source of the later canonical Greek griffin type which appears in other arts in the seventh century [*Fig. 96*]. By the time of the Kelermes mirror [*Fig. 95*] this monster had been adopted by artists to depict the *gryps* fought by Arimasps. The identification would have been encouraged by the monster's name, probably of eastern origin, which carried with it expectations of a hooked nose and rapacious ways. Whether descriptions of the eastern *gryps* also included ears we cannot know – I rather doubt it, just as I doubt whether the forehead knob has to do with anything other than Syrian origins. In Greek art the ears grow longer, like a hare's, and the knob taller and more like a piece of furniture, while as a protome it acquires a long snaky neck [*Fig. 101*],[9] and by the classical period also a spiny mane. As remarked, the first occurrences of the beast facing an Arimasp are the Scytho-Greek mirror [*Fig. 95*] and the mid-sixth-century Athenian cup [*Fig. 94*]. Throughout this period, and later, the griffin continues to enjoy a life of its own as a decorative motif, and in the classical period attacks other animals, as do lions, and just occasionally fights a lion in peripheral or non-Greek art, in Black Sea lands.[10] Thus it regained its integrity as an independent monster, and was only occasionally called upon to fight Arimasps, perhaps mainly for artists such as vase painters responding to a subject that might appeal in the Black Sea markets – these mainly of the fourth century BC [*Fig. 97*].[11] It remains a most favoured subject for classical artists in a decorative role, but the lion-eagle regains a yet more distinguished function as the symbol of the Church of Christ in Dante.[12] The griffin/gold story generated a snowball of fantasy in later writers, copying and improving on each other, with which artists could not keep pace.

There is, however, a further slight problem with their early history, since it has been observed that the story of the Arimasps fighting griffins for their gold is remarkably like that of the Indians stealing gold from the ants (= marmots), which we discussed in Chapter Two and found to be, in its way, authentic. Indeed, Aelian has the griffins themselves digging the gold as they built their nests, and Indians acting as Arimasps stealing it. So it might be that the ant story gave rise to the more graphic griffin story, in the imagination of an easterner or Greek;[13] Goethe made the ants and griffins associates.[14] This would further diminish the appropriateness of the 'griffin' fossils, and spare us trying to make a connection between them and the Greek orientalizing griffins. A by-then familiar monster and a northern people of familiar (assumed) aspect replaced unfamiliar ants and Indians.

One lesson of this should be to encourage wariness in the use of commonly accepted words, such as 'griffin', which carry narrative baggage not appropriate in all or even most, contexts. We may lose much in ignoring interesting local origins and character, and in saddling monsters of whatever period and place with conventional names – 'dragon', 'sphinx', 'siren'. The process of finding an image for a name presents a pattern which we shall see was followed in the creation and then mythical identification of other monsters. This is the way the Greeks gave visual identity to creatures of their myth-historical past, opponents of their heroes, prompted perhaps on occasion by the physical evidence of fossils, but more often by the inspiration won from the arts of the near east in the eighth and seventh centuries BC. These we turn to now, à propos of sphinxes, sirens, the Chimaira and gorgons. Other mixed animals like sea monsters, and man-animals from centaurs to satyrs, are special cases, but also to be considered here, though some were timeless and not essentially tied to a distant heroic past. The phenomenon is not one paralleled in the arts of the near east or Egypt where there are archetypal images of monsters and where, especially in the east, any certain identification in a specific myth narrative is exceptional.[15]

102. Ivory panel from Nimrud showing a sphinx trampling a man. Probably Phoenician, 8th cent. BC. (ND 13867)

103. Athenian Geometric cup with a frieze of figures including sphinx-like creatures. About 700 BC. Diam. 12.5 cm. (Athens, National Museum 784)

The human-headed lion – the 'sphinx' – is a creature well known to the arts of both Egypt and the near east. In Egypt it was commonly wingless but in the east it was usually winged. It has various functions, not least as a symbol of royal power in Egypt where it may be given a portrait head. A common iconographic group is of the sphinx trampling down a human foe; this appears also in the near east [*Fig. 102*] and may affect its role in Greece, where the trampling is taken for lifting a body.[16] The creature had already appeared in Greek Bronze Age art. In the Levant it seems to represent a 'cherub' and is of either sex. It reappears in Greece at the end of the eighth century, derived from Syrian art, and its usual role is as one of a frieze of animals and monsters, with no obvious function or identity. It generated monsters such as the two we see on the Athenian Geometric cup [*Fig. 103*], which are simply generically supernatural but with no particular function.[17] A special type, common in Crete, is male and helmeted. However, it may be that the eastern scenes of it over-running a human figure gave rise to its use in Greece as a death demon, and as guardian of a tomb, functions which it could exercise from the late seventh century on, without disturbing its more secular and decorative role. However, the creature was soon to be called upon to play a name role also in heroic myth.[18]

104. Impression of a chalcedony scarab with a sphinx seizing a young warrior. L. 18 mm. About 500 BC. (London, British Museum 1933.10–15.1)

The land of Thebes was ravaged by a monster which carried off the young men; this is a familiar folktale involving a locally threatening monster or demon. The carrying-off was a function which helped identify the Theban monster with the human-headed winged lion, in its role in foreign art of trampling a man. The human head had narrative value too since the creature uttered a riddle which, unanswered, guaranteed the death of those sent out from Thebes to confront it. This is another folktale element – the riddle to be solved to avoid death – which was grafted on to the episode. The hero Oidipous outwitted it, solved the riddle and killed the creature. We do not know how old the story is, but we can see that its elements are relatively commonplace, part of which may have originated in the discovery of monstrous and human remains. The attacking sphinx remains a subject for Greek art whether or not it is to be taken as the Theban, from gems [*Fig. 104*],[19] to sculpture – on the throne of Olympian Zeus.[20]

Oidipous' adversary was called *phix* in its homeland Boeotia, where there is a mount Phikion (T.459), but elsewhere generally *sphinx*, both words being of uncertain derivation: *sphingein* means to bind tight, perhaps then 'grasping'. The Boeotian poet Hesiod was calling it Phix by about 700 BC, and placing it in a family tree with other monsters of myth. Greek artists later decided that the human-headed winged lion, by then long familiar in their art, was a suitable model for it, and that it should be female (like its name); the name 'Sphinx' was accordingly applied, and has been ever since, with or without the context of the Oidipous story. Indeed, most representations of the sphinx in Greek art thereafter have nothing to do with the story but are decorative, or related to its funerary associations. The first use of the name in art (as *theichs*, poorly written, probably meant for *phix*)[21] is on an Athenian vase of little before 550 BC, and on another rather later as *sphichx*;[22] on both the creatures are simply decorative, but the name implies earlier association with the Theban story, which is shown, without the names, on uninscribed cups of the same date where the creature is seen pursuing youths; these must surely be the

105. Athenian red figure amphora by the Achilles Painter. A youth, probably Oidipous, argues with the Sphinx. H. 33.2 cm. About 450 BC. (London, British Museum E331, from Nola)

Thebans but with no suggestion of a riddle. Scenes with a probable Oidipous also appear before the end of the sixth century, and often later [*Fig. 105*].[23] Thus the creature's career in myth is established, without disturbing its other roles, funereal or decorative. From the early fifth century on sphinxes are occasionally given human breasts to accentuate their femininity, and the male sphinx was long forgotten except in the Persian east, where it may be regal as it was in Egypt. But the 'Riddle of the Sphinx' is Greek in origin, not Egyptian, however it may be popularly applied.

The fact that the Oidipous with the riddling monster was the same as the Oidipous of the tragic family life, killing his father, marrying his mother, blinding himself, with doomed children, is an interesting reflection on the vagaries of Greek myth. In dealing with the tragic Oidipous the poet Sophocles was obliged also to refer to his monster-slaying, which seems and is a quite alien episode. The functions and origins of the two stories were totally different, their coincidence in one figure a product of the locality.

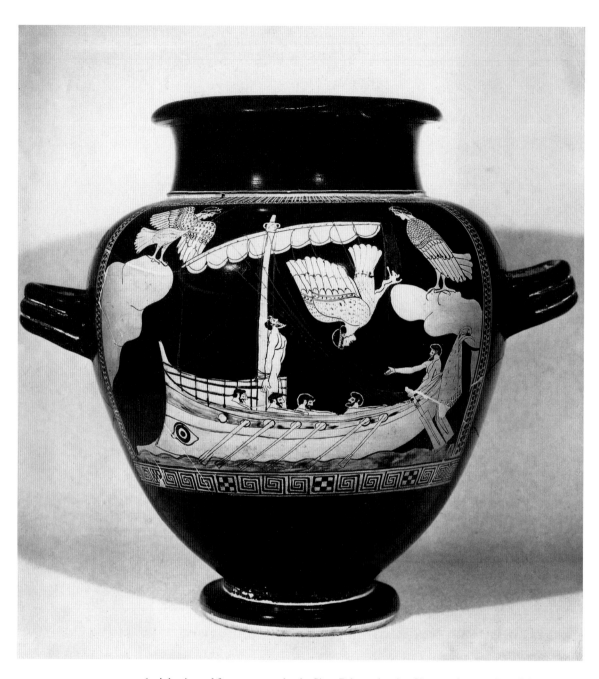

106. Athenian red figure stamnos by the Siren Painter showing Sirens trying to seduce Odysseus, who is tied to his mast as his crew (their ears stopped) row by. H. 35.3 cm. About 470 BC. (London, British Museum E440, from Vulci)

Sirens have a similar though simpler history. Human-headed birds were well known to Egyptian and eastern arts and appeared from an early date in Greek orientalizing arts in no narrative context.[24] Rivers (recall the Rhine Maidens) and seas are haunted by musical female demons who may be beneficent but may as readily lure sailors on to rocks. If this is done by their singing, then it is well that they have human heads, and if possible human arms if they are to handle musical instruments. It may have been a matter of choice whether they were deemed marine like mermaids or avian, and Homer did not describe the Greek versions but located them on an island. The Greeks chose the birdlike in the early sixth century, when it became a matter of devising images for the Sirens who attempted to drive Odysseus' ship on to rocks [*Fig. 106*].[25] Their singing was an important and defining element, and as musicians they appear also in Greek art as mourners. Creatures of the same physical form had other funereal roles, as bearers of dead bodies, Harpies, and so could mimic the sphinxes in this function. In myth they are rapacious spoilers of King Phineus' feast, but for this they are given a wholly human form, winged.[26]

It is often the case that monsters or demons may be described in poetry or any oral tradition in terms which denote their horrific or supernatural character, but which were not necessarily accompanied in the imagination of the teller by any

107. Herakles leads a female monster, breathing fire. On an Athenian black figure jug by the Athena Painter. H. 22 cm. About 500 BC. (Boston, Museum of Fine Arts 98.924)

108. Athenian black figure cup by the Heidelberg Painter showing Bellerophon on Pegasos confronting the Chimaira; armed witnesses. H. 14 cm. (Paris, Louvre A478)

plausible image. Indeed, many could not be, and may be composed of fire, water and dung; it would have taken a Greek of more than Hindu ingenuity to devise an image for demonic and often mutating creatures such as Lamia or Empousa, which are at any rate very much the stuff of folktale and had no place in heroic story or, as a consequence, in heroic iconography. On the other hand, there are in art some monsters we cannot name, such as the bitch breathing fire and led on a chain by Herakles on some vases of around 500 BC [*Fig. 107*], and recurring in a rustic setting in Boeotia some years later. There is a name and story here still lost to us.[27]

The Chimaira presents a slightly different case: a fire-breathing monster, associated with a cave in a volcanic area of Lycia, that has to be killed by Bellerophon riding his winged horse Pegasos. In early literature (Hesiod, Homer) it is described as a lion in front, a serpent behind, and a chimaira (she-goat) in the middle, the last having the fiery breath. It seems that the geophysical location determined the fire-breathing function and the name, while Bellerophon's Lycian connection cast him as the appropriate hero to deal with it. Presumably some earthy exhalation with or without heat recalled the creature's bad smell, and this was a recommendation for applying the name; otherwise one might think that the goatee beard had suggested flames, but a she-goat has none. Then the lion and serpent are added by story-tellers, not artists, as archetypal threatening monsters without too much concern for anatomical plausibility, unless perhaps the Chimaira was thought of as having three bodies or necks and heads, like a Kerberos.

Orientalizing art came to the aid of the artist almost as early as the first descriptions we have in literature (the story itself must be much older). The eastern winged lion was again recruited. It was an eastern conceit on occasion to embellish the extremities of creatures with other animal forms, a fashion dominant also in the Animal Style of the northern steppes. Thus the tip of a wing might grow a head, and for the Chimaira this is a goat's head; in some Greek representations in art the fact that its neck was once a wing is not forgotten. In Syria a lion's tail may have a bird's head instead of a tuft; in Greek art such extremities were usually decorated with a snake's head (thus the divine aigis, or Hermes' caduceus wand), and so the Greek Chimaira has a snake tail [*Fig. 108*].[28] For a brief period at the end of the seventh century artists tried to be completely true to the literary prescription and made the whole rear of the creature into a serpent, without the lion's hind legs [*Fig. 109*]. This totally immobilized it, offending Greek logic even about monsters, and was soon abandoned. But if it was indeed the literary description that determined this abortive image, we have a very early instance of literature dictating a detail in art.[29]

109. Serpentine gem from Melos with a Chimaira, its rear all serpent. About 600 BC. W. 26 mm. (Munich, Münzsammlung A1322)

The gaze of the senior Gorgon sister, Medusa, could turn men to stone; a story readily inspired by humanoid rocks or primitive statues. She is pursued and decapitated by the hero Perseus, who was provided with a magic cap of darkness, winged shoes, and a bag (*kibisis*) for the head. In the story her powers were clearly defined, but not her appearance, and as soon as Greek artists attempted narrative they had no hint or tradition to follow. An Athenian artist of before the middle of the seventh century gave the sisters a head like an orientalizing cauldron, but drawn like a facing griffin's head and fringed with lion-headed snakes, themselves

110. The Gorgon sisters on this Athenian vase of about 660 BC have heads like cauldrons; a unique attempt to create the petrifying gaze of Medusa. (Eleusis Museum)

111. The Gorgon Medusa shown as a horse, being decapitated by Perseus who looks away from her fatal stare. On a Boeotian relief vase. About 650 BC. (Paris, Louvre CA795)

112. Impression of a cornelian scarab showing a Gorgon, winged, with a horse's body, wrestling with a lion. L. 14 mm. (Unknown whereabouts)

resembling the treatment of bronze cauldrons [*Fig. 110*].[30] This was a fine fantasy. It was agreed that their bodies should be humanoid and later they were generally also winged. Another artist chose a grotesque human head, rather like a mask of the type met in dedications in Greek sanctuaries, but also gave her a horse body out of respect for the fact that she had mated with Poseidon, who had taken the form of a horse for the encounter [*Fig. 111*].[31] Medusa's horse body lingered here and there in Greek art, as on gems where there is no Perseus narrative [*Fig. 112*],[32] but the decision about the head had by then been taken by Corinthian artists in the mid-seventh century, and again depended on the example of the orient.

The solution was basically a frontal lion's head, and the source probably eastern monsters, such as Pazuzu, who have various animal/monster bodies, but a frontal

113. Syrian bronze head of the demon Pazuzu, from Nimrud, with lion's head, horns and lolling tongue. H. 4.3 cm. 7th cent. BC. (Oxford, Ashmolean Museum 1951.33)

114. Athenian black figure plate by Lydos, with the Gorgon Medusa's head. Diam. 24 cm. About 560 BC. (Munich, Antikensammlungen 8760)

lion head with open jaws, lolling tongue, and often little horns [*Fig. 113*].[33] In Greek art the horns are an occasional additive, the mane and locks are stylized into snakes, and the upper part of the face – the eyes and ears – are allowed to look human. This remains the essential gorgon face throughout the archaic period [*Fig. 114*],[34] only later losing its demonic, leonine quality, and gradually turning into an ordinary, even beautiful female face, remembering only the reduced snake locks and adding hair-wings. The result of her encounter with Poseidon was, in the story, the birth of the winged horse Pegasos and of an odd hero called Chrysaor, who both emerged at the moment of her death through decapitation. In art they spring from her severed neck and we cannot say whether or not the scheme was inspired by eastern two-headed monsters; probably not – there was little alternative, and the east had done enough to inspire this image for a potent monster of the heroic past. The head, the gorgoneion, was long to continue as a device in art, in early temple pediments, on shields, but also on jewellery and in drinking cups, probably too familiar to be visually terrifying except by association with its story.

In story-telling, spoken or written, a monster may be made the more horrific by being multiple, poisonous or invulnerable. The last was held true of the Nemean Lion faced by Herakles, and was probably not an original attribute since in early

115. Laconian black figure cup by the Hunt Painter showing the dog of Hades, Kerberos. Herakles, who holds the chain, is shown only by his leg, hands and club, at the right border. About 540 BC. W. 19 cm. (London, Erskine Collection)

116. Corinthian aryballos. Athena holds a phial for the Hydra's poisonous blood while Herakles and Iolaos attack the monster. H. 14.7 cm. About 590 BC. (Basel, Antikenmuseum BS 425)

scenes the hero uses a sword or spear on it. The invulnerability is demonstrated in art only once or twice by showing his sword deflected by its hide,[35] and is implicit in his subsequent wearing of the lionskin like a corselet, or a shield on his arm.

In art multiplication is more effective, but where literature may give the dog of Hades, Kerberos, a hundred heads, art settles for three or less. Snaky extremities are impressive, on Kerberos [*Fig. 115*][36] and often elsewhere, as on the divine aegis worn by Athena. Multiplicity gives the Hydra faced by Herakles many heads, self-renewing (except for one). Its poisonous blood, known in story, can only perhaps be alluded to in art where Athena seems to be keeping some of it in a phial, for Herakles to tip his arrows [*Fig. 116*].[37] Most of Herakles' monster adversaries are ordinary animals of the hunt, with special properties added in literature rather than art (the stag, bull, boar, the man-eating horses of Diomedes).[38] For these the artist did not need to go beyond common experience to devise the images.

117. Detail from an Athenian vase of about 660 BC. Sea monsters with triple lion heads and fish bodies. (Boston, Museum of Fine Arts, L.6.67)

We met the Greek sea monster, *ketos*, in Chapter Two, investigating the probable origin of the story about the one at Troy, and its possible unique skeletal image in art [*Fig. 7*]. Other origins for the story and creature must also be admitted, especially where there is the prospect of someone being swallowed by one. The great white shark swims the waters of the Mediterranean, and whales, real or fossilized, were known, and their bones exhibited in various places. One of Herakles' exploits was to rid the sea of monsters, especially the western seas, and this sounds like knowledge of the sea-bound rather than rock-bound. In seventh-century art sea monsters are shown with a gaping lion forepart and a fishy tail [*Fig. 117*].[39] It is this creature, rather than the fossil, that threatens Hesione in later sixth-century art, where Herakles may be shown even entering its jaws, to cut off its tongue [*Fig. 118*]. The same type serves as a familiar to sea deities, and as a mutant form of the sea-goddess Thetis when she wrestles with Peleus.

With the fifth century the artist begins to look for fresh inspiration, and devises a creature with a long wrinkled snout, tall ears, gills, a long spiny mane, and a long fishy body ending in a fish tail. Early examples are sometimes provided with a pair of lion forelegs, recalling the archaic beast, but later these are generally replaced by flippers. This is far more of an amalgam than the other monsters we have

118. Athenian black figure cup showing Herakles entering the jaws of the sea monster, seizing its tongue. Hesione, its prey, waits at the left, hand on head in dismay. (Toronto, Royal Ontario Museum 52.155)

considered. It owes something to the lion, in its legs, probably to the crocodile for its snout, but a crocodile has no ears (which are rather like the griffin's with which it shares the spiny mane in the classical period), the mane also recalls the seahorse, which could also model for the general proportions of the snout, and the snout can sometimes turn up like a pig's, and then resemble the treatment of the curled lip of the Babylonian dragon of earlier days.

This new-look *ketos* continued to serve to threaten Hesione, and also Andromeda, to be killed by Perseus, as well as remaining a familiar for sea gods and as a decorative motif [*Fig. 119*]. The Andromeda episode was sited on the Levant

119. Thetis or her sister riding a sea monster carries a new helmet for Achilles. From an Apulian red figure pelike. About 350 BC. (Ruvo, Museo Jatta J1500)

120. Silver coin of Akragas showing, beneath a crab, Skylla as a wild woman naked to the hips, where there are the foreparts of two ravening dogs, and with a sea monster body. Diam. 27.5 mm. Late 5th cent. BC.

coast at Joppa (Jaffa, near Tel Aviv), a fishing port where the monster's bones (jawbones of a whale) were exhibited (T.509), and eventually brought to Rome by M. Scaurus. The artists' magnificent re-creation of the monster, not at all like a whale, was long lived, and in art served even as Jonah's whale, despite its narrow neck, though it was given a more capacious belly. Jonah too sailed from Joppa and his 'whale' can as readily be translated as 'shark' in Hebrew as in Greek. Joppa may even have been a home whaling port for distant voyages into the Atlantic; it was a place for tales of life-threatening encounters with big fish in both Hebrew and Greek story-telling. In the Hellenistic period the classical image travelled east, eventually to enter Indian art; in Europe it personified the Sea giving up its dead at the Last Trump,[40] while the slaying by Perseus provided a model for St George and the Dragon, also rescuing a king's daughter in Palestine. This is not the only monster devised by Greeks to illustrate their past which was to serve others for centuries later in a variety of roles.

Skylla was a monster of the cavernous shore, accommodated in various genealogies of monsters, but primarily a scourge for Odysseus who has to pass both her and the whirlpool Charybdis. In Homer Skylla barks like a dog, has twelve legs, six long necks and heads with triple rows of teeth, which project from her cave to snatch passers-by.[41] Twelve legs and six heads sounds like a multiple humanoid, and the multiple rows of teeth like a shark (they were also attributed to Herakles to explain his gluttony!). There was no scope here for Greek artists, but since Skylla could also have a more heroic ancestry she was shown from the early fifth century on as a woman above the waist, with the foreparts of dogs or of the usual *ketos* monster just described issuing from her hips, and sometimes with a *ketos* body and tail [*Fig. 120*]: almost 'normal', and in the animal legs picking up a motif long popular in various ancient arts from Europe to India. She appears most often in the Greek art of south Italy, near her presumed lair.[42]

Man-monsters, usually with animal heads or foreparts on human bodies, had long been familiar in the east and Egypt. In the early Iron Age there is a fine clay man-horse from a cemetery at Lefkandi in Euboea of the ninth century BC [*Fig. 121*],[43] and on through the seventh century BC these creatures are presented as hunters, often shouldering a branch from which hangs their catch. However, by about the middle of the seventh century they are seen assaulting women, then being fought by Herakles [*Fig. 122*][44] and identifiably fighting the Lapiths, a Thessalian race. They are, by then, 'Centaurs', since they are so identified and named in myth, but were they 'Centaurs' before these narrative contexts appear, or just rustic hunters deriving from a folk tradition? Their name gives nothing away (except a hint of 'bull' in the ...*taur*, which is not helpful), and early authors who name them do not hint that they are other than humanoid. In myth they are generally unruly and drunken. In Thessaly, probably their original home, they break up the wedding of Peirithoos the Lapith king and attack the women, but are defeated, at the feast and then in battle, by the Lapiths and their king's comrade, Theseus. The classic presentations of the story are in the west pediment at Olympia and the south metopes of the Parthenon. Herakles has to fight them because they resented his use of their wine cellar, though invited by one of their number, Pholoe; this was in the Peloponnese. A single centaur, Nessos, tried to make off with Herakles' bride Deianeira after carrying her over a stream in Aetolia. But centaurs were not all bad, and Cheiron had a reputation as a healer and served as mentor to various heroes – notably Achilles, officiating at various episodes in his family history – the match between his parents, Peleus and Thetis, and their wedding [*Fig. 123*]. He got involved in the fight with Herakles and was wounded in the leg. The fact that there seems to be a gash in the leg of the ninth-century clay centaur [*Fig. 121*] would, if truly identifying Cheiron, push far back the association of the creature with 'Centaurs', but we cannot be quite sure, and it seems likely that the form preceded the identification, while it long remained a generic symbol of rusticity as well as playing its role in myth. Cheiron, being respectable, may be allowed human forelegs and dress [*Fig. 123*],[45] while some other early centaurs are also given human forelegs – essentially men with the rear-end of a horse. The same surgery creates the man-bull who personifies rivers, notably Acheloos, who may have simply a human head rather than upper body also, like a centaur. But there is another, more evocative man-bull to consider.

The Minotaur is a creature whose story could well have been generated and associated with Knossos by the discovery of Minoan representations of bull-headed men [*Fig. 124*],[46] and the various bull-games shown on wall paintings and other artefacts from the old labyrinthine site. But when artists first came to represent the monster in the archaic period, before the mid-seventh century, it is as a bull with a human forepart and not in the Minoan mode, shown on yet another relief vase, from the Greek islands, from the same class as the Medusa of [*Fig. 111*].[47] In other words, it conformed with the construction of a centaur, and as such had several predecessors in Greek art, back to the Bronze Age, but without any discernible myth associations since they are individual figures and not in any narrative context. However, the bull-headed-man type was also adopted at almost the same time[48] and was dominant thereafter [*Fig. 125*],[49] even for the baby

121. Clay figure of a centaur, parts found in two graves at Lefkandi in Euboea. H. 36 cm. 9th cent. BC. (Eretria Museum)

122. Athenian black figure kantharos by the Sokles Painter showing Herakles fighting two centaurs who are armed with branches. H. 25.5 cm. About 550 BC. (Berlin, Staatliche Museen 1737, from Vulci)

123. The centaur Cheiron, with a human forepart and legs, attends (left) with other divine guests the wedding of Peleus and Thetis on an Athenian black figure dinos painted by Sophilos. He has plenty of game for the feast, slung from his branch. About 570 BC. (London, British Museum 1971.11–1.1)

124. Impression of a seal of lapis lacedaemonius from the Dictaean Cave in Crete, showing a bull-man. 15th cent. BC. Diam. 24 mm. (Oxford, Ashmolean Museum, Kenna 322)

125. Detail of an Athenian red figure vase of the L.C. Group showing Theseus and the Minotaur. About 390 BC. (Athens, National Museum 12541)

126. Pasiphae nurses her child, the baby Minotaur, patting him on the back, on an Etruscan red figure cup by the Settecamini Painter. About 375 BC. (Paris, Cabinet des Médailles 1066)

Minotaur with his mother Pasiphae, but only in Etruscan art which admitted such oddities more readily than did Greek [*Fig. 126*].⁵⁰ To mate with her bull Pasiphae had Daidalos make her a hollow cow, shown in later Greek art with a door in its flank for her to climb in.

Other animal-headed men in Greek art are not all re-creations of an heroic age. Odysseus' companions being turned into animals by the witch Kirke may seem to be, but are shown simply part-translated [*Fig. 127*].⁵¹ Archaic art, especially of the East Greek area, proliferates with animal-headed demons, who may even fight each other, but who own no mythical identity [*Fig. 128*].⁵² Humanoid grotesques encountered in far distant lands have nothing particular to do with the past but are simple travellers' tales.⁵³

127. (*above*) The naked witch Kirke mixes her potion for the companions of Odysseus, already part turned into animals. Odysseus comes to the rescue from the left. On an Athenian black figure cup. About 550 BC. (Boston, Museum of Fine Arts 99.518)

128. Impression of a chalcedony scaraboid showing a dog-headed man fighting a donkey-headed man. H. 19.5 mm. About 500 BC. (London, British Museum 1929.6–10.3)

129. Detail from an Athenian red figure cup by Epiktetos. A satyr goes to war, blowing a trumpet, carrying a light shield, but not forgetting his wine jug. About 520 BC. (London, British Museum E 3)

The temptation to include any detailed account of satyrs here must be resisted. They are essentially hairy horse-men, with, at first, horse tails and ears, occasionally legs, then taking on more goat-like aspects. They serve the god Dionysos and so are in effect contemporary beings, which is what much of their very human behaviour, even with what appear to be mortals, might imply. But in earlier days they went to war against the Giants with their god [*Fig. 129*].[54] They helped provide the physique for the myth figure Marsyas, a piper who challenged Apollo and generated relics (his pipes and flayed skin), but who belongs to the non-Greek world of Anatolia. Another satyr-like figure, Silenos, was involved with an historical Phrygian king, Midas, but in the story the encounter happens in Midas' rose gardens in Thrace.[55] Satyrs and especially their senior (Pappo)silenos are hairy; I show the latter as portrayed by an actor in Athens, with mask and hairy suit, beside a stage Herakles [*Fig. 130*].[56] We may well imagine that the flayed skin of Marsyas which was exhibited was the hide of some large ape. The neighbouring Assyrians were given to flaying and exhibiting the bodies of their enemies, and we may recall the skins of two 'hairy women' dedicated in the Temple of Juno at Carthage by Hanno, returned from an island off west Africa.[57] The satyrs also interact with the image of another demon, the Arcadian god Pan, who starts as all-goat and gradually humanizes – completely in the Classical period, but retaining goats' legs and bestial features in later art [*Fig. 131*].[58] From him the satyrs come to adopt goat-tails and sometimes legs. These are not images of a remote past but rather of a haunted present. Nevertheless 'real' centaurs were found in Arabia, some caught and sent alive to Caesar in Egypt, their pickled bodies sent back to Rome and kept in the royal granaries.[59]

Wings on the usually un-winged were another sign of the supernatural and old. They could be given to deities: Artemis, Nike, Eros, even Athena; to various personifications such as Death, Sleep, Strife; and to other demons, animal-headed and the like – in East Greece pigs can fly. An ordinary figure of myth is rarely so

130. Detail from an Athenian red figure vase by the Pronomos Painter with actors: a Herakles and a Silenos, with their appropriate masks and costumes. About 400 BC. (Naples, Museo Archeologico 3240, from Ruvo)

131. Marble group from Delos of Aphrodite and Eros dealing with an amorous Pan. He has a brutish face, goats' horns and legs. About 100 BC. H. 1.29 m. (Athens, National Museum 3335)

132. Laconian black figure cup by the Typhon Painter. An anonymous monster. Diam. 17 cm. About 530 BC. (Cerveteri Museum 67658)

equipped, such as three-bodied Geryon, and many may be expected to fly at any rate – the sons of Boreas (the north wind), Gorgons, Pegasos. Snake-legs are the perquisite of creatures of the earth, notably giants but also some nymphs. There are plenty of Greek artists' fantasies which are not too easy to name [*Fig. 132*].[60]

Giants are monsters too, if only for their size, a natural quality to attribute to creatures of the remote past, and easily abetted or inspired, as we have seen, by discovery of their outsize bones – the fossils of various massive creatures. In art they are shown at the size of their divine adversaries and, only from the classical period on, often with snake legs. Sometimes, in archaic art, a giant encountered by Herakles will be shown larger, but generally when he is seated or recumbent, and here considerations of filling space and of isocephaly intrude. Polyphemos had one eye, not a feature for most early art where the head is shown in profile anyway, and only apparent in frontal views of the Hellenistic period on. Now too, in a period of greater realism and expression of landscape settings, a giant may at last be shown gigantic *vis-à-vis* the heroic, in painting and sculpture. Of this the most splendid is the great marble group of the blinding of Polyphemos installed for the Emperor Tiberius in his grotto resort at Sperlonga, sixty miles south of Rome [*Fig. 133*].[61]

Talos, the Cretan giant who walked round the island thrice every day for Minos and was made of bronze by Hephaistos, was exceptional. He had a single artery, from his head to where it was plugged at the ankles. The concept clearly derives from processes of the *cire perdue* casting of statues. He had to be succoured by the Argonauts when Medea pulled out the plug [*Fig. 134*].[62]

133. Reconstruction of a marble group from Sperlonga showing the giant Polyphemos being blinded by Odysseus and his companions. Copy of a work of about 200 BC.

134. Athenian red figure crater by the Talos Painter showing the brazen giant collapsing into the arms of the Dioskouroi. Malign Medea with her box of poisons watches from the left. About 400 BC. (Ruvo, Museo Jatta)

Siamese twins are real enough. Those known to Greek myth and literature are not seen in art,[63] though Geryon is constructed as a three-bodied man with variously two or six legs, even wings. Multi-bodied creatures are not uncommon in myth worldwide and some could be generated by observation of confused burials. Hermaphrodites too are real enough, and were deemed monstrous but with a prophetic faculty;[64] yet they too have a heroic model, a child of Hermes and Aphrodite [*Fig. 135*].[65] The Pygmies who fight the cranes are remote in place rather than time, shown at first as little men, later as real dwarfs.[66]

135. An onyx cameo of Hermaphrodite holding out her dress to admire his erection. 1st cent. BC. H. 17.5 mm. (Once Ionides Collection)

136. A bronze coin of Tanagra showing Dionysos in a temple, with a Triton below. Minted in the reign of Antoninus Pius (AD 139–161).

Not all creations of past monsters relied on the imagination of graphic or other artists. There were some physical concoctions on display which were associated with events of the remote past, such as the headless Triton (man-fish) at Tanagra (T.449), decapitated by the women it attacked (or by the owner of flocks: he managed to get the beast drunk). A Triton on coins of Tanagra [*Fig. 136*] may allude, but he has his head.[67] For the artists a Triton was a conventional image not at all affected by the inventions of showmen. These must be on a par with modern (or at least recent) fairground exhibits of mermaids and the like – stitched together out of various animal parts. Pausanias gives a graphic description of the composition of one displayed in Rome (T.450).[68] Real animals too could be identified with the mythical if they were far enough away. Monkeys especially were taken for satyrs, and baboons could be called sphinxes. Pausanias has a story of 'satyrs' on an Atlantic island torturing an old woman, illustrated on an Attic vase of the early fifth-century.[69]

CHAPTER SIX

Imaging the Past: The Hero and the Heroic

THE CLASSICAL GREEK had little doubt that he was himself very like his heroes. They may have been a bit taller, stronger and more handsome, but there is little or no inkling of this in an art which increasingly idealized the natural world, including the human image. Some heroic and divine figures may be shown a head or so taller than the obviously mortal, than athletes or the like, but there was no regular enlargement, and a slightly more than lifesize statue would be a natural choice for a figure or group designed to impress a mortal viewer. For Homer the goddess Artemis is taller than her nymphs. From the classical period on the mortals shown attending deities, as worshippers, are shown much smaller on votive reliefs, but for artists' purposes it is clear that the physique and appearance of heroes and heroines could be taken to have been the standard, mortal. The images of an Achilles or Helen were indistinguishable from those of contemporary Athenians. The latter must have found this reassuring, and a confirmation of their views about the relevance of the heroic past to the often less than heroic present, without reflecting that this was the artists' choice and not accurate reporting.

Generally there is little differentiation between the figures on Olympus and those of the heroic age, other than dress – Helen or Aphrodite may be more svelte, Hera more matronly, Poseidon more unkempt, Dionysos effeminate – and there are age differences which are sometimes the product of artistic choice rather than the story. Several gods are regularly shown younger and beardless after the archaic period – Apollo, Dionysos, Hermes; Eros regresses from being a classical stripling to a baby putto. Only Herakles is accorded a true portrait, by the sculptor Lysippos in the fourth century BC – low-browed, a mop of curly hair and jutting beard, bull-necked [*Fig. 137*]. A few gods are allowed wings, especially in archaic Ionia; demons like the Gorgons may fly, but not heroes except for poor Ikaros (who failed) and, naturally, the wind gods. Otherwise winged caps or shoes are supplied, for Hermes and Perseus. This is not a world teeming with animal-headed or multi-limbed deities, but simply of the modified humanoid.

There is, however, a problem here, and it may be that this emphatic humanizing of the divine or heroic is sometimes a conscious, but desired, disguise for other concepts. The god Dionysos may often seem something of an outsider, but his

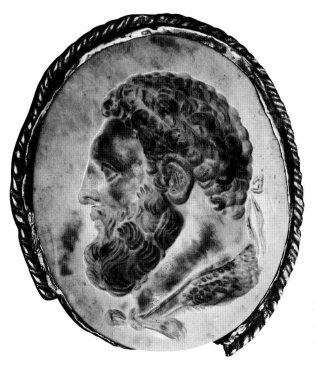

137. Portrait of Herakles, in the
Lysippan manner, on a late Hellenistic
chalcedony gem. H. 27 mm.
(Private Collection)

name is read in Bronze Age texts and his worship spanned the Greek world. In
Euripides' play *Bacchae* he is described as white-skinned, red-faced, with long
blonde hair; but he is made to say that he has changed his divine form for a mortal
one, and in the play Euripides, with some other classical authors, has him
essentially bull-horned or bull-faced. There is a darker side to Greek thought and
religion than the bright humanity presented by Greek artists, although this was the
commonplace and must have been the image generally accepted by most Greeks,
and so by us.

Nor should we be too sanguine about taking the images on Greek vases as
accurate representations even of classical Greeks. On vases the conventions of
painting dictated black hair for most, but where the conventions could be
abandoned, when the painting is on a white ground with colour or for later panels
and wall painting, we see a lot of fair hair, and we know from texts that fair hair and
blue eyes were admired, while the pictures do not suggest a dominantly stocky,
wavy-haired race.

The same considerations applied no less to representation of dress. The use of
modern dress for the heroic and divine is nothing exceptional; it has been the
standard practice in western theatre and art until relatively modern times, with
Shakespeare's Henry V continuing to be dressed as an Elizabethan, Veronese's
Alexander and Darius dressed as Renaissance noblemen. If Bronze Age artefacts
revealed significant differences in dress and armour from the classical – the bare-
breasted, corseted women are the most obvious example, the men with loincloths
and belts, and the figure-of-eight shields [*Fig. 138,139*] – these were nonetheless

138. Bare-breasted women with flounced skirts on a gold ring from the Acropolis Treasure at Mycenae. 17th cent. BC. L. 34 mm. (Athens, National Museum 992)

139. Inlaid bronze dagger blade from a Shaft Grave at Mycenae. A lion hunt: the men wear loin cloths and carry rectangular and large figure-of-eight hide-covered shields. 18th cent. BC. (Athens, National Museum)

140. Detail from an Athenian red figure vase by the Painter of Bologna 279 showing Greeks fighting Amazons. Of the latter, one at the centre has a corselet tailored to her breasts; others are dressed as Greek hoplites or in Scythian patterned dress. About 450 BC. (Basel, Antikenmuseum BS486)

resolutely ignored in re-creating the image of a Helen, Ajax or Agamemnon. The traditional stories for the most part did not involve problems over dress and equipment, and we shall look at the few exceptions below.

The Amazons are a special case, providing a modern battleground for iconographers, anthropologists and feminists. They were probably inspired by real-life warrior women who fought beside their nomad menfolk and whose burials have been found on the northern and eastern steppes, but there was never any exclusive regiment of women. The common lack of male facial hair among many Asian nomads may have contributed something. These woman-warriors who lived far to the north and east, beyond Anatolia, and who were fought by Herakles, were womanly in physique if not behaviour. The Greek 'without a breast' (*a-mazon*) derivation of their name is false and it was ignored in Greek art: it was alleged to help them to draw a bow – which it clearly does not, to judge from modern sportswomen. (False etymologies were a very fruitful source for Greek myth.) The Amazons are shown as women, dressed as Greek warriors although their corselets may sometimes be tailored to their breasts [*Fig. 140*],[1] and their helmets may often be of a lighter variety, as they are also for Athena who, though a warrior goddess, had next to nothing to do with Amazons; she generally absents herself in scenes where her hero Herakles fights them but is at his side in most other encounters. Otherwise, Amazon dress could be inspired by their apparent homelands – at first

141. From an Athenian red figure vase by Myson. Theseus and Peirithoos carry off the Amazon Antiope who wears a Scythian costume and cap, and carries a bowcase and battle axe. About 490 BC. (Paris, Louvre G197, from Vulci)

142. Paestan red figure vase by the Painter of Naples 2585 showing the Judgement of Paris. Hermes, Hera, Athena and Aphrodite surround Paris, who is dressed as a Persian prince. About 330 BC. (Sciclounoff Collection, from Castellamare)

like that of the Scythians of the south Russian steppes, with patterned sleeves and trousers [*Fig. 141*],[2] later like that of Persians. The Persian dress in particular allowed their assimilation to Greece's new eastern enemies, though the equation was not usually made explicit, for all that war with Persians, like war with Troy, was a paradigm for some of Greece's fifth-century conflicts with the east.[3] In the same way, from the later fifth century on, Trojan heroes, hitherto treated as though they were Greeks, may be accepted as true easterners and shown in Persian dress [*Fig. 142*].[4] The Amazons' battles and tombs in Athens have already been discussed in Chapter Three; in fifth-century Athenian art they can be shown mourning their kin, a privilege not normally accorded to enemies in Greek art.[5]

The Amazons fight as hoplites in the vase paintings but were also formidable on horseback, as befits their nomad/steppe background, and with the bow, carrying the eastern bowcase (*gorytos*). They also fight with a battle axe [*Fig. 141*], which was not a weapon in common use in Greece, but was still wielded by easterners in the historic period. Indeed, familiarity with the battle axe in the hands of Amazons in art led to an interesting instance of art instructing life, when Xenophon remarks that the north Anatolian tribes met by his men, in their famous *anabasis* march to the sea, used battle axes 'like those the Amazons carry': that is, like the ones they saw in art.[6]

143. Warriors carrying 'Dipylon shields' from Athenian Geometric vases. 8th cent. BC.

The axes lead us to discussion of other heroic weaponry. Homer's descriptions of tower-like shields, and the representations of figure-of-eight shields in Minoan and Mycenaean art [*Fig. 139*], were of objects quite unfamiliar to later Greeks; none could have survived except in images, and they never attempted to depict them. In the fanciful 'Alexander Romance', first concocted for uncritical consumption in the last centuries BC and much improved in later centuries, Alexander the Great was shown Ajax's 'seven-ox-hide' shield at Troy, and marvelled at its size.[7] The story was prompted by knowledge of Homer's descriptions rather than by any relic, and in the Romance Alexander scoffs also at the width of the River Scamander, and

144. Bronze shield from the Idaean Cave, Crete. The type with a lion-head boss is Syrian, as is the style, but it was made in Crete. Notice the 'Dipylon shield' carried at the left. 8th cent. BC. Diam. 83 cm. (Heraklion Museum 7)

thinks the heroes lucky to have a poet who so eloquently exaggerated their prowess.

However, the hide shields stretched on a wicker frame, and so with curved outlines, were still in use in the eighth century BC, stylized in Geometric art into what we call the Dipylon shield [*Fig. 143*]. A generation ago scholars were intent on discovering myth and the heroic in early Greek art, and the shields were held to be an indication of an heroic scene. This is generally now discounted,[8] and specific heroic or myth scenes are no longer confidently recognized in Greek art until near 700 BC. I shall revert to the shield's possible successors.

However, Homer describes the Shield of Achilles, made for him by the craftsman god Hephaistos to replace that lost when he gave his first set of armour to Patroklos, who was then killed by Hektor.[9] It was large and round, therefore roughly of the hoplite type which came into use by around 700 BC, but fitted with a baldric like the older shields, not an arm-grip. It was elaborately decorated, and although elements can be plausibly derived from knowledge of the decoration of shields, on cups and other metal objects of orientalizing type – Syrian, Phoenician and within the Greek world, especially Crete [*Fig. 144*][10] – nothing has been found

145. A warrior bears another from the battlefield, probably Ajax with Achilles. Both have large 'Boeotian' shields with elaborate blazons. On an Athenian black figure vase by Exekias. About 540 BC. (Munich Antikensammlungen 1470)

of such complexity either overall or in detail. It is likely that familiarity with such art prompted the description, but that the scenes described owe most to a poetic imagination – blind Homer's contribution to the tradition, some might think. The representations of heavenly bodies and constellations outdid anything yet known in eastern art, and depiction of city life, including a detailed account of a lawcourt in action, simply tries to translate into the visual the sort of setting which Homer describes at length in the *Odyssey* for the 'real' city of the Phaeacians. The siege scene can be paralleled on an eastern cup, but the nearest we get to the detailed farming activities described is in Egyptian painting. Achilles' shield was of a type that never existed, nor could exist, but wondrously combines poetic imagination with a few traces of the arts of the time of Homer and his predecessors.[11] Achilles' original shield, also made by Hephaistos, was described only later, by Euripides, who makes it slightly more plausible – less complicated and with a sun-chariot at the centre.[12]

146. Silver coin of Thebes showing a 'Boeotian' shield. The reverse shows the infant Herakles
strangling the snakes sent to destroy him by Hera. Early 4th cent. BC.

How, then, was a Greek artist to depict what was arguably the most famous piece
of armour of myth-history, recorded for him only by a poet? We shall see that
details of Homer's text had but the slightest effect on art for a long time, but the
way archaic artists treated Achilles' and other heroic shields does raise an
interesting question about the possible deliberate creation of a shield-type deemed
heroic. It is the so-called Boeotian shield, which is oval, with side cut-outs, and in
outline possibly deriving from or translating the old Dipylon shield. It appears
often as an heroic shield, and often with an elaborate blazon [*Fig. 145*].[13] Was it a
translation by the artist of what he knew to be an early shield into a form more
compatible with the new hoplite shields? If so, we have a possibly unique example
of the creation of an image for an exclusively heroic object. I have my doubts. The
shape derives from that of a real, though lighter shield, the 'Dipylon'. In art it is
depicted realistically, and given a baldric rather than the arm-grip of a round
hoplite shield, since it is heavier, probably imagined as having a wooden frame
covered with hide or metal. There are even some bronze arm-grips found in
Boeotia which might fit it, and it appears carried by Persian soldiers in the fifth
century – Persian artists and armourers would not have copied an unreal invention
of Greek artists. Moreover, it is regularly used as a coin device in Boeotia in the
classical period [*Fig. 146*]. I suspect that it did exist, even if only as ceremonial or
élitist armour, carrying a certain whiff of antiquity, perhaps of the heroic, though it
derived from no heroic shield ever found or described.[14]

    There is, however, one military activity which may appear in eighth-century art
and which, it has been argued, depicts behaviour proper only to the Bronze Age as
either remembered or, more probably, demonstrated in the epic record, which was
yet to be set down by Homer. It is the exercise of the *apobates*, a warrior who jumps
down from a chariot to fight on foot. It was the normal practice on the Trojan plain
and may be depicted, though not in an actual battle, on a very few eighth-century
Euboean vases [*Fig. 147*]. The suspicion may, however, linger, that what we are

147. The neck of a Geometric vase from Eretria. In the figure friezes a warrior jumps down from each chariot. Late 8th cent. BC. (Eretria Museum)

shown is an awkward depiction of a warrior without a shield mounting a standing chariot and not jumping off it. As a traditional exercise the apobatic continues on into the classical period, best shown on the Parthenon Frieze. But eighth-century Greeks probably did not, and classical Greeks certainly did not, use chariots on the battlefield like their Bronze Age predecessors, while the heroes at Troy used them to get around the action, not to fight from, as did Hittites, Egyptians and, maybe, Mycenaeans. The land of Greece does not lend itself much to such tactics, though the Trojan plain might; in our period we hear of chariot warfare only in Cyprus and Cyrenaica. It is not possible to explain this in terms of continuity of practice rather than as a military exercise using a racing chariot, but the nature of the debt to the past, if there is one, is difficult to define. In Geometric battle scenes the examples in which a chariot is present are extremely rare and equivocal.[15] All this does not illustrate an Homeric world though it may conceal intimations of the heroic, such as linger for centuries in Greek art devoted to the everyday. The iconography of mourning the dead has been adduced as a parallel phenomenon to the *apobates*, but I think this is easier to explain in terms of continuity of behaviour.[16]

Hoplite warfare involving ranks of men with round hoplite shields and long thrusting spears began in the first half of the seventh century and became the normal battlefield practice. Artists seldom show the full hoplite ranks, and most battles in art are duels or mêlées, such as might develop once the hoplite ranks had broken, but which more obviously recall heroic practice [*Fig. 148*].[17] That the heroic mode is retained is simply an indication that most such scenes were meant to be heroic, even when the figures are not identified, and being 'myth-historical' as

148. On a Corinthian vase by the Chigi Painter a hoplite phalanx is breaking up into individual duels. H. of frieze 2 cm. (London, British Museum 1889.4–18.1)

well as generic they mainly reflect the practice of presenting modern activities in heroic guise. This may be enough to explain the *apobates* exercises too, which were real enough in the classical period although not on the battlefield: they evoke the heroic. The same goes for generic scenes of warriors departing in chariots, which were, after all, well known pieces of equipment throughout Greek history on the race track or in a formal procession, even if not on the battlefield.

There were several famous pieces of heroic equipment described in some detail by the poets. In archaic Greek art Achilles' shield is at best a rather grand Boeotian [*Fig. 145*]. Only in the first century BC did artists attempt to present it in Homeric terms. The Tabulae Iliacae are multi-figured stone reliefs which depict the *Iliad*, book by book, like a strip cartoon. Some figure the shield, and there are related reliefs from the same workshop which present the shield alone [*Fig. 149,150*].[18] They are singularly unconvincing and inadequate interpretations of the Homeric description. Alexander borrowed heroic armour from Troy for his eastern campaign, and his depiction on a Roman gold medallion shows him with what can only be regarded as a version of Achilles' own shield [*Fig. 151*], which of course he could not have taken since it was not there.[19] A proper response to Homer's poetic vision of the shield can only be attempted by an art in tune with poetically cosmic, rustic, civic, landscape and heroic formulae, which were not developed in the west until the Renaissance. A combination of these with Neo-classicism has produced several noble attempts at the Shield of Achilles, which succeed only in so far as they either ignore most of the scenes that Homer described, or try so hard to be comprehensive that the results are quite confusing [*Fig. 152*].[20] Literary descriptions do not translate easily into real images.

One other literary shield, that of Herakles, described in the *Aspis* poem (lines 139–320), which was written in the sixth century BC but ascribed in antiquity to

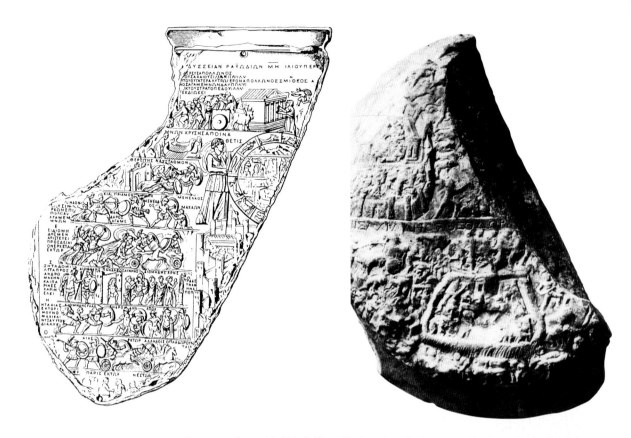

149. Fragment of a marble Tabula Iliaca. Each register depicts events from separate books of the *Iliad*, fully labelled. To the right are the walls of Troy and above them Thetis displays the new shield for her son Achilles. On it is the zodiac at the rim and an assortment of other motifs in friezes. 1st cent. BC. (Lost)

150. Fragment of a marble version of the Shield of Achilles (related to *Fig. 149*). 1st cent. BC. Diam. 17.8 cm. (Rome, Museo Capitolino Sala d.Col. 83a)

Hesiod, also inspired no ancient artist. Yet it is more plausibly based on the type of decoration that a hoplite shield of the period might have carried, though hardly all at once: a central Phobos (Fear) like the by-then traditional gorgoneion, personifications of Panic, Slaughter and the like, which were beginning to appear in art, animal fights, the Lapith and Centaurs myth and others, deities. Less plausible elements of the decoration, probably derived from Homer's view of Achilles' shield, are a harbour, and rustic and civic scenes.[21] Blazons attributed to the shields of the heroes who fought at Thebes form an important part of the dramatic narrative in Aeschylus' play, *Septem*; they were devised for this purpose and only incidentally might seem at all plausible for any period.

Generally the battle and siege episodes of myth were conducted and depicted in contemporary guise. There were very few exceptional pieces of major equipment,

151. Gold medallion from Aboukir showing Alexander the Great carrying a decorated shield which may be taken as a Shield of Achilles. 2nd cent. AD. Diam. 5.1 cm. (Baltimore, Walters Art Gallery 59.1)

152. The Shield of Achilles, re-created by John Flaxman in 1821. It was designed as a tribute to the Duke of Wellington. Flaxman made many original interpretations in drawings of Homeric episodes and read Homer aloud to his friends. Diam. 95.5 cm. (Bronze copy in Oxford, Ashmolean Museum)

153. The Trojan Horse, with Greek heroes climbing from it and concealed within it. On the neck of a relief vase from Mykonos. About 650 BC. (Mykonos Museum 2240)

such as the Trojan Horse [*Fig. 153*],²² which was probably inspired by Assyrian wheeled siege towers, adapted by Greek story-telling to inspire a machine for infiltration of a walled city. Late Bronze and early Iron Age figurines of horses, made on the potters' wheel with fat cylindrical bellies, may have helped the invention. I wonder whether a similar source helped the story of Pasiphae's hollow cow in which she mated with the beautiful bull to produce the Minotaur.²³

To turn to lesser equipment: belts are not conspicuous items of dress for the archaic and classical periods, except for some metal-faced belts for women, current in Anatolia and in the Ionian cities down to the sixth century [*Fig. 154*]. They were Phrygian in origin, and in Greek cities they were dedicated to goddesses, preferably Artemis and Hera, for whom they were appropriate offerings from a young bride.²⁴ A simple cord served at the waist of the classical *chiton* or *peplos* robe, to judge from pictures and statues. The belt of Ares which Herakles got from the Amazon Hippolyte has some substance in the few representations we have [*Fig. 67*],²⁵ but no detail. What passed for the famous belt was shown in the Argive Heraion (T.81). I suspect that it was an archaic Anatolian bronze belt; several of these were dedicated at Ephesus, which has strong Amazon associations also. Having lost her belt, an Amazon is shown, in one of the famous classical statues made for Ephesus, using a broken rein of fifth-century type as a replacement [*Fig. 155*].²⁶

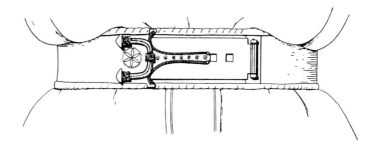

154. Reconstruction of an Ionian woman's bronze belt with a leather backing. (Chios Museum, from Emporio)

155. Copy of the statue of a wounded Amazon, the original of about 430 BC. She wears a broken rein as a belt. H. 2.04 m. (New York, Metropolitan Museum 32.11.4)

156. Detail from an Athenian red figure vase by the Kleophrades Painter. Hektor is led away from Ajax (on the other side of the vase) having received a belt in exchange for his sword. About 490 BC. (Würzburg, Martin von Wagner Museum 508)

Imaging the Past: The Hero and the Heroic · *171*

Other heroic belts, 'bright with purple', are gifts between heroes remarked in Homer.[27] When a fifth-century artist shows one in the hands of a glowering Hektor [*Fig. 156*], Ajax having received in exchange Hektor's silver-studded sword, it is just a broad ribbon such as no contemporary Greek wore, except perhaps round his head.[28] The exchange was made poetically poignant by the fact that the sword would be the instrument of Ajax's suicide, the belt that which bound Hektor's body to Achilles' chariot.[29]

It seems, from what has been said in previous chapters, that the Greeks' pursuit of their past *in corpore*, through tombs and possibly even in relics rather than in story, was well established by the eighth century BC. When did the interest manifest itself also in images? Before the late eighth century there is very little in Greek art that we can positively identify as a representation of a deity, let alone a hero engaged in a narrative event. There are a possible few in Cypriot art,[30] and there were many Greek-speakers in Cyprus, but the arts in Greece were mainly innocent of human-figure decoration, except for some in Crete where the links with the Bronze Age past were more persistent. In Greece the rebirth of an art of human and animal images proved to be a slow and intermittent process.[31]

This is not the place for a close study of the beginnings of myth-narrative or divine images in Greek art, but their emergence at a time when writing, and attention to tomb or hero cults, were occupying the imagination of artists, priests and rulers, is probably not a matter of coincidence, although it is clear that this attention was not the only or even perhaps the main stimulus, and the innovations appear over a period of some two generations.

The identification of figures through detail of dress or attribute and the depiction of narrative were constrained by styles of art, and the Geometric figures, painted or cast in bronze, offered very little opportunity. The orientalizing arts, which gave birth to images for the monsters we discussed in the last chapter, provided the same impetus for depiction of the divine and of narrative by humanoid figures. It was, however, as much a matter of approach and of the opportunities offered by new, more detailed, techniques of representing figures, as of copying eastern models, as it had been with the monsters. The one obvious and much quoted example – the use of the eastern lion-fighter motif to depict Herakles – is also virtually unique, although there is a number of generic fighting formulae also adopted which could be used for specific occasions of myth.[32] It was, however, through such scenes, that the world of myth-narrative became part of the everyday visual experience of the Greeks, and the fact that it was 'in modern dress' simply accentuated its relevance. A very high proportion of the figurative art of Greece was devoted to such subjects. In Athens they were probably most accessible as vase decoration, at least from the sixth century on. This provided a plentiful and relatively cheap source, apart from what was apparent anywhere in Greece on more expensive goods, and what was on public view, depicted on temples.

157. A startled Zeus giving birth, from his head, to a fully armed Athena. Hephaistos, who effected the delivery with his axe, starts away. On an Athenian cup by Phrynos. About 560 BC. (London, British Museum B424, from Vulci)

To enquire how much more of early story-telling and depiction of the remote past depended on observation of the foreign or even of the everyday, transmuted, is an invitation to almost endless speculation. There is very little to justify the assumption that Greek portrayal of some figures of myth or of the foreigner were moved by conceptions of the truly primitive, the 'cave man',[33] rather than from views of what was simply wild, or rustic (animal skins for giants), or close to the animal world (centaurs, satyrs, even Pan), or too un-Greek and therefore barbarian. Herakles starts in Greek art as an heroic bowman or hoplite, without club and lionskin, and although the latter may seem primitive, in their origins they are not – the lionskin is regal and magic, and the club probably a royal mace – sometimes even described and shown as metallic.[34] Herakles could be thought of thereafter as a rather wild and wilful strong man but never as primitive. The animal elements of Pan, satyrs and centaurs do not prevent them being depicted as mainly civilized in all but behaviour to mortals, while the only 'cave man'-like figures I know are the early, hairy Arimasps on the Greco-Scythian mirror [*Fig. 95*].

We are concerned mainly with depiction of the more bizarre events which were to tax the ingenuity of the Greek artist, but the quest may involve consideration also of the origins of the stories themselves, a vast subject. We have met several examples already in earlier chapters; I add a few here. A fully armed Athena emerging from the head of Zeus looks silly in art, along with the idea that his head was split open by Hephaistos [*Fig. 157*]. It is not easy to imagine what foreign

158. Interior of an Athenian red figure cup in the manner of Douris showing Herakles with club and bow sailing in his cauldron.
About 480 BC. (Vatican Museums, from Vulci)

159. Gold bowl from S. Angelo Muxaro, Sicily. 7th cent. BC? Diam. 14.6 cm. (London, British Museum 1772.3–4.70)

image could have inspired it, and originally it was probably a totally non-visualized concept, implausibly rationalized by Hesiod and the artists, dressed up with various ritual (the split head of a sacrificial animal) and folktale elements; worldwide there are stories of births from improbable parts of the body.[35] Observation of the tearing of battlefield corpses by birds was the source of pictures and poetry, even at the very start of the *Iliad* 'their limbs to dogs and vultures gave', and in Greek Geometric art. If the victim is immortal, like the Titan Prometheus, the punishment, by Zeus' eagle, has to be administered daily and his entrails renewable.

Herakles sails the Mediterranean in a bowl given him by the sun, looking like an eastern cauldron in Greek art [*Fig. 158*],[36] while the notion that he brought back the cattle of Geryon in it could easily have been encouraged by the many Syrian phialai in the Greek world which were commonly decorated with a frieze of bulls. I show a gold version made in Sicily in a mixed Greco-oriental style [*Fig. 159*].[37]

160. Cast of a bronze medallion of the emperor Caracalla. Herakles, at the right, is seated at a feast. Above is his massive cup, dedicated in the Forum Boarium at Rome. AD 205–207. (Paris, Cabinet des Médailles)

Herakles challenging the sun could be inspired by an eastern scene of an archer beneath a winged sun disc.[38] Herakles' sailing cup was kept at the Ara Maxima in Rome (T.543) and is prominent on some Roman medallions and coins [*Fig. 160*]; a rare instance of a relic depicted.[39] Herakles' death, from a poisoned cloak, recalls that of King Kreon's daughter, from Medea's lethal gift of dress and crown; might the discovery of burials, with the skeleton still wrapped in shreds of the dress that seemed to have eaten the flesh, have been enough to inspire such stories?

We have seen that in general the Greeks did not invent new forms for objects which served gods or heroes but relied upon the familiar and contemporary. However, invention was required for some. A thunderbolt is understandably winged and spiky (the lightning) but also sometimes of a rather floral aspect, suggested by the shape of the archaic lotus pattern. The aigis worn by Athena, but belonging originally to Zeus, was a magic goatskin, but is shown with scales, as of a snake, and the curly edges are stylized into snake heads, which was a common Greek practice in art for such extremities. The same process introduced snakes to the caduceus (*kerykeion*) carried by Hermes, Iris and hero heralds, since it started as a simple cleft stick. The Dionysiac thyrsos wand was originally a fennel stem with ivy wound around its tip. That it was not commonly met in 'life' is shown by the way artists come to turn the tip into what in early art it at any rate resembles – a pine cone.

There is just one more area to explore in the matter of re-use of the past although it is generally not possible to affirm that the phenomenon had much to do with a deliberate attempt at re-creation. It was a matter of style rather than subject, and passes as 'archaism' in art history. We may exclude the type of archaism which is

161. Archaizing marble relief of the 1st cent. BC showing Dionysos and the three Seasons (Horai). H. 32 cm. (Paris, Louvre MA968)

detectable in fifth-century art, since this is no more than a continuation of the styles of the archaic period, old-fashioned and only lightly adjusted to the new subject matter of the classical world. It is rather mannered, and the artists generally called Mannerists. It appears most obviously in vase painting, but from the later fifth century on there is more archaism also in sculpture. Much of this can be explained by the fact that many archaic statues were still visible, and their style would have seemed venerable and worth imitating for cult images or the like.[40] Otherwise the Greeks were not sentimental about retaining out-of-date styles. Some have thought that the Corinthian helmet (which covers the face and can be worn 'up' on the head to show the features) was not made and worn after the earlier fifth century, though it was shown regularly in art; this seems the result of a misreading of the slighter evidence for it from an age when many more helmet types were current, and it certainly survived in an adapted form for wearing in Hellenistic Greece and Republican Italy.[41]

There seems little if anything in the ordinary visual experience of the Greeks which both deliberately and accurately reflected a remote past by style; this was done better by counterfeit if at all, and was probably not looked for. But there is one other area of style which might, misleadingly, seem to embody a deliberate reflection of the past, largely because it is called 'heroic' – nudity. The 'heroic

162. A fifth-century BC bronze head of a youth embedded in a rough wall block excavated from a late building in Athens.

nude' was indeed a Greek creation, but it was not imposed on the image of the hero or divine; it emerged from the practices of Greeks of the archaic and classical periods, and certainly not of the 'heroic' Bronze Age; and in these periods it only denoted the heroic by accident, as it were, since it was as readily demonstrated in life as in art, depicting contemporary behaviour. This was, indeed, very different from that of other peoples of the ancient world of like climate and status, and they criticized it, but it was not a device to distinguish only a hero or god, and it was decidedly for the male only until artists learned also to exploit realistic female nudity, as a sensual additive to statues of an Aphrodite or paramour.[42]

A residual Greek delight in sheer pattern in anatomy or dress could on occasion displace the current idealized realism of the major arts of the fifth and fourth centuries. This is quite unlike the more conscious archaism which recurs at the end of the Hellenistic period, which again is an artistic movement, no little engendered by the interests of Roman patrons, having little to do with any particularly conscious attempt to recapture appearances of remote antiquity [*Fig. 161*]. When an early classical bronze head was set in lead in a rough stone block, presumably for display, and presumably in a building of the Roman period, this seems not to be a deliberate display of an 'heirloom' of the past, since its style was one still commonly copied in the later period; what it does signify, however, remains anyone's guess and we need to know more about the context of its discovery, but it makes an evocative picture [*Fig. 162*]. It was found in the recent excavations for Athens' new Metro.[43]

The detection of archaism that results from observation of Bronze Age arts still visible above ground or from objects found is very much an archaeological affair. Although there is no serious continuity in the decorative arts from the Bronze Age to the Iron Age, except in the reworking of old patterns into new Protogeometric forms, there are some interesting echoes in the full Geometric period of the eighth century. It is difficult not to believe that many of the Geometric scenes, especially of chariots and in the disposition of filling ornament, do not owe something to observation of the very similar treatment of the same or similar subjects on the latest of the Bronze Age arts, and in the same medium – painted pottery.[44] In Crete, where the Bronze Age was perhaps more accessible and conspicuous, there seem to be several throwbacks, and over a long period. Much was simply a matter of continuity.[45] The Late Bronze Age burials were often in clay tubs (*larnakes*), and these could be re-used or even imitated. Re-cycling was a regularly attested activity by thrifty Greeks of all periods, but on occasion it must have been inhibited by consideration of what was appropriate in the handling of what might be ancestral or heroic relics. The Cretans knew themselves to be newcomers – Dorians – and the Dorian ancestral hero was not Minos.

Dependence on observation or knowledge of Bronze Age architecture is difficult to judge. Much may be illusory or the result of some sort of continuity,

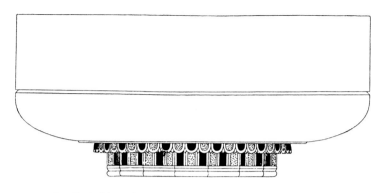

163. Capital from the grave monument of Xenvares on Kerkyra.
Early 6th cent. BC. W. 80 cm. (Corfu Museum)

though hardly in the practice of monumental arts, rather than from observation.
The *megaron* form adopted for Greek temples from the eighth century on may
resemble the *megara* houses and palaces of the Bronze Age, but these were
differently proportioned and for a different purpose. They are rectangular, with
columned porches, the Bronze Age ones having a squarish main room with a
hearth. Doric capitals which appear in the later seventh century only roughly
resemble Bronze Age capitals, though there are floral rings below the *echinus*
capitals that might derive from observation of either architectural or decorative
Bronze Age forms [*Fig. 163*]. The 'palm capital' could have other sources, notably
its original home in Egypt, and, for its reappearance in the Hellenistic period, its
currency in the Persian empire. But the case for dependence on Bronze Age forms
for these types of capitals has been argued.[46] If true, any consciously 'heroic'
connotations are hardly apparent in the contexts in which they are used. On the
whole architecture did not lend itself to archaism in the way that sculpture did.[47]
Yet a Greek artist is able to introduce something of the supernatural into divine
architecture, at least once. An Athenian cup [*Fig. 164*] shows what seem to be the
stables of Poseidon; the artist Amasis has given them a long colonnade which is
roughly Doric with a frieze of metopes above. Half of these are decorated with
figures, as they would be on many Greek buildings, but in one of them the figure is
climbing out of his frame, surrealistically, to join other manikins in the harnessing
scene.[48]

Borrowing appropriate decoration could not have been inhibiting. Some of the
new figure decoration on Cretan vases seems inspired by the past;[49] for example,
the monsters and animals on a vase from a Knossian grave [*Fig. 165*].[50] There was a
premature orientalizing period of decoration in the island in the later ninth century
(the so-called Protogeometric B style) which introduced many new patterns, some
of them, however, more Minoan than oriental.[51] And as late as the sixth century
some of the simpler vase patterns seem to have been derived from the same source
[*Fig. 166*].[52] The artists who made these adaptations may have been aware of the

164. From an Athenian black figure cup by Amasis showing the stables of Poseidon. One of the figures decorating the metopes is sufficiently animated to climb down (*detail below*). About 540 BC. (New York, Metropolitan Museum 1989.281.62, gift of Norbert Schimmel Trust 1983)

165. Monsters on a vase from Knossos. Late 9th cent. BC. (Heraklion Museum)

166. Cretan vase from Taucheira, a Greek colony on the Libyan coast. The leaf pattern and scrolls on the neck and shoulder are essentially Minoan rather than archaic Greek though the vase is of the 6th cent. BC. (Tocra Museum 921)

167. Impression of a grey stone gem showing a contorted winged goat. About 600 BC. W. 15 mm. (London, British Museum, Walters no. 203)

168. Corinthian imitation of the Bronze Age stirrup-vase shape. Early 6th cent. BC. (London, British Museum 1970.9–10.2)

great antiquity of what they were copying, but we must judge it improbable that they regarded their models as in any way ancestral.

In Crete especially, Bronze Age artefacts are often found in later tombs.[53] The commonest finds are the sealstones, and although some of the figures on them, notably the 'Minotaurs' [*Fig. 124*], might have been influential, they were not otherwise copied. It was a different matter in the seventh century BC on the island of Melos where there had been important Bronze Age settlements. Here the Bronze Age seals were copied, for their shapes (lentoid and amygdaloid, like a lens or an almond) although not their material, which was harder than anything the Greeks were then able to work. Occasionally too the devices were copied, for example the twisted animal bodies [*Fig. 167*], but for the most part the subjects were contemporary, orientalizing. These are the 'Island Gems', which continued in manufacture and use into the sixth century, when new styles and shapes (scarabs), and the techniques of handling harder stones were adopted from the east. The phenomenon seems primarily an artistic one rather than consciously nostalgic, but we cannot be sure.[54]

Other isolated 'throwbacks' like a sixth-century Corinthian copy of a Bronze Age stirrup vase [*Fig. 168*] are simply the product of an observant or curious potter, not heroic equipment.[55]

CHAPTER SEVEN

Conclusion

IT WILL BE EASIER to assess the nature of the Greeks' attitudes to their past and the extent to which they were prepared physically to re-create it, once the practices of some other ancient peoples are considered. A certain curiosity about the past can probably be assumed for any people who have achieved even a limited degree of self-consciousness, which is a stage of behaviour and thought far older than awareness of what passes as ethnicity in modern literature. In settled societies an interest in the past seems almost a prerequisite for an interest in the future and in any concept of progress. Nomad societies may seem relatively more rootless and vague in their sense of the past, except sometimes where their burial grounds are concerned, as with the Scythians, but on the whole the nomads do not enter much into this story. And peoples who have lived, and sometimes continue to live, so close to an environment which they do not seek or need to modify, may take a timeless view of their past, a Dream Time, and although very strictly bound by traditional practices, may evince no great interest in exploring or preserving physical records of the origins of those practices, rather than recording them in timeless symbols. Not for them, or the nomads, long genealogies of gods and heroes, or even kings. Story-telling is the prime factor in all cases, so we are very much at the mercy of surviving literature from the literate, while others remain for us dumb, but in this book we are looking at the tangible evidence for the past, which can be identified, imagined or even forged.

One of the first things that is apparent in making such comparisons is how much the Greek experience, made available to us in the archaeology and literature of their Iron Age, depends on its virtual severance from any real knowledge of the Bronze Age past, except for what was orally transmitted in a garbled form or observed on the ground, while the civilizations of the Nile Valley, Mesopotamia and China could see and understand their past history, in story and in monument, back almost to the very beginnings of urban life. Even India could reach more easily into its pre-Aryan past. There is a further problem in making comparisons. The Greek record is unique in antiquity for bringing us so close to the experience and thus the concepts of a major part of the population, and not just its upper classes. This is the result of being a very small 'country', much subdivided, and never, in the period that concerns us most, dominated by any single religious, military or political élite. There was possibly too a much smaller 'underclass', proportionally, than in many other places. It is unlikely that we shall ever learn as much about the lower classes and slaves of old civilizations outside Greece, as we do about the Greek; little enough has so far been gleaned from archaeology, except for the localized phenomenon of the workmen's villages in upper Egypt, and the surviving literature is generally less informative on the matter.

THE FOREIGNERS

Egypt offers us surprisingly little. Herodotus' record of the stories told him by Egyptian priests and scribes does not go beyond the traditional superstitions. These are not the only ways in which Egypt's record differs profoundly from those of others we consider. Both divinity and the dead seem to have played a major role in the behaviour of the living. There is no Egyptian 'heroic age' rather than stories of contests between the gods and the definition of their roles and powers, some of which have heroic tones. And heroes and their families, a major source for Greek interest in their past, are not at all apparent, except sometimes in accounts of the exploits and reputations of certain old kings. These may be attested in texts, and monuments may revive old Pharaoh names, most obviously in the many late scarabs which allege issue from the reigns of such as Ramses II. Old monuments remained standing, and often still in use, beside the new. Archaic forms can be deliberately observed, and sometimes copied in art, but the overwhelming success of the idiom created in the third millennium BC seems not to have given such archaizing the status that comparable practice evoked in Greece – notably in the re-creation of a golden, classical age to be admired by the Romans. Old artefacts, rather than monuments or inscriptions that could simply be erased or added to, seem not to have attracted attention.

The single exception concerns Osiris whose origins and story are in significant ways different from those of the major gods, and whose life and death seem almost as closely related to the experiences and hopes of the Egyptian people as Herakles' are to those of the Greeks. Plutarch tells a version of the story which is much affected by what he knew of Greek practice with relics. Osiris was killed by Typhon, meaning Seth, his wicked brother, the Red God. He dismembered the body which was distributed all over Egypt, but Isis searched for all the parts and gave them proper burial.[1] There is record of the parts, often duplicated, all over Egypt and associated with Osiris worship, although the 'relics' themselves seem not to have been the object of cult. So this is not quite like Greek practice, nor did it need to be a model for it.[2] The Osiris relics might well have been fossil bones and we know that such were collected in Egypt. The most notable hoard was of blackened fossils, found in the thirteenth century BC, which seem to have been associated with the god Seth.[3]

Mesopotamia is more responsive. We have to take with it extensions west into Syria and parts of Anatolia, and east into Persia; but the prime record lies in the lands of the two rivers, mountainous in the north, more desert in the south, but everywhere offering possibilities of considerable agricultural wealth, especially with the assistance of controlled irrigation, which here required somewhat more thought than it did on the banks of the Nile. Sumerian, Assyrian, Babylonian, Elamite and eventually even Achaemenid Persian imperial behaviour displays a certain continuity of life and thought, abetted by writing which, despite differing languages and scripts, never retreated into total unintelligibility as did the Minoan and Mycenaean in Greece. Thus, the Assyrian king Ashurbanipal (mid-seventh century) could collect in Nineveh a library of old texts, which he seems to have treated with an editor's zeal: 'I have read intricate tablets inscribed with obscure Sumerian or Akkadian, difficult to unravel, and examined sealed, obscure and confused inscriptions on stone from before the Flood'.[4] Comparable collections, including statues and reliefs in what might seem libraries or museums, appear to indicate an interest close to that of the Greeks, but the parallel is misleading. The libraries of the Greeks were few, and differently motivated; we have had little need even to mention them in earlier chapters. At best, we know that some administrations, religious and civil, kept lists of priests and magistrates and Olympic victors, but these were continuing records and few could have gone back far even into the archaic period. Collections of oracles were for local historical or personal purposes. Far later historians were busier in creating such lists and even incorporating into them the annals of the east and Egypt.

In Mesopotamia we are dealing with serious and detailed historical or religious documents. In Greece there was constant recourse to Homer and the other early poets such as Hesiod who, with Homer, 'gave the Greeks their gods', or in other words codified much of what was current in a rich oral tradition, and filled the gaps. In Mesopotamia, if we search the literary tradition, there are epics too; they encompass a complicated genealogy of the divine, cosmogonies (including the Flood), and exploits of kings, such as Gilgamesh, who, in their dealings with the divine and supernatural, come closer to the stories of Greek heroes than they do to the legend-histories of Greek kings, the Trojan War and the like.[5] Gilgamesh is modelled on a third-millennium king; the Greeks had no such remote ancestry to recall and elaborate, indeed by then they had barely arrived in Greece.

The supernatural exploits of the eastern kings, whether Mesopotamian Gilgamesh or Syrian kings in the Ugaritic epics, might seem to give grounds for monument identification and relic collections, just as the god, king and hero stories did in Greece, but we have no evidence for it beyond the fact that the locale was familiarly Mesopotamian or Syrian. Maybe it is simply that the texts we have are not of the type to record them, and archaeologists have been unable to recognize evidence for them, but this is rather hard to believe. Many exploits took place in identifiable locations whose associations with epic could hardly have been overlooked by later populations, unless they were of a markedly different temper of mind, or more preoccupied with what higher authority obliged them to believe, than we can easily credit or imagine.

We simply do not know how far Greek attitudes to their past were echoed or anticipated in the east. Where we do have evidence for treatment of past monuments the circumstances are very different from the Greek, although they might have offered much the same opportunities, which seem to have been ignored. The Assyrian royal annals represent what has been called a 'dialogue between past and future kings'.[6] They could be updated and re-edited, and formed a corpus of precedent not unlike the Homeric poems, but based on what passed as a true account of historical events in realistic and familiar situations, which might counsel or inspire future generations, much as Homer was used by some later Greeks, though very differently. There was indeed opportunity for some reflection:

> Mount thou upon the ruined mounds of ancient cities and walk around; behold the skulls of those of earlier and later times. Who is the evildoer, who is the benefactor?[7]

Arnold Toynbee remarked that 'Archaism is a symptom of diffidence, and, in the post-Assyrian age, the Babylonians, like the Egyptians, were both proud of and disconcerted by the antiquity of their civilization...intimations of mortality'.[8]

When a new building was planned, or the renewal of an old one, care was taken to dig down to earlier foundations so that the new might be linked to the old, and in the proper identification of what had gone before. This usually took the form of recovering the foundation or building texts which would have been interred in generally predictable places in the old building, but might also include inscribed monuments and statues. Generally these would be left in the new building or incorporated in some way as a demonstration of continuity. Thus, Nabonidus: 'I deposited with my own inscription an inscription of Hammurabi, an ancient king, written on an alabaster tablet which I found inside a ruined temple; I placed them forever.'[9]

All this was more a matter of religious necessity than archaeological nostalgia. The record is best studied in the neo-Babylonian empire of the seventh and first half of the sixth centuries, and a prominent figure is Nabonidus, who is sometimes credited with some exceptional archaeological zeal. Rarely, these monuments to past achievement, along with the booty from campaigns, were kept apart in what then begin to resemble museums. One such was an annex to Nebuchadnezzar II's palace in Babylon, which remained in use and receiving new acquisitions into the reign of Nabonidus.[10] The monuments it contained went back to third-millennium Sumer and the majority can be taken to have been booty from the campaigns of Babylonian kings. But the spirit in which they were collected involves something deeper than display of captured treasures – which for the most part they were not, since the treasures of pecuniary value would have been for palace display or use, or for recycling through melting down of precious metals. Rather they were religious and historical monuments, and possession of them implied possession also of the powers they embodied. The statues of the god were even identified with the gods themselves, and their removal or dispatch elsewhere indicated a relocation of divine power and support;[11] in the same spirit the power of an enemies' gods might be harnessed by taking their images. There are only vestigial examples of such practice in Greece, usually with hero relics, and probably not with divine or heroic images. At best some Greek relics are given healing properties, but this was never a prominent function.[12] Closest perhaps is the association of the Palladion statue with the fate of Troy, which might easily have been an eastern story, given the powers attributed to statues in the east: one of the many Anatolian aspects of the Troy story which have yet to be properly explored. At Babylon were to be seen (together surely with much more that did not survive to be excavated) inscribed statues and reliefs of the fourth and third millennia BC, a Kassite mace, several ninth-to-seventh-century Assyrian reliefs, inscribed clay cylinders and a virtual library of literary tablets.

When Babylon fell to the Persian Cyrus in 540 BC it too suffered looting, but was to become a Persian capital of considerable importance, and remained a depository for historical documents. Among the finds is remarked a copy of the Persian Darius' famous relief and inscription at Bisitun (520 BC), which he had 'sent in all directions among the lands'.[13] Cyrus' own new capital, at Susa in Persia, had been an Elamite capital where a comparable collection to the Babylonian had been made long before. Some are inscribed to indicate that most were plunder from Mesopotamia after campaigns in the late second millennium BC, but they were not ordinary treasure. They include inscribed victory reliefs from yet earlier days (the stele of Naram-Sin from Sippar, of before 2200 BC), the famous lawcode of Babylonian Hammurabi, and other reliefs and statues of gods and kings; 'essential strands in the fabric of life, binding the past to the future and preserving evidence of divine sanction and authority'.[14]

China offers a significantly different record. The Chinese, before the Christian era, were neither cursed nor blessed with an organised pantheon of gods and heroes and the story-telling that goes with them, rather than a sophisticated form of ancestor-worship, and a number of well defined but mythologically minor deities (Kuan-Yin and others) who were a continuing presence and were much inspired by new Buddhist teaching. This allowed a more reassuring sense of continuity with the past and a far better historical sensitivity. In the later centuries BC there was a determined effort to make sense of the many records of the past, including the documents found in the house of Confucius, and to make of them a real history of the Chinese people, to far back into the Bronze Age, if only with authentic king lists. This was accompanied by the creation of a mainly Taoist divine bureaucracy including deified mortals. Here, as in Mesopotamia, it may be that this scholarly historical awareness provided the right climate for acquisition of relics of the historical past. The Greeks had been attempting the same thing since the fourth century BC, in both general and local histories, but could never get to events before their Iron Age without becoming entangled in myth-history; whence the attempt by many of them to rationalize it.

The land of China was replete with remnants of the past, mainly objects since the architecture tended to be rather impermanent (except, of course, the Great Wall) and renewed rather than replaced, but many of the objects found could be accurately placed in their history and there was no call for the invention of relics. An important class of object thus recovered was of bronze ritual vessels, cauldrons and bells, many of them inscribed and so datable. Texts show that they were being recovered and recorded from the second century BC on, but there must have been many available before they attracted any real antiquarian interest. Some dated back to the thirteenth century BC, and occasional finds were optimistically placed in impossibly earlier dynasties; but this was mainly an activity of centuries AD, when the bronzes could be copied and even moulded for the casting of new pieces, and fake antique inscriptions added. Most such finds were kept in temples but some private collections were also formed. The old vessels suffered a change in use also, from containers for grave offerings to use for incense in cult.[15]

China is and was no less a major source of fossils, and details of the canonical form of the Chinese dragon may well derive from finds, which are certainly associated with dragons in folklore.[16]

THE GREEKS

None of this selective and superficial review of non-Greek attitudes to the past strikes much of a chord when we recall what we have discovered about the Greek use and re-creation of their past, historical or mythical, most of which operated at a far lower level than the imperial. The difference must, as already intimated, be explained by a combination of the totally different histories of the peoples involved, of their totally different social and religious structures, and of their environment. In the Greek there is much that is difficult to describe as other than childish, with responses appropriate to the credulous, except when it came to weaving their myths and superstitions into a more timeless literary appraisal of the human condition, from Hesiod and Homer through the playwrights. The easterners seemed more focused, even more practical, in their use of the past, though no less anxious to recover it physically wherever opportunity offered.

The appeal of the authentic relic is universal and eternal; by now Beatles' memorabilia are as sought after as Beethoven's, more expensive, and no doubt as often forged as were the relics of an Achilles or the Buddha. The Greeks were equally ready to buy relics of historical philosophers and poets (T.104) – lamps, sticks, writing tablets. Every aspect of their heroic age was explored by them and identified on the ground or by relics; for the heroes themselves their conception,[17] birth, homes, exploits and death could all acquire some material testimony.

169. Theseus raises the rock beneath which lie the sandals and sword by which his birth as an Athenian prince is proved. On an Athenian red figure lekythos by the Sabouroff Painter. About 470 BC. (Stockholm, National Museum A1701)

It is perhaps too easy to see in what we have reviewed nothing more than an ingenious attempt by the Greeks to bend the material world, and what was made of it by artists, to illustrate what was believed about their remote past. It is possible, however, that the natural (fossils and landscape) and artificial (ruins and relics), were themselves to no small degree responsible for many details, and sometimes more than just details, of that picture of the past. Many cultures had stories of their remote ancestors, but it is quite exceptional for the earliest humanoid race that has to be dealt with by the gods or heroes to be treated as of gigantic stature.[18] In Greece the mythographers record first the Titans who have to be dealt with by the Olympian gods, and their stories are very similar to those about rival gods in other early and eastern cultures. They are followed by the Giants, who are given a similar background, being also the children of Earth and Sky, and have to be dealt with in a like manner. But they seem almost an intrusion into the record of the relations between men, gods and other supernatural beings, and even superfluous, given the Titan stories. They have no interesting functions, such as are attributed to the Titan Prometheus, they are just big and belligerent. The artisan giants, like the Kyklopes, are a different breed. The Giants were not the product of any more complicated narrative associations, foreign or native, but mainly of local observation of phenomena which required explanation in purely Greek terms. Greece is richer in fossils than Egypt, even than most of Mesopotamia. So was it a matter of the many discoveries of what were naturally taken to be the remains of giant humanoids that generated the story of the Giants, sons of Earth, and their nature (volcanic, fiery, serpentine), rather than that the fossils lent credence to already established tales? The former is, to my mind, the more likely. For other natural phenomena, such as landscape details, it might have been that there was a tale already waiting to be illustrated by a novel interpretation, but many might as easily have been the very genesis of the story, such as the petrifaction of figures like Niobe or the Phaeacian ships. This would indicate another source of inspiration for some myths, dependent on observation and not on traditional tales with names attached, nor on borrowings from the foreigner.

For most ruins and potential relics, such as weapons, there could usually be an available name or tale to recruit, but many may as well have generated their own stories, or variants on old stories. This is most apparent where the source is a foreign image which may suggest a whole episode (Herakles and the Sun, perhaps) or significant detail (the invulnerable lion and lionskin). The common appearance in Greek story of *gnorismata* – physical tokens by which persons, generally lost children, can be identified [*Fig. 169*],[19] seems on a par with their response to the appeal of the physical relic. This Greek ability to create myth from varied physical sources was a very close match to their ability to illustrate it in object or image. It seems also to have been a very Greek attitude positively to pursue such proofs of the past to justify status and power, and eventually to attract and entertain the even more credulous. I have mentioned 'the tourist trade' more than once. We can see its genesis with the travels and collecting of the first Roman generals who fought on

Greek soil, and it developed rapidly once Greece became a Roman province. It was an important factor behind much that Pausanias records yet it is also clear that in his time a great deal was still taken very seriously indeed. Intelligent Romans were not deceived about the Greek ability to attribute improbable antiquity to 'antiques'. Pliny noted the Greeks' obsession with their own glorious past.[20] The emperor Titus 'viewed the wealth of the temple [of Aphrodite in Cyprus], the presents of eastern kings, and the collection of rarities, which the genius of the Greeks, fond of tradition and the decorations of fabulous narrative, affected to trace from remote antiquity'.[21] But both Greeks and Romans long continued to seek out and admire this spurious past. We should not dismiss it too readily, for it played an important part in the Greeks' own creation of national identity and pride, and had been at times a major factor in determination of far more serious matters. The stock of Greek myth created a Greek identity as surely as any dynastic or religious unity did for other peoples. Moreover, it is a most vivid reflection of the Greeks' use of the past to further the ambitions of the present and to mould the future.

This book has dwelt on the physical evidence for the Greeks' re-creation of their past, but it has involved also their treatment of it in images, which did not present it as in any respect antiquated, but allowed it to refer immediately to the contemporary world in appearance and therefore also in its preoccupations. An extension of this, not considered in any detail here but another facet of the same attitude of mind, is Greek theatre. Already in the sixth century gods and heroes could be impersonated by actors and priests appropriately dressed and provided with identifying attributes. These at first served cult processions – such as a Dionysos with his rout of satyrs on a wheeled ship passing through the streets of Athens, and probably other ritual occasions which are less well recorded for us in text and picture than the inescapable Dionysiac. It could even happen in a purely political context, where the tyrant Peisistratos is led to Athens by a country girl dressed up as Athena. All this led inevitably to the acting of related mythical occasions – first the return of Hephaistos to Olympus by Dionysos and his attendants; thence to more formal dancing and acting of stories which were sung in dithyrambs and choruses, and all this a short step away from tragic as well as comic (the satyr play) performances of mythical subjects. Stage dress was simply contemporary dress, with some exaggeration for effect – boots and masks. The setting is religious still but much subordinated to the secular. Words, song and music come to complement the dumb images and physical paraphernalia through which the Greeks made their past alive and relevant to their present. Even on the stage the display and use of objects had a strong narrative function.[22] Beside it goes the occasional assimilation of prominent figures to heroes, without as yet the positive identification which comes with attributing divinity to royalty, especially from Alexander the Great on [*Fig. 170*].[23] Kings were gods elsewhere in the ancient world, but did not also adjust divine or heroic story to illustrate or enhance their

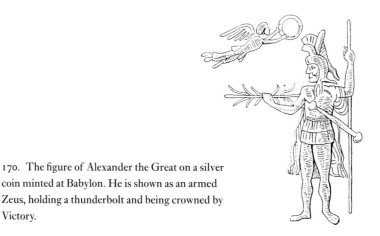

170. The figure of Alexander the Great on a silver coin minted at Babylon. He is shown as an armed Zeus, holding a thunderbolt and being crowned by Victory.

record. This was happening already by the sixth century BC in Greece, through the identification of a state with its most prominent god or hero, and thereby the identification and, where need be, invention of myth to demonstrate authority or comment on events in the by-then traditional Greek way of exploiting the past to comment on the present.[24]

All this is possibly the principal factor that makes the genesis and development of Greek myth so little like those of other early peoples: apart from the inevitable folktale elements, it was more closely embedded in both the Greek environment and the memory, however distorted, of comparatively recent history; it was unhindered by explicit written records and therefore infinitely flexible in the hands of authors and artists; and it was exercised by a people who had the good fortune, bestowed by their country and its history of relative freedom from authoritarian rule, to be able to exercise at all levels of society a remarkable liberty of choice and enquiry. What has been surveyed in the preceding chapters, devoted to the physical evidence, is but a vestigial view of what must have been widespread in Greek lands and society, and which we can glimpse only through the courtesy of such texts as have survived, and of our own interpretation of the very little that excavation has uncovered. Yet we seem often to be dealing with the genesis as much as with the mere illustration of what the Greeks thought of their past and the tales they told about it.

Abbreviations

AA	*Archäologischer Anzeiger*
AJA	*American Journal of Archaeology*
Ancestors	C. Antonaccio, *An Archaeology of Ancestors*. 1995
ABV	J.D. Beazley, *Attic Black-Figure Vase-Painters*. 1956*
ARV	J.D. Beazley, *Attic Red-Figure Vase-Painters*. 1963*
BCH	*Bulletin de Correspondance Hellénique*
Boardman, *AGGems*	J. Boardman, *Archaic Greek Gems*. 1968
Boardman, *ARFH* I, II	J. Boardman, *Athenian Red Figure Vases. A Handbook. The Archaic Period*. 1975; *. . . The Classical Period*. 1989
Boardman, *Diffusion*	J. Boardman, *The Diffusion of Classical Art in Antiquity*. 1994
Boardman, *EGVP*	J. Boardman, *Early Greek Vase Painting*. 1998
Boardman, *GO*	J. Boardman, *The Greeks Overseas*. 1980/1999
Boardman, *Vases*	J. Boardman, *The History of Greek Vases*. 2001
BSA	*Annual of the British School at Athens*
FGrH	F. Jacoby, *Die Fragmente der griechischen Historiker*. 1923–1958
FHG	C. Müller, *Fragmenta Historicorum Graecorum*. 1841–1870
GRBS	*Greek, Roman and Byzantine Studies*
Jeffery, *LSAG*	L.H. Jeffery, *The Local Scripts of Archaic Greece*. 1961, 1989
JHS	*Journal of Hellenic Studies*
LIMC	*Lexicon Iconographicum Mythologiae Classicae*
Mayor	A. Mayor, *The First Fossil Hunters*. 2000
NCP	F. Imhoof-Blumer and P. Gardner, *Ancient Coins. A Numismatic Commentary on Pausanias*. 1887
OJA	*Oxford Journal of Archaeology*
Para	J.D. Beazley, *Paralipomena*. 1971*
Pfister	F. Pfister, *Der Reliquienkult im Altertum*. 1909–1912
Powell, *Coll.Alex.*	J.U. Powell, *Collectanea Alexandrina*. 1925
Trendall, *LCS*	A.D. Trendall, *The Red-Figured Vases of Lucania, Campania and Sicily*. 1967

* for later references consult T.H. Carpenter, *Beazley Addenda* (1989) and *www.beazley.ox.ac.uk*.

Notes

PREFACE (pp. 7–16)

1 Plato, *Phaidros* 229b–230a.
2 Renate Tölle's *Genealogische Stammtafel zur griechischen Mythologie* (1967) attempts to offer a comprehensive chart of all Greek divine and heroic genealogies and their linkages, without pretending to reduce the pattern to 'history'. There is a more detailed study mainly of names and places by C. Parada, *Genealogical Guide to Greek Mythology* (1993).
3 Once the Spaniards had brought horses to Central America the Maya started mounting their gods on them.
4 S. Moser, *Ancestral Images* (1998) ch. 2. In Aeschylus, *Prometheus Vinctus* 447–458, such an existence is described as a foil to the blessings of civilization that Prometheus offered.
5 A full study of Hesiod's work on genealogies in M.L. West, *The Hesiodic Catalogue of Women* (1985) ch. 3.
6 The view of the Greek past that is the subject of this book is that of the Greeks themselves, not of the modern archaeologist-historian. For an account of the latter and his problems see I. Morris' engaging essay 'Periodization and the Heroes' in *Inventing Ancient Culture* (eds. M. Golden and P. Toohey, 1997) 96–131. *A New Companion to Homer* (eds. I. Morris and B. Powell, 1997) has useful essays on Homer and myth, folktale, history, art, though necessarily no more authoritative than many such in the past, or to come; this is a subject much affected nowadays by new evidence, which is a positive gain, and by new theories, which may need more rigorous testing than proving. K. Dowden, *The Uses of Greek Mythology* (1992) is a useful account of the purposes of Greek myth; and F. Graf, *Greek Mythology* (1993) of its origins and development; neither take account of the possible physical origins for some stories and details, and the archaeological and literary pursuits of the subject still remain largely discrete. In the footnotes in this book I have confined references to sources which I think are worth looking up.

CHAPTER ONE (pp. 17–32)

The Function of the Past in Greece: Our Sources

1 S.I. Johnston, *The Restless Dead* (1999), for Greek problems with ghosts and the like.
2 Herodotus 1.4.
3 Lineage boasting in Homer: M.L. Lang, *Classical Quarterly* 44 (1994) 1–6.

4 Antigone's dilemma was anticipated at the end of Aeschylus, *Septem*.
5 On the voting at Troy on vases, *LIMC* I, 326–327; our *Fig. 2* is pl. 244, Aias I, no. 84; *ARV* 369,2. The other side has Ajax and Odysseus coming to blows (*ARFH* I, fig. 247).
6 Herodotus 5.90.
7 W.H.C. Frend, *BSA* 57 (1962) 193–196, fig. 8.
8 *Anthologia Palatina* 6.297, by Phanias.
9 And *Iliad* 2.793; of old Aisyetes, otherwise unknown, but his tomb remembered (T.583).
10 From H. Schliemann, *Ilias* (1880) 657, fig. 1514.
11 *Iliad* 24.602–617; T.134; below, Chapter Four.
12 Pfister, 540–544, on relics in Homer.
13 G.L. Huxley, *Pindar's Vision of the Past* (1975).
14 On Thucydides' 'Archaeology', S. Hornblower, *Commentary on Thucydides* I (1991) 7–8.
15 Thucydides 1.11,20,21.
16 The anachronisms are well explored by P. Easterling in *JHS* 105 (1985) 1–10. References to writing, mainly avoided in Homer but not in the plays, are not really anachronistic, and some apparent references to coinage may rather be to the use of signets.
17 Aristotle himself, a good observer, would have promoted such compilation. On Aristotle as an antiquary, G.L. Huxley, *GRBS* 14 (1973) 271–286.
18 The example shown was built probably in the 9th cent. BC, enlarged in the following two centuries, and even with a Roman building eventually attached. See M. Guido, *Sardinia* (1963) 122, pl. 36.
19 Herodotus 4.55.
20 Cf. M. Davies, *The Epic Cycle* (1989) 48, 59; *Epicorum Graecorum Fragmenta* (1988) 32, 47. Achilles in Scythia: G.F. Pinney in *Ancient Greek Art and Iconography* (ed. W. Moon, 1983) 127–146.
21 Discussed by T.S. Scheer in *Klio* 78 (1996) 353–373.
22 *Anthologia Palatina* 6.342, 358.
23 Strabo 19 on the value of the study; 298–299, 554–555, on Homeric geography. D. Dueck, *Strabo of Amasia* (2000). A new edition is in preparation; see *Studia Troica* 3 (1993) 201–231 for the Trojan section.
24 Discussed by S. Carey in *Journal of the History of Collections* 12 (2000) 1–13.
25 Appian, *Mithridatica* 116–117.
26 Contrast the more relaxed and, for the traveller, entertaining but not didactic, travelogue of Herakleides (3rd/2nd cent. BC; edited by F. Pfister, 1951), which writes about the people and the logistics of travel rather than

monuments, but is sadly fragmentary.

27 On Pausanias, C. Robert, *Pausanias als Schriftsteller* (1909) cannot be neglected. There have been several recent studies, notably K. Arafat, *Pausanias' Greece* (1996), with ch. 2 on 'Pausanias and the past'; E.L. Bowie and S.E. Alcock in *Pausanias historien* (ed. J. Boyen, 1994); W.K. Pritchett, *Pausanias Periegetes* I (1998), II (1999); S.E. Alcock et al. (eds.), *Pausanias. Travel and Memory in Roman Greece* (2001).

28 Pausanias 8.4.7.

29 'Quelques aspects du 'culte des reliques' dans les traditions de la Grèce ancienne', *Bull. de la Classe des lettres et des sciences morales et politiques* (Académie royale de Belgique) 75 (1989) 58–99. An engaging essay by J.B. Hainsworth in *Minos* 20–22 (1987) 211–219.

CHAPTER TWO (pp. 33–43)

Fossilized History: Them Bones

1 A.B. Lloyd, *Herodotus Book II. A Commentary* (1975), on 2.12, for yet earlier observations of the shells.

2 Pindar, *Olympia* 9.42–46; called 'men of stone' from a false etymology of the word *laos*, 'people' (*las* 'stone'). Apollodorus 1.7.2, for the whole story.

3 The Hindu *shalgram* is a black stone full of ammonite fossils, worshipped as Vishnu at Salagrama on the River Gandhaki (north of Patna), because a spiral shell is one of the god's emblems. K. Oakley has an interesting paper on the folklore of fossils worldwide in *Antiquity* 39 (1965) 9–16, 117–125.

4 The proportional differences in different species of what is basically the same skeleton was explored long ago by W. D'Arcy Thompson, *On Growth and Form* (1917).

5 Mayor, 123, fig. 3.5.

6 On their estimated sizes, Pfister, 507–509. Diodorus (1.24.2) saw the problem that if they were of the period of earliest man (10,000 years before, on Egyptian reckoning) they should not have been fought by Herakles a generation before the Trojan War.

7 Plutarch fr.7, Sandbach.

8 Loss or dedication of a finger, *pars pro toto*, is a recognized activity and not only in Greece: Frazer, on Pausanias 8.34.2; W. Burkert, *The Creation of the Sacred* (1996) 34–40. Adorants would bite off the toes of the mummified St Xavier at Goa and keep them as relics.

9 Mayor, 116–129, 199–202, on ancient observations of the size of heroes and giants, based on the fossil bones found.

10 G.N. Curzon, *Leaves from a Viceroy's Notebook* (1926) 363–364.

11 References for the Dun Cow in J. Westwood, *Albion. A Guide to Legendary Britain* (1985) s.v. Index; to which Arthur MacGregor kindly directed me. The cow also left a footprint in stone, and an 18th-century antiquary, Browne Willis, was said to have boots that were made from the Cow. Marcus Lynch of Warwick Castle also kindly supplied me with information on the Cow, referring to W. Field, *The Town and Castle of Warwick* (1815) 24–27, 232–233; and *Cooke's Guide to Warwickshire*

(1870) 99–101. [*The Book of the Dun Cow* is a mystic compilation of different origin.]

12 The skeleton of a giant 17 ft. high was shown in Lucerne town hall, composed of bones from a fossil mammoth: Oakley, op.cit., 123.

13 Quintus Smyrnaeus 12.449–480.

14 Mayor, 157–165, on the Corinthian vase (her fig. 4.2) and the Samos skull (fig. 4.3). The vase, Boardman, *EGVP* fig. 402. It is by no means a straight copy of a fossil skull, however; see Mayor in *Archaeology Odyssey* March/April 2002, 49–50.

15 Mayor, ch. 3.

16 Plutarch, *Theseus* 13. Pallas was also the name of a Giant, slain by Athena, who used his skin to shield her body: Apollodorus 1.6.2. The Pallantidai as Giants, Sophocles fr. 24. Pikermi – Mayor, 83–91.

17 J. Schoo, *Vulkanische und seismische Aktivität des ägäische Meeresbecken in Spiegel der griechischen Mythologie* (1937).

18 Alternative candidates for placing under Etna were the Giants Enkelados (Virgil, *Aeneid* 3.571–582) or Briareus (Callimachus, *Hymn* 4.141–144). For earthquakes and Giants, A.B. Cook, *Zeus* III (1940) 1–29. Typhon and Hesiod, see M.L. West, *Hesiod Theogony* (1966) 251, 393.

19 Mayor, 196.

20 Mayor, 127, Map 3.2.

21 The fight with these 'sown men' (*spartoi*) is avoided in art except on one Sicilian vase; *LIMC* V, 872, no. 42. The fight with the serpent is commonplace.

22 Mayor, 222, 266; the story was rationalized by the Aristotelian Palaephatus.

23 Apollonius Rhodius 3.1278–1407.

24 Pindar, *Olympia* 1.46–51. The fossil and story, Mayor, 104–110. Any relationship to the importance of a ram's shoulder-blade in sacrifice is tenuous; cf. W. Burkert, *Homo Necans* (1983) 99–100. Shoulder-blades were used worldwide as writing material since they were the only broad flat bone in vertebrates.

25 Mayor, 169–170, for the Athens find; 170–191 for others.

26 Ptolemaeus Chennus, ap. Photius, *Bibliotheca* 151b.

27 Herodotus 3.102–105. They are not the winged creatures of Sophokles fr. 29.

28 From *Encyclopaedia of Indian Natural History* (ed. R.E. Hawkins, 1986) 367: long-tailed marmot.

29 And Strabo 705–706. The Budé edition of the Pliny passage (1947, 152–153) discusses the Indian evidence. M. Peissel, *The Ants' Gold* (1984) for observations in Baltistan; the excavated earth was sifted for gold by the locals. Mayor, 129–135, for the 'dragons' of India seen by Greeks (Apollonius of Tyana, 1st cent. AD); her figs. 3.9–11 from India are fossil skulls that could pass as antlers. Further references to monster ants in M. Davies and J. Kathirithamby, *Greek Insects* (1986) 44–46, and fully discussed for their oriental associations by J.D.P. Bolton, *Aristeas of Proconnesus* (1962) s.v. index.

30 Chapter 30 of A. Layard's edition of the *Marvellous Adventures* (1895). Ants are called Pismires because ant-hills smell of urine. Much of his story is garbled Herodotus. The ant-lion (*myrmekoleon*) of late antiquity and mediaeval bestiaries who found gold is a different matter; it may be the honey-badger who digs honey from ground nests.

31 Mayor, 182–183; H. Kyrieleis, in *Early Greek Cult Practice* (ed. R. Hägg, 1988) 215–221.

32 The Samos fossils and monsters, Mayor, 54–61. A.B. Cook, *Zeus* III (1940) 3. For the name, Callimachus, *Aetia* fr.1. Compare the modern Greek word for a horse – *alogon* – 'irrational'.

33 Mayor, 71, for fossil 'footprints'.

34 Euripides, *Hekabe* 1269–1273; Strabo fr. VII.55; Apollodorus, Epit. 5.23. Pfister, 326–328, for animal graves which gave their names to locations.

CHAPTER THREE (pp. 45–78)

Homes Fit For Heroes

1 *ARV* 1300.4; K. Schefold, *Die Göttersage in der klassischen und hellenistischen Kunst* (1981) 91.

2 R.D. Cromey, *JHS* 111 (1991) 165–174, disallows a Pelasgian as 'Gigas', but any Pelasgian has to be a giant to shoulder such a load; and since it is undressed rock it is hardly for any new classical building, as he suggests. No 'real' giant is named Gigas in Greek art and literature, so this is more an epithet than a proper name. Martine Denoyelle confirms that the tree really does seem leafless; white-painted details sometimes leave ghost traces, but not, it seems, here. This complicates the identity, unless it is a reminder that this is the tree burned by the Persians, but which revived.

3 Herodotus 6.137 quotes Hecataeus on the Pelasgians in Athens.

4 J.M. Hurwit, *The Athenian Acropolis* (1999) 73–74, a possible column base and terrace.

5 *Odyssey* 7.80.

6 Hurwit, op.cit., 74–79, 105, 142.

7 *Troades* 1088.

8 From *La Grèce. Vues pittoresques et topographiques, dessinées par O.M. Baron de Stackelberg* (Paris, 1834).

9 Euripides, *Iphigenia in Tauris* 845–846.

10 *The Archaeology of Ancestors* (1995) = *Ancestors*; chapter 2 for a full account of attention paid to Bronze Age tombs, without specific identification with heroes; chapter 3, the identified cults. Unfortunately, it omits Crete, which may be a special case but is very illuminating. M. Deoudi, *Heroenkulte in homerischer Zeit* (1999) gives a useful gazetteer, and description of the sites and evidence, which can now be used beside *Ancestors*.

11 Pfister, 627–643, also listed by location.

12 On the power of names, S. Pulleyn, *Classical Quarterly* 44 (1994) 17–25.

13 Pfister, 347–423, gives a full discussion of the text evidence.

14 Byron also called Gell 'classic' and 'coxcomb' in versions of the lines which appear in his *English Bards and Scotch Reviewers*. His letter on Troy is to H. Drury, of 3 May 1810. See *Lord Byron. Selected Letters and Journals* (ed. L.A. Marchand, 1982) 35–36, 243. W. Gell, *The Topography of Troy* (1804).

15 H. Schliemann, *Ilios* (1880) 653, fig. 1512; J.M. Cook, *The Troad* (1973) 88–89.

16 Ibid., 159–165. For the Tomb of Protesilaos (T.97) at Elaious over the straits, see now C.P. Jones, *JHS* 121 (2001) 144–146, pl. 1.

17 *Studia Troica* VI (1996) 256–257, figs. 9–10; J. Boardman, *Persia and the West* (2000) 37.

18 Discussed by L. Burn in *Antike Kunst* 28 (1985) 102–104 with pls. 23.1 and A.1 (colour); A. Griffiths, *JHS* 106 (1986) 58; *ARV* 763,2.

19 *ARV* 240, 44; C. Bérard, *Antike Kunst* 7 (1966) 93–100 on this (pl. 23.2) and other scenes with satyrs destroying herms. *Das griechische Satyrspiel* (eds. R. Krumeich et al., 1999) 62–63, pl. 13b. The marks on the tumulus side have been taken for flames, which is most unlikely; they more probably indicate the results of the satyrs' attack.

20 Cook, op.cit., 107–108, 133–134; J.V. Luce, *Celebrating Homer's Landscapes* 127–129.

21 *Odyssey* 24.80–84. Luce, op.cit., 135–141, also reporting recent German exploration of the site: M. Korfmann, *AA* 1989, 474–479. Cf. *Studia Troica* 2 (1992) 181–182 for speculation about the tombs of Achilles and Paris.

22 Pausanias has Hektor's bones later taken to Thebes for burial: T.443.

23 Cook, op.cit., 132–134. Caesar – Lucan, *Bellum Civile* 9.975–979, quoted by Cook; and op.cit., 105, 128, 129, 152, for other surmised heroic tomb locations in the Troad.

24 G.E. Bean, *Aegean Turkey* (1966) 58–61, fig. 5. Probably 6th-century: R.V. Nicholls, *BSA* 53/4 (1958/9) 64.

25 Bean, op.cit., 63, fig. 8. Cf. T.160 for another Lydian 'throne'.

26 On the political motivation behind the latter see D.M. Leahy, *Historia* 4 (1955) 26–38.

27 Pfister, 423–428.

28 On the tomb, *Ancestors* 127–130. K. Fittschen in *Alexander the Great: from Macedonia to the Oikoumene* (Veria Congress 1998; 1999) 57–60, on the monument base. Alexander's loyal Boeotian cavalry made an offering to Zeus Soter in 329 BC, having returned from the Asian campaign: M.N. Tod, *Greek Historical Inscriptions* II (1948) no. 197; could this have been the monument? I am grateful to Olga Palagia for the suggestion. The Roman cult, S.E. Alcock, *AJA* 105 (2001) 266.

29 *Ancestors* 104–109.

30 Menidi – P. Wolters, *Jahrbuch des deutschen archäologischen Instituts* 14 (1899) 116, fig. 24; *Ancestors* 51. Cf. A.M. Snodgrass, *Annali. Istituto Universitario Orientale. Napoli (AION)* 10 (1988) 19–26 on the 'archaeology of the hero'. R. Hägg in *Gifts to the Gods* (eds. T. Linders and G. Nordquist, 1987) 93–100, on the types of Geometric and Archaic offerings made at such tombs: they are in no way extraordinary. The Mycenae sherd, Jeffery, *LSAG* 173, dated about 475 BC; O. Kern, *Inscriptiones Graecae* (1913) pl. 8.

31 Curses on those who disturb the grave: J.H.M. Strubbe in *Magika Hiera* (eds. C.A. Faraone and D. Obbink, 1991) 33–59.

32 On re-use and amends, D.C. Kurtz and J. Boardman, *Greek Burial Customs* (1971) 196–197.

33 R.W. Hutchinson and J. Boardman, *BSA* 49 (1954) 215–228.

34 J. Boardman, *BSA* 62 (1967) 65–66, fig. 2. The 'hut-urns', R. Hägg, *Opuscula Atheniensia* 18 (1990) 95–97.

35 J.N. Coldstream in *Praktika tes Akademias Athenon* 71 (1996) 236–262, doubts general re-use of the chamber tombs, though one or two seem unarguable (and cf. J.K. Brock, *Fortetsa* (1957) 4–5). He also cites evidence for minor offerings at old disturbed tombs. The relative scarcity of Bronze Age *larnax* burial fragments in the cemeteries of Knossos is less important than the fact that any are there at all. Minoan chamber tombs needed minimal if any adjustment for later use.

36 There are valuable essays on hero and tomb cult in volumes edited by R. Hägg: *Ancient Greek Cult Practice from the Epigraphical Evidence* (1994); *...from the Archaeological Evidence* (1998); *Ancient Greek Hero Cult* (1999).

37 S.E. Alcock on post-classical tomb cults in *AJA* 95 (1991) 447–467, suggesting new incentives; in *Placing the Gods* (eds. *eadem* and R. Osborne, 1994) 247–261, she reflects on how some shrines may appear to be re-activated in later periods (this depends on what might be very lacunose archaeological evidence), and the many we know nothing about (a common blind spot for archaeologists).

38 On the tourist trade, L. Casson, *Travel in the Ancient World* (1974) Chapters 14–19.

39 *Ancestors* 112–117.

40 *Ancestors* 228–235.

41 On founder cults and the colonists' attitudes to their local ancestry and traditions see I. Malkin, *Religion and Colonization in Ancient Greece* (1987) chs. 6, 7; and *The Returns of Odysseus* (1998) for the effects on myth and cult of the western journeys.

42 *Ancestors* 183–186 for the Hyperboreans; P. Bruneau and J. Ducat, *Guide de Délos* (1983) 144–145, fig. 30, 149.

43 On Amazon graves, Pfister, 127.

44 E.B. Harrison, *AJA* 85 (1981) 294–311.

45 *Ancestors* 155–166.

46 *Ancestors* 147–152. The publication, J.M. Cook, *BSA* 48 (1953) 30–68.

47 J. Knauss, *Antike Welt* 28 (1997) 381–395; *Argolische Studien* (1996).

48 *Odyssey* 3.278–285. The statues – B.S. Ridgway, *The Archaic Style in Greek Sculpture* (1993) 69–70. The plaque – Boardman, *EGVP* fig. 192; *BSA* 49 (1954) 198.

49 *Ancestors* 169.

50 *Ancestors* 170–176. The new cult, probably archaic, helped provide testimony for the origin of the Olympic Games. The same may be true for the cult of Opheltes at Nemea, and the Nemean Games (ibid., 176–177); his tomb was shown there (T.216).

51 *Ancestors* 178–181.

52 *Ancestors* 181–182.

53 P. Cartledge, *Sparta and Laconia* (1979) 112. *Ancestors* 182–183 for other rather tenuous Spartan hero associations.

54 Kurtz and Boardman, op.cit., Index s.v. Cenotaph.

55 *Odyssey* 4.584.

56 H. Schliemann, *Ithaka, der Peloponnes und Troja* (1869) 19–21 and map. *Odyssey* 13.13–14, 96–112, 216–217, 349–351. The possibility that Homer's Ithaca is not the same as modern Ithaca, a topic for dispute years ago, can be safely ignored.

57 J.V. Luce, *Celebrating Homer's Landscapes* (1998) 191–196. The dedications at the Cave of the Nymphs were reported by the late J.M. Cook and were of pottery, but no details are available. An interior view, W.B. Stanford and J.V. Luce, *The Quest for Odysseus* (1974) fig. 82 (exterior, fig. 72).

58 Schliemann, op.cit., 45–47.

59 S. Benton, *BSA* 34/35 (1935) 45–73, describes the 1930/1 excavation of the cave, and gives a slightly garbled account of its earlier history (46–47); for the inscribed pottery and mask, ibid., 54–56. The mask is here restored after another example from Ithaca, *BCH* 29 (1905) 148, fig. 11. The stone inscription: Jeffery, *LSAG* 231. *Ancestors* 152–155, for a general account of the cave; and Luce, op.cit., 224–228.

60 *Ancestors* loc.cit. says the tripods are in a 4th-century context but at best they had been arranged finally beside a 4th-century wall when the cave space was regularized, and this says nothing about when they arrived in the cave.

61 I. Malkin, *The Returns of Odysseus* (1998) ch. 3, and in *Gaia* 5 (2001) 11–27, making the good point that nymphs serve Greeks as welcoming deities in foreign parts where there is no existing and named Greek divine presence. Luce (op.cit., 226, 228) hints much the same explanation for the tripods, or that Homer saw them and worked them into the story, which is closer to my view.

62 S. Casson gives a lively account of Homer's visit to Ithaca in *Antiquity* 16 (1942) 77–81.

63 Strabo 59. The excavator (Benton, op.cit., 55–56) says 'Finds die out towards the end of the first century A.D.', but does not specify what they are. Strabo's comment seems to have been overlooked by recent commentators; it is out of context, in his Introduction.

64 The find is published in M.R. Popham et al., *Lefkandi* II.2 (1993), for the architecture, burials and the burial urn (ch. 6, by H.W. Catling). (*Lefkandi* II.1 for the pottery, and II.3, forthcoming, for the other finds.) General accounts in *Cambridge Ancient History Pls. to Vol. III* (1984) 246–247; *Archaeological Reports for 1981–82* 15–17; *Antiquity* 56 (1982) 169–174.

65 Older Egyptian alabaster vases taken to Spain by Phoenicians in the later eighth century; Boardman, *GO* 213.

66 Thus, S. Morris, *Daidalos* (1992) 140.

67 On a possible parallel at Thermon, I. Morris, *Archaeology as Cultural History* (2000) 225–228. The conversion of palace to tomb has no eastern parallel, and though each eastern king built his own palace, those of his predecessors were not 'cancelled'.

68 I. Morris in *Culture et Cité* (eds. A. Verbanck-Piérard and D. Viviers, 1995) 59–61.

69 N. Spencer, *OJA* 14 (1995) 286–289, with references.

70 *Ancestors* ch. 5 argues the hero/ancestor dichotomy.

71 The gravestone of Heropythos: H.T. Wade-Gery, *The Poet of the Iliad* (1952) 8–9; Jeffery, *LSAG* 344, 47. On genealogical thinking in Greece, R.L. Fowler, *Proceedings of the Cambridge Philological Society* 44 (1998) 1–19.

72 P. Cartledge, *Sparta and Lakonia* (1979) 341–346.

73 Pfister, 347–357, with other 'heroic' structures. W.K. Pritchett lists the ruins mentioned by Pausanias in *Pausanias Periegetes* II (1999) ch. 3.

74 Euripides seems to imply that Semele's home, ruined by Zeus' thunderbolt, was still visible in Thebes: *Bacchae* 6–8.

75 Pliny, *Historia Naturalis* 36.85; Diodorus 1.61 said that it had disappeared, through destruction or erosion.

76 J.N. Coldstream, *BSA* 95 (2000) 284–288; the temple probably not earlier than the 5th century.

77 *NCP* pls. Mx, GGxv.

78 J. Boardman, *Antiquaries Journal* 39 (1959) 195–196, pls. 34, 35.

79 Eleusis: G.E. Mylonas, *Eleusis* (1961) 59–60; an 8th-century building, perhaps for cult, was destroyed in the early 7th century, and a new structure with an altar was built in front of the 'ruins' in the 6th century.

80 On the association of Mycenaean centres with later cult, K. Tausend, *Gymnasium* 97 (1990) 145–153. Cf. C. Rolley in *The Greek Renaissance of the Eighth Century B.C.* (ed. R. Hägg, 1983) 113–119; E. Thomas in *Archäologische Studien in Kontaktzonen der antiken Welt* (ed. R. Rolle, 1998) 205–218, believes in a degree of continuity, noting the Mycenaean palace megaron plan used for later temples. On grounds for the placing of cult places see essays in *Placing the Gods* (eds. S.E. Alcock and R. Osborne, 1994), especially that by C.M. Antonaccio, 79–104, on relationship to Bronze Age remains. *Cultural Poetics in Archaic Greece* (eds. C. Dougherty and L. Kurke, 1993) also has much of relevance, notably Part One (I. Morris and C.M. Antonaccio).

81 For Pylos now, traces of a 7th/6th-century temple: T. Brenningmeyer, *AJA* 104 (2000) 330.

82 The continuity argued by some French scholars is improbable; comment in *Ancestors* 185 with n. 165.

83 J. Boardman in *Studien zur Mythologie und Vasenmalerei* (edd. E. Böhr and W. Martini; Festschrift K. Schauenburg, 1986) 129–131.

CHAPTER FOUR (pp. 79–126)

Realia et Naturalia

1 By Pausanias' day even classical armour, seen in paintings, looked odd: T.489.

2 *Iphigenia in Tauris* 823–826.

3 P. Kalligas in *Stele* (*eis mnemen N. Kontoleontos*, 1980) 351–357; pls. 157, 158. For the former also, Jeffery, *LSAG* 449, no. 11a.

4 A.B. Cook, *Zeus* III (1940) 898–900; K.P. Oakley, *Folklore* 82 (1971) 207–211. I am indebted to Zosia Archibald for information and photographs. It was acquired by Cook in the 1940s, found at Ephesus but with no closer detail of location. Scholars have associated it with the cult statue in a very speculative manner.

5 *Acts of the Apostles* 19.35.

6 W.K. Pritchett lists military dedications by heroes in *The Greek States at War* III (1979) 245–247.

7 Arrian, *Anabasis* 6.10.2.

8 Theocritus, *Idyll* 24.4–5.

9 Aristomenes was treated as heroic, but was probably historic, though ancient and modern authorities are not sure about which of the first three Messenian Wars he fought in (from late 8th to early 5th century): G.L. Huxley, *Early Sparta* (1962) 89–93; P. Cartledge, *Sparta and Laconia* (1979) 114, 127, 153.

10 Unlike the Roman, where the sacred shields of the Salii were preserved, and recognizable from old representations: J.P. Small, *Mélanges. Ecole Française de Rome. Antiquité* 103 (1991) 247–264.

11 I.R. Arnold, *AJA* 41 (1937) 436–440.

12 Pausanias 1.15.4.

13 Pausanias 2.24.7.

14 The buildings are best described in L.E. Lord, *Hesperia* 7 (1936) 496–538, as fourth-century guard houses. There is mortar between the blocks, possibly from a repair. And cf. R.A. Tomlinson, *Argos and the Argolid* (1972) 35–36, fig.9. A sophisticated scientific attempt at dating places the pyramid in the third millennium BC, which is impossible for such masonry: P.S. Theocharis et al., *Journal of Archaeological Science* (24 (1997) 399–405. I am indebted to Richard Tomlinson for comment and photographs.

15 Apollodorus 1.9.27.

16 *Odyssey* 8.555–563.

17 G.L. Huxley, *Early Sparta* (1962) 99, n. 34.

18 W.B. Dinsmoor in *Charisterion Orlandou* IV (1967/8) 151–155 (Herodotus 9.121). And for the Stoa of the Athenians at Delphi.

19 K. Philips, *AJA* 72 (1968) 3.

20 David Ridgway suggests to me a plain torque such as are found in 8th-century tombs in south Italy: e.g., *Atti. Società di Magna Grecia* 18–20 (1977–79) 34, fig. 12; 83, fig. 32.

21 H.-V. Herrmann, *Olympia* (1972) 76, fig. 45.

22 *Odyssey* 4.131–132.

23 On the stands as heirlooms, H.W. Catling, *Report of the Department of Antiquities, Cyprus* 1984, 69–91; 86, pl. 11.5, for the Lefkandi wheels. For *Fig. 54*, idem, *Cypriot Bronzework in the Mycenaean World* (1964) 207–208, pl. 36a.

24 *NCP* pl. Qi-iv.

25 T. Dohrn, *Die Ficoronische Ciste* (1972); Boardman, *Diffusion* 263–264.

26 Boardman, *Vases* 248. There are many late archaic Attic examples in clay. Athenaeus 487b records the use of the word for a cup by Paphians (Cyprus).

27 *ARV* 196.1bis; Boardman, *ARFH* I, fig. 146.

28 J. Boardman, *JHS* 99 (1979) 149–151.

29 *Iliad* 11.632–637.

30 *LIMC* I, 556–557; C. Robert, *Jahrbuch des deutschen archäologischen Instituts* 34 (1919) 72–76. For the class, U. Hausmann, *Hellenistische Reliefbecher* (1959).

31 Boardman, *GO* 176–177, 276; I. Malkin, *The Returns of Odysseus* (1998) 156–160, for a full discussion. J.-L. Lamboley, *Gaia* 5 (2001) 29–39, takes the Nestor to be the hero, who might have been worshipped in nearby Campania, making this a forged relic, which seems unlikely. The cup was probably inscribed in Euboea, where a similar one has been discovered.

32 J.B. Carter, *JHS* 118 (1998) 172–177. The type was discussed by H.W. Catling in *Lefkandi* I (ed. M. Popham, 1979) 249–250, and *Knossos North Cemetery* (ed. J.N. Coldstream,

1996) II, 565. Cf. Boardman, *GO* 113–114; H. Matthäus, *AA* 2000, 521–523.

33 *Iliad* 6.169.

34 Trendall, *LCS* 415, no. 360.

35 A.J. Evans, *The Palace of Minos* IV (1935) 672–674.

36 Herodotus 5.58.

37 On Herodotus' epigraphical interests, S. West, *Classical Quarterly* 35 (1985) 278–305; W.K. Pritchett, *The Liar School of Herodotus* (1993) 116–121, 162, and 144–191, answering West's scepticism about Herodotus' accuracy. Pausanias (5.17.6), or his source, seemed well able to cope with the mid-sixth century inscriptions on the Chest of Kypselos at Olympia, some of them *boustrophedon*.

38 G.L. Huxley, *GRBS* 8 (1967) 88–91.

39 A. Toynbee, *A Study of History* vols. VII–X abridged (1957) 250–251. See now L. Casson, *Libraries in the Ancient World* (2001).

40 N. Kourou in *Cyprus in the 11th Century* (ed. V. Karageorghis, 1994) 203–226 for maces and sceptres.

41 Boardman, *EGVP* fig. 207.

42 C. Bérard, *Museum Helveticum* 29 (1972) 219–227, also on the 'spear-sceptre' in the Eretria *heroon*.

43 Y. Sakellarakis in *Neue Forschungen in griechischen Heiligtümern* (ed, U. Jantzen, 1976) 283–308, with lists; E. Thomas in *Forschungen zur Ägäischen Vorgeschichte* (Bonn, 1984) 231–239, thinks they imply some form of continuity from the Bronze Age, but it is probably more a matter of simple survival.

44 J.N. Coldstream, *Knossos North Cemetery* II (1996) 625, pl. 264, fig. 154: 18.f3; III, 540, n. 1083 on adjustments made to the stone for mounting. I am indebted to Nicolas Coldstream for the photographs.

45 Trendall, *LCS* 415, no. 359; *LIMC* V, 73, no. 2461; G.W. Bond, *Euripides Heracles* (1981) 170.

46 Plutarch, *Quaestiones graecae* 48, stolen from Argos and put in a shrine of Odysseus (who had a Spartan wife) at Sparta. Polyaenus, *Strategemata* 1.5, taken by Demophon.

47 For the Palladion in ancient art, *LIMC* II, 965–969, 1019; the two Palladia, *LIMC* III, 397, 401 (no. 32 = our *Fig. 69*, *ARV* 1516,1), 408. The gem (*Fig. 69*) is J.D. Beazley, *Lewes House Gems* (1920) no. 57. H.A. Shapiro, *Mediterranean Historical Review* 7 (1992) 48. On the Palladion shrines in Attica, N. Robertson in *Religion in the Ancient World* (ed. M. Dillon, 1996) 383–476; there was a lawcourt *epi palladio*.

48 *LIMC* II, 631–632.

49 M. Crawford, *Roman Republican Coinage* (1974) pl. 53.448/3; C. Ampolo, *Parola del Passato* 25 (1970) 200–210; good pictures in *AJA* 64 (1960) pl. 34. The cult – I. Malkin, *Religion and Colonization in Ancient Greece* (1987) 69–72, the cult transfer to Massilia.

50 Callimachus, *Aetia* fr. 31b-e (K. Pfeiffer, *Callimachus* II (1949) 110–111).

51 Pfister, 340–346, for a good account of the heroic-age statues. On Daidalos, J. Boardman in *The Materials and Techniques of Greek Sculpture* (ed. O. Palagia, 2002).

52 J. Boardman, *Greek Sculpture. Classical Period* (1985) 213–214; ...*Late Classical Period* (1995) 29. The Amazons as a

group, W. Gauer in *Tainia* (Fest. R. Hampe, eds. H.A. Cahn. E. Simon, 1980) 201–226; cf. *Fig. 154*.

53 Callimachus, *Aetia* fr.100.

54 George Huxley reminds me of a four-eared, four-handed Apollo at Sparta: Sosibios, *FGrH* 595 F25.

55 The phenomena are discussed by M. Donderer in *Österreichisches Jahrbuch* 61 Beiblatt (1991/2) 192–275 (sculpture); 62 (1993) 93–134 (architecture).

56 H. Blanck, *Wiederverwendung alter Statuen* (1969); 80–81 for the warrior statue base from the Acropolis. Our *Fig. 72* = *Inscriptiones Graecae* I2 530, II2 4168; A.E. Raubitschek, *Dedications from the Athenian Acropolis* (1949) no. 121. E.B. Harrison in *Marble: Art Historical and Scientific Perspectives* (1990) 163–184, on the repair, re-use and re-working of older statues.

57 Pausanias 1.18.3, 2.17.3. Tomb inscriptions of the historic period too could be usurped by descendant namesakes: *idem* 8.9.9.

58 R. Olmos, 'El amor del hombre con la estatua', in *Kotinos* (eds. H. Froning et al.; Festschrift E. Simon, 1992) 256–266. R. Kassel on talking statues in *Zeitschrift für Papyrologie und Epigraphik* 51 (1983) 1–12.

59 A. Jacquemin in *Nature et Paysage* (ed. G. Siebert, 1996) 121–128.

60 See essays in *Peuples et pays mythiques* (eds. F. Jouan, B. Deforge, 1988).

61 V. Scully, *The Earth, the Temple and the Gods* (1962) is the most optimistic study of the phenomenon; reviewed by the author in *Burlington Magazine* 1964, 469. On myth and landscape, R. Buxton, *Imaginary Greece* (1994) 80–114. On relevance in other periods and places, R. Bradley, *The Archaeology of Natural Places* (2000).

62 For representations of caves, heroic and other, on Greek vases see G. Siebert in *Nature et Paysage* (ed. *idem*, 1996) 47–57.

63 S. Owen, *JHS* 120 (2000) 139–143; I am grateful to Sara Owen for the photograph.

64 A.C. Brown, *Before Knossos* (1993) 57, fig. 47.

65 J. Boardman, *The Cretan Collection in Oxford* (1961) 1–5.

66 Y. and E. Sakellarakis, *Archanes* I (1997) 50–51.

67 But Homer's Scheria may not be modern Corfu. On identifications see W. Hansen in *A New Companion to Homer* (eds. I. Morris and B. Powell, 1997) 455–456.

68 *Iliad* 24.614–617; cf. Sophocles, *Antigone* 823–832. *LIMC* VI, 911–912; *Fig. 75* is no. 11: Trendall, *LCS* Suppl. II, 223, 340a.

69 G.E. Bean, *Aegean Turkey* (1966) 53–55, for the Niobes on Sipylos, with pictures. Ibid., 58–61, for other local heroic monuments. The rock Niobe was identified by H.T. Bossert; see *Forschungen und Fortschritte* 13 (1937) 343–344 and his *Altanatolien* (1942) figs. 154–156; a distant view in *Archiv für Orientforschung* 13 (1939) 189, fig. 10. The Kybele may be the sanctuary of Mother Plastene mentioned in Pausanias 5.13.7. The Hittite relief at Karabel was taken for Ramses II, 'Sesostris': Herodotus 2.106, who rejects the notion that any such reliefs are of Memnon. For the true identity of the Karabel relief see J.D. Hawkins, *Anatolian Studies* 48 (1998) 1–31. On Greek petrifications, P.M.C. Forbes Irving,

Metamorphosis in Greek Myths (1990) 139–148, 283–299.

70 For Aigeus' leap from the Acropolis, Pausanias 1.22.4.

71 K. Clinton, *Myth and Cult* (1992) 37, and 87–89.

72 For the hill, Frazer on Pausanias 1.44.4. The Megarians celebrated their dead in the Persian war on a local monument: M.N. Tod, *Greek Historical Inscriptions* I (ed. 1, 1946) no. 20.

73 G.P. Stevens et al., *The Erechtheum* (1927) 104–110, 487.

74 Euripides, *Ion* 281–282.

75 Olga Palagia drew my attention to this. C. Collard et al., *Euripides. Selected Fragmentary Plays* I (1995) Erechtheus 370.45–57.

76 The matter is fully discussed in U. Kron, *Die zehn attischen Phylenheroen* (1976) 43–48. J.M. Hurwit, *The Athenian Acropolis* (1999) 203–204. Zeus-Erechtheus in Hyginus, *Fabulae* 46.

77 C.A. Faraone, *Talismans and Trojan Horses* (1992) discusses. More fully, U. Kron in *Kotinos* (eds. H. Froning et al.; Fest. Erika Simon, 1992) 56–70. W.K. Pritchett, *Pausanias Periegetes* I (1998) 97–121, 142–147, has a full discussion of the mainly text evidence for all such phenomena and other objects 'fallen from heaven'. Pliny, *Historia Naturalis* 2.149 dwells on meteorites.

78 Cited by Frazer on Pausanias 10.4.4.

79 For the volcanic inspiration of images in Virgil see A. Scarth, *Classical World* 93 (2000) 591–605.

80 C.A. Salowey in *Archaeology in the Peloponnese* (ed. K. Sheedy, 1994) 77–94, on what may have been taken for Herakles' waterworks.

81 *NCP* pl. Bi,ii,v.

82 *NCP* pl. X.xiv-xvi.

83 Early reference to the palm, Homer, *Hymn* 3.115–118.

84 Pindar, *Olympia* 3.13–16, has Herakles bring his olive wreath from the Danube.

85 *Idyll* 18.45–49.

86 H. Baumann, *Greek Wild Flowers* (1993) 71–72, fig. 121. The mark is really IAI.

87 Theocritus, *Idyll* 10.28 (see A.S.F. Gow, *Theocritus* II (1952) 201). Virgil, *Eclogues* 3.106–107. The 'hyacinth' sprang from the blood of Apollo's boy, Hyakinthos, and the same story of the AIAI cry was told of it (Ovid, *Metamorphoses* 13.394–398).

88 J.D. Beazley, *Etruscan Vase Painting* (1947) 53–54, l. 11.4; Gow, op.cit., pl. 8a.

89 *Ajax* 430.

90 S. Sherwin-White, *Ancient Cos* (1978) 16–17. It is possibly a post-antique identification.

91 On watery Argos in Geometric art, J. Boardman in *Ancient Greek Art and Iconography* (ed. W. Moon, 1983) 22 and n. 59.

92 *LIMC* IV, 797–798; V, 207–210.

93 Schol. Plato, *Symposium* 215B, *Republic* 399E, *Minos* 318B.

94 For origins of springs and rivers, Pfister, 358–361.

95 O. Keller, *Die antike Tierwelt* II (1913) 313 for dumb frogs; also in Cyrene, and there are quiet pigs in Macedonia and quiet cicadas in various places: Aelian, *Historia animalium* 3.35. C.T. Seltman, *Greek Coins* (1955) 40, also saw the Seriphos joke.

96 Otherwise regarded as the revenge of Aphrodite: Apollodorus 1.9.17.

97 On the Trojan associations especially see C. Higbie in

Athena in the Classical World (eds. S. Deacy, A. Villing, 2001) 105–125; she promises a fuller study of the document.

98 Phalaris, next mentioned, had a bronze bull of the period which was mischievously held to have been a device for the roasting of his victims. We need not doubt the bull at least.

99 I am indebted to Maria Stamatopoulou, who has studied Thessalian burials, for comment on this.

100 For Amyklai, Stesichorus in the sixth century (fr.216 Davies), and Pindar, *Pythia* 11.21–23. For Mycenae, Homer, Aeschylus and most other sources.

101 *passim* and *Troades* 1020–1021, *Andromache* 159–160, 173–176.

102 T. Polanski, *Oriental Art in Greek Imperial Literature* (1998) for remarks on these and other obsessions with Egypt.

103 Diodorus 1.62.1–4.

104 *LIMC* V, 792, on the coiffure.

105 *ABV* 144,8. F. Lissarrague, *L'autre guerrier* (1990) 21–29 for a good account of Memnon and Greek art. Twice (ibid., 27) he is given Scythian trousers but is never distinguished facially from any other hero. Also on his non-blackness, C. Bérard in *Not the Classical Ideal* (ed. B. Cohen, 2000) 395–402. *LIMC* VI, s.v. Memnon.

106 *Odyssey* 11.522.

107 Lissarrague, op.cit., 27, fig. 3; *CVA* Gela III, pl. 23.

108 *Iliad* 22.209–213.

109 G.N. Curzon, *Tales of Travel* (1923) 85–122 'The Voice of Memnon'. For the history of the statues, E.A. Gardiner, *Journal of Egyptian Archaeology* 47 (1961) 91–99. A. and E. Bernand, *Les inscriptions grecques et latines du Colosse de Memnon* (1960): pl. 7 top = our *Fig. 91*. If identity as Memnon depended on similarities with a royal throne name it might have happened at an early date; otherwise, from the 'song'. The Persian Cambyses (late 6th cent. BC) has also been blamed for hurting the statues, but the earthquake is more likely, and the 'song' was attested only after it. On the origin of Memnon, R.D. Griffith, *Classical Antiquity* 17 (1998) 212–234.

110 Herodotus 2.102–109; A.B. Lloyd, *Herodotus Book II. Commentary* II (1975) 16–37, at 26–27 on the Hittite reliefs. Also, Diodorus 1.52–58.

111 Mayor, 182.

112 Euripides, *Bacchae* 13–22.

113 On Dionysos, Herakles and India see P.A. Brunt, *Arrian* II (Loeb Library, 1983) 435–442. Arrian, *Anabasis* 4.28, for Alexander and Aornos. Diodorus 2.38–39, for a full ancient account of Dionysos and Herakles there.

114 Lucian, *Dionysos* 6.

115 For the Dionysiac in India, Boardman, *Diffusion* 137–140. J. Eskenazi, *Art of Gandhara* (1999) 12–13.

116 Boardman, *Diffusion* 141–143.

117 T. Severin, *The Ulysses Voyage* (1987). For Odysseus in the west see I. Malkin, *The Returns of Odysseus* (1998), which contains much of relevance here, and for far more than Odysseus.

118 Thus, J.M. Hall, in *Ancient Greek Hero Cult* (ed. R. Hägg, 1999) 49–59. On Orestes, D. Boedeker, in *Cultural Poetics in Archaic Greece* (eds. C. Dougherty and L. Kurke, 1993) 164–177.

Imaging the Past: Here be Monsters

1 *The Notebooks* (ed. I.A. Richter, 1952) 167.

2 *gyps*, for a vulture, is theoretically an unrelated word. In story griffins are given some roles readily derived from vulture behaviour: and cf. the griffin vulture *Gyps fulvus*. An ibex horn is kept as a 'griffin's claw' at St Cuthbert's, Durham: *Mythical Beasts* (ed. J. Cherry, 1995), 84.

3 *LIMC* VIII, pl. 340.2; M.F. Vos, *Scythian Archers in Archaic Attic Vase-Painting* (1963) pl. 1, no. 13. I am grateful to Catherine Lesseur for the museum photographs.

4 Boardman, *EGVP* fig. 325.

5 Boardman, *GO* 260–261, fig. 303, 282; L.K. Galinina, *Die Kurgane von Kelermes* (1997); reviewed, J. Boardman, *Colloquia Pontica* 6 (2002) 449–451.

6 Boardman, *ARFH* II, fig. 380; *LIMC* VIII, 528–534. The object in the field of Mayor, fig. 1.6 (a scene from a Greek vase), is not a gold nugget but a filling ornament of the type commonly seen on such vases.

7 Mayor, ch. 1, with fig. 1.13 (our *Fig. 98*).

8 M.R. Popham and L.H. Sackett (eds.), *Excavations at Lefkandi, Euboea. A Preliminary Report* (1968) 18, fig. 35. I am indebted to Don Evely and the British School at Athens for the photograph.

9 See *Cambridge Ancient History Plates to Vol. III* (1984) 231–232.

10 Boardman, *Diffusion* 189–190, fig. 6.7.

11 The iconographical origins of the Greek griffin have been much discussed; most fully in an unpublished Oxford thesis by Iz de Moor. See also E. Akurgal in *Kotinos* (eds. H. Froning et al.; Fest. E. Simon, 1992) 33–52; Boardman, *GO* 66–67, 79. The eagle beak may be given a single lower fang in Syrian art, and teeth in some archaic Greek: J. Boardman, *Greek Emporio* (1967) 203, perhaps just borrowed from the leonine jaw.

12 *Purgatorio* XXIX. In later folktale the griffin became extinct because it disdained to enter the Ark. For the later accounts of this and other monsters see Cherry, op.cit., and J. Nigg, *The Book of Fabulous Beasts* (1999) – with the texts.

13 Thus, J.P. Bolton, *Aristeas of Proconnesus* (1962) 65–67, 80.

14 Nigg, op.cit., 308, 310.

15 J. Black and A. Green, *Gods, Demons and Symbols of Ancient Mesopotamia* (1992) is a useful and well-illustrated source.

16 The motif was originally Egyptian, the 'sphinx' signifying the Pharaoh. It is copied in near eastern art, in Phoenicia and Syria, the sphinx then being winged: e.g., G. Markoe, *Phoenician Bronze and Silver Bowls* (1985) 36, 244 Cy2 (bowl from Cyprus), 374 Comp. 22 (griffins, ivory from Nimrud); G. Herrmann in *Images as Media* (ed. C. Uehlinger, 2000) pl. 35.5 (Nimrud ivory) = our *Fig. 102*.

17 Boardman, *EGVP* fig. 72.

18 *LIMC* VIII, Sphinx, for the origins and development of the type. A. Dessenne, *Le Sphinx* (1957) especially for the non-Greek.

19 Boardman, *AGGems* ch. 7 for several examples; the one shown, with the youth fighting back, is exceptional: ibid., no. 251, cf. no. 252 where a griffin unusually takes on the role.

20 Vienna I 1536; *LIMC* VIII, pl. 816.319.

21 M.L. West, *Hesiod. Theogony* (1966) 256. *ABV* 106,1; *LIMC* VIII, pl. 808.222.

22 Ibid., pl. 799.82.

23 *ARV* 989.31; *LIMC* VII, Oidipous.

24 E. Hofstetter, *Sirenen im archaischen und klassischen Griechenland* (1990); *LIMC* VIII, Seirenes.

25 *ARV* 289.1; Boardman, *ARFH* I, fig. 184.

26 *LIMC* IV, Harpyiai; cf. Boardman, *EGVP* figs. 417, 479.

27 Ibid., fig. 253; *ABV* 524.1; *LIMC* V, 120; J. Boardman in *Stips Votiva* (Papers...C.M. Stibbe, 1992) 7–8. Aristophanes would have taken this for a mutation of Empousa – a fire-breathing bitch (*Frogs* 290–294).

28 Boardman, *ABFH* fig. 39; *ABV* 66.54, from Kameiros.

29 *LIMC* III, Chimaira; pl. 207.98, 99 (our *Fig. 109*) for the snake rear, a form which appears also on an Attic black figure vase. D. Ohly, *Athenische Mitteilungen* 76 (1961) 1–11, and J. Boardman, *JHS* 88 (1968) 3, for such creations. Cf. the 6th-century bronze blazon from Melfi, *Archeo* 199 (2001) 28.

30 Boardman, *EGVP* fig. 208.

31 Boardman, *Vases* 41, fig. 47.

32 Boardman, *AGGems* 27–28, nos. 31[112]–33, pl. 2.

33 Boardman, *GO* 79, fig. 81. A fine stone head, Sotheby's, New York, 12.6.01, no. 112.

34 Boardman, *ABFH* fig. 69; and *Vases* 196, figs. 34, 214, 215. *LIMC* IV, Gorgo, for fullest illustration of the Medusa development.

35 E.g., on *CVA* Oxford III, pl. 32.4.

36 Boardman, *EGVP* fig. 427.

37 Boardman, *EGVP* fig. 365.

38 J. Boardman in *Le Bestiaire d'Héraclès* (eds. C. Bonnet et al., 1998) 27–35 for the animals and possible eastern sources, which are judged slight; and in *OJA* 1 (1982) 237–238 for the Hydra's poison.

39 Boardman, *EGVP* fig. 211.

40 For the history of the *ketos* image, J. Boardman, in *BCH* Suppl. 14 (1986) 447–453 – in the east; in *Monsters and Demons in the Ancient and Mediaeval Worlds* (eds. A. Farkas et al., 1987) 73–84 (pl. 25.15 = our *Fig. 119*; Boardman *ABFH* fig. 179; pl. 22.3 = our *Fig. 118*); *LIMC* VIII, Ketos.

41 *Odyssey* 12, 85–97.

42 *LIMC* VIII Skylla.

43 *BSA* 65 (1970) pls. 8–10.

44 Boardman, *ABFH* fig. 122; *Para* 72.

45 Boardman, *ABFH* fig. 24, the whole vase. *LIMC* III, Cheiron, no. 41.

46 J. Boardman, *Greek Gems and Finger Rings* (1970/2001) colour, p. 48.10.

47 Basel, Ludwig 601; M.E. Caskey, *AJA* 80 (1976) pl. 6.22; *LIMC* VI, pl. 321.33.

48 On a Sicilian vase: *LIMC* VI, pl. 316.6.

49 *ARV* 1457.10.

50 *LIMC* VI, pl. 321.41.

51 *ABV* 190; Boardman, *Vases* 200, fig. 217. *LIMC* VI, pls. 24–27 for others.

52 Boardman, *AGGems* pl. 20.293.

53 E. Bianchi in *Acme* 34 (1981) 227–249, on *l'homo monstruosus*, mainly in Herodotus and Pliny. R. Wittkower in

Journal of the Warburg and Courtauld Institute 5 (1942) 159–197 for the legacy in later art.

54 *ARV* 70.3; Boardman, *ARFH* I, fig. 66.

55 Herodotus 8.138. The Phrygians of Asia Minor derive from Thrace.

56 Boardman, *ARFH* II, fig. 323; *ARV* 1336.1. On the costume, A. Pickard-Cambridge, *The Dramatic Festivals of Athens* (ed.2, 1968) 186.

57 Pliny, *Historia Naturalis* 6.200.

58 *LIMC* VIII, Pan; J. Boardman, *The Great God Pan* (1997) figs. 46–47.

59 Phlegon, 34–35. T.568 for reports of dead Nereids.

60 Boardman, *EGVP* fig. 435; M. Pipili, *Laconian Iconography* (1987) 69.

61 R.R.R. Smith in *The Oxford History of Classical Art* (ed. J. Boardman, 1993) 199–201; B. Andreae, *Odysseus* (1982).

62 *ARV* 1338.1; Boardman, *ARFH* II, fig. 324 for further details.

63 Boardman, *EGVP* 54; *Vases* 193–194.

64 Diodorus 4.6.5.

65 J. Boardman, *Engraved Gems. The Ionides Collection* (1968) no. 62.

66 V. Dasen, *Dwarfs in Ancient Egypt and Greece* (1993); *LIMC* VI, Pygmaioi.

67 *NCP* pl. X.vii-viii.

68 On artificial monsters, from antiquity to today, Mayor, ch. 6.

69 Pausanias 1.23.6. *ABL* 266,1; by the Beldam Painter, Boardman, *ABFH* fig. 277. I am not quite convinced that the woman is hermaphroditic as M. Halm-Tisserant argues in *Kernos* 2 (1989) 67–82. Monkey satyrs: Aelian, *de Natura Animalium* 16.21; Diod. 1.18.4; Pliny, *Historia Naturalis* 5.44, 8.216; Solinus 27.60, cf. 31.5. 'Sphinxes' – Diodorus 3.35.4, and Solinus 27.59.

CHAPTER SIX (pp. 157–182)

Imaging the Past: The Hero and the Heroic

1 Boardman, *ARFH* II, fig. 16; *Vases* 97; *CVA* Basel III, pl. 5.1.

2 *ARV* 238.1.

3 On Amazons and Athenian history, J. Boardman in *The Eye of Greece* (eds. D. Kurtz and B. Sparkes, 1982) 1–28; and in *Vases* 206–208. *LIMC* I, Amazones, for a range of pictures of all periods.

4 A.D. Trendall, *The Red-Figured Vases of Paestum* (1987) 319, pl. 206.

5 A. Ajootian, *AJA* 105 (2001) 256.

6 *Anabasis* 4.16.

7 Pseudo-Kallisthenes 1.42.11–12 Kroll; R. Stoneman, *The Greek Alexander Romance* (Penguin, 1991) for the Romance. Sophocles has Ajax' son take away the great shield and put only his other arms in his grave: *Ajax* 575–577.

8 J. Boardman in *Archaic Greek Art and Iconography* (ed. W.G. Moon, 1983) 27–29, on the reality of the shield. J.M. Hurwit, suggests a compromise with 8th-century warriors

using the shield because it 'made them feel like heroes', and even adducing its likeness to a double-axe in shape: *Classical Antiquity* 4 (1985) 121–126. It was so flimsy compared with the hoplite shield that the Geometric warriors would not have felt heroic for long, and in vase scenes the Dipylon shield is regularly defeated by the hoplitic.

9 *Iliad* 18.478–608.

10 Boardman, *GO* 58–60 for such shields.

11 There are many modern studies of the shield, notably: K. Fittschen, *Der Schild der Achilleus* (Archaeologia Homerica II.N.1, 1973); P.R. Hardie, *JHS* 105 (1985) 11–31; E. Simon in *Beschreibungskunst-Kunstbeschreibung* (eds. G. Boehm and H. Pfotenhauer, 1995) 123–141.

12 *Electra* 452–469, followed by description of the decorated helmet, corselet and sword.

13 *ABV* 144.6.

14 Boardman, op.cit. (n. 8), 29–33, on the Boeotian shields.

15 G. Ahlberg, *Fighting on Land and Sea in Greek Geometric Art* (1971) esp. 84–88; eastern battle scenes which are a possible source of inspiration for some Geometric Greek are replete with chariots and fighting from chariots. A Geometric amphora from Paros, recently found, has a chariot beside a fight (*Archaiologike Ephemeris* 2000, 288, fig. 6). An archaic burial at Eleutherna in Crete hints at the sacrifice of someone (a prisoner?) at the tomb, recalling Polyxena at Achilles' tomb and a common eastern practice (info N. Stambolidis). Homer's poems record various eastern practices, and are not themselves the model for archaic Greek behaviour, as some scholars used to argue.

16 On the eighth-century *apobates*, E. Rystedt in *Opuscula Atheniensia* 24 (1999) 89–98; also for the mourning scenes, for which see J.L. Benson, *Horse, Bird and Man* (1970); K. Sheedy, *Athenische Mitteilungen* 105 (1990) 117–151, for Egyptian parallels (rather than models, I think).

17 Boardman, *EGVP* fig. 176.

18 A. Sadurska, *Les Tables Iliaques* (1964) pls. 5–7, 9. Hardie, op.cit., 23, fig. 1 and pl. 1d.

19 Hardie, op.cit., 24–25, is unduly sceptical; the medallion, pl. 2a; A. Stewart, *The Faces of Power* (1993) fig. 130 (he does not discuss the shield).

20 *John Flaxman R.A.* (ed. D. Bindman, 1979) 145–147; N. Penny, *Catalogue of the European Sculpture in the Ashmolean Museum* III (1992) 64–66.

21 Fittschen, op.cit., 18–23.

22 For the whole vase, Boardman, *Vases* 41, fig. 46.

23 Shown in later art as a cow with a side entrance: *LIMC* VII, pls. 130, 131.

24 Boardman, *GO* 90–91.

25 Trendall, *LCS* 415.359; *LIMC* V, 73, no. 2461.

26 J. Boardman, *AJA* 84 (1980) 181–182.

27 *Iliad* 6.219, 7.305. The purple may be the decoration of ivory plaques on the belts; cf. *Iliad* 4.141–142.

28 *ARV* 182.5; J. Boardman, *Antike Kunst* 19 (1976) 5.

29 Sophocles, *Ajax* 1028–1039.

30 For these V. Karageorghis in *Four Thousand Years of Images on Cypriote pottery* (ed. *idem* et al., 1997) 73–79.

31 Boardman, *Vases* ch. 5.

32 Boardman, *Vases* 193–202, for the beginnings of myth scenes; and for a well-illustrated conspectus of early scenes, G. Ahlberg, *Myth and Epos in Early Greek Art* (1992).

33 As S. Moser, *Ancestral Images* (1998) 28–38.

34 *LIMC* IV, 729; V, 184–185. The skins of the big cats were worn by Homeric heroes off parade (*Iliad* 10.23–24 – Agamemnon; 29–30 – Menelaos; 177–178 – Diomedes), and by Artemis and Dionysos. For Stesichoros (fr. 229 Page) Herakles' skin and club might make him like a brigand, but the poet (who even doubted Helen at Troy) does not reflect the common view.

35 *ABV* 168; Boardman, *ABFH* fig. 123. M.L. West, *Hesiod. Theogony* (1966) 401–402. A.B. Cook, *Zeus* III (1940) 726–739 has an interesting account of explanations, ancient and modern, for the story. The practice of trepanning has also been thought a possible source of inspiration: R.D. Barnett in *The Aegean and the Near East* (Studies...H. Goldman, 1956) 236–237. On mythical conceptions and births see J. Boardman, forthcoming (Fribourg conference).

36 *ARV* 449,2. *LIMC* V, Herakles no. 2552, cf. 2550 on pl. 92.

37 G. Markoe, *Phoenician Gold and Silver Bowls* (1985) 214–215, 341. J. Boardman in *Le Bestiaire d'Héraclès* (eds. C. Bonnet et al., 1998) 33. The bulls are copied on the interiors of some Attic Geometric cups: Boardman, *Vases* 23, fig. 16.

38 J. Boardman in *Festschrift für Nikolaus Himmelmann* (eds. H.-U. Cain et al., 1989) 194, with pl. 33.3. Shefton, cited ibid., thought the bowl motif might be inspired by Phoenician 'cup-palmettes'.

39 *Syria* 44 (1967) 336–338, pl. 16.1,2; O. Palagia, *OJA* 9 (1990) 51.

40 Mannerism on vases: Boardman, *Vases* 95; T. Mannack, *The Late Mannerists* (2001) ch. 2. The Greek-style archaism seen in Persian Imperial arts is a totally different matter: J. Boardman, *Persia and the West* (2000) 110–111 and *passim*.

41 P. Dintsis, *Hellenistische Helme* (1986); B.S. Ridgway in *Tamanskii relief* (eds. E. Savostina and E. Simon, 1999) 41.

42 Briefly on heroic nudity, J. Boardman, *Greek Art* (1996) 158–160. N. Himmelmann, *Ideale Nacktheit in der griechischen Kunst* (1990).

43 *The City beneath the City* (eds. N.C. Stampolidis and L. Parlama, 2000) 198–203. I am indebted to the two editors named for permission to reproduce the picture.

44 J.L. Benson, *Horse, Bird and Man* (1970) pl. 13.1–2 for comparisons.

45 Explored by G.S. Korres in *Pepragmena III Diethnous Kretologikou Synedriou 1971* I (1973) 412–476, distinguishing *epibiosis* (survival) from *anabiosis* (rebirth). He concentrates on survival of motifs and practices.

46 B. Wesenberg, *Kapitelle und Basen* (1971) 48–49, 61–62 (fig. 95 = our *Fig. 163*); R.V. Nicholls in J.M. Cook and R.V. Nicholls, *The Temples of Athena (Old Smyrna)* (1998) 146–147, 187–192, 199–201.

47 It has been argued that the Chian Altar at Delphi is a Hellenistic replica of the late archaic structure, even to details of mouldings and inscription: P. Amandry in *Chios* (eds. J. Boardman and C.E. Richardson, 1986) 205–218. The Roman rebuilding of the altar at the Samos Heraion copied the archaic but added Hellenistic ornament. This is not the same as archaizing in style.

48 E. Simon and A. and M. Hirmer, *Griechischen Vasen* (1976)

pl. 70 below, right; *Para* 67.

49 J.N. Coldstream, in *Studies in honour of T.B.L. Webster* (eds. J.H. Betts et al., 1988) II, 23–41; *Praktika tes Akademon Athenon* 71 (1996) 236–262.

50 H. Sackett, *BSA* 71 (1976) 117–129; Boardman, *EGVP* fig. 23.

51 Ibid., figs. 146–151 (Protogeometric B).

52 Boardman, *EGVP* fig. 276. J. Boardman and J. Hayes, *Excavations at Tocra* II (1973) 36–37; and in *Pepragmena II Kretologikou Synedriou* I (1967) 135–136.

53 Korres, op.cit. (n. 45).

54 J. Boardman, *Island Gems* (1964); *JHS* 88 (1968) 1–12; *Greek Gems and Finger Rings* (1970/2001) 118–122, 384; pl. 242 is our *Fig. 167*.

55 Boardman, *EGVP* fig. 376.

CHAPTER SEVEN (pp. 183–192)

Conclusion

1 *de Iside et Osiride* 18.

2 H. Beinlich, *Die 'Osirisreliquien'* (1984); critically reviewed by L. Panatalacci in *Chronique d'Égypte* 62 (1987) 108–123. I am indebted to John Baines for references. Mayor, 151–152. When Diodorus writes of Osiris killing multi-bodied creatures, like Greek Giants, he is probably following the equation of Seth with Typhon (T.60).

3 Mayor, 177–178.

4 A. Kuhrt, *The Ancient Near East* (1995) 523–524, quotes.

5 S. Dalley, *Myths from Mesopotamia* (1991) for translations and a careful commentary.

6 Kuhrt, op.cit. (n. 4), 474–476, for a good description of the process and what it meant.

7 From a Mesopotamian 'Dialogue of Pessimism' cited by T. Jacobsen in H. Frankfort et al., *Before Philosophy* (Penguin, 1949) 233; W.G. Lambert, *Babylonian Wisdom Literature* (1960) 149, 76–78.

8 A. Toynbee, *Mankind and Mother Earth* (1976) 161, writing of Nabonidus.

9 R.S. Ellis, *Foundation Deposits in Ancient Mesopotamia* (1968) 32; and 15–16 on building over old foundations.

10 On the principles of collection and function, G. Goossens in *Revue d'Assyriologie* 42 (1948) 149–159; lists of the finds in E. Unger, *Babylon, die heilige Stadt* (1931) ch. 23 'Das Schlossmuseum'. Nabonidus' activity and motivation: Kuhrt, op.cit. (n. 4), 598–600.

11 E. Matsushima in *Official Cult and Popular Religion in the Ancient Near East* (eds. idem et al., 1993) 209–219.

12 Pfister, 338–339, 510–514, on the healing and other properties of relics.

13 U. Seidl, *Archäologische Mitteilungen aus Iran* 9 (1976) 125–130; *Zeitschrift für Assyriologie* 89 (1999) 101–114.

14 For the Susa 'museum', P.O. Harper in *The Royal City of Susa* (eds. eadem et al., 1992) 159–182.

15 I am indebted to Jessica Rawson for references and

discussion of Chinese matters. See her article 'The many meanings of the past' in *Die Gegenwart des Altertums* (eds. D. Kuhn and H. Stahl) 397–421; and S.E. Erickson's 'Investing in the antique; Bronze Vessels of the Song Dynasty', ibid., 423–435; N. Bernard on the literary sources for finds of bronze vessels in *Journal of the Institute of Chinese Studies of the Chinese University of Hong Kong* 6 (1973) 455–530.

16 Mayor, 39. Fossil 'dragon bones' were ground up for medicine.

17 Pfister, 365–366, on locations of *gamoi*.

18 Later Jewish (cf. T.102) and Irish folktales have races of giants which probably derive from the many individual and localized giants. For the former, M.L. West, *The East Face of Helicon* (1997) 117. 'Giants' are regularly invoked anywhere to explain colossal natural or man-made structures.

19 *ARV* 844.145.

20 *genus in gloriam sui effusissimum (Historia Naturalis* 3.43).

21 Tacitus, *Historiae* 2.4.

22 O. Taplin, *Greek Tragedy in Action* (1978) ch. 7. In general on early impersonation of the divine and origin of theatre as understood from images, Boardman, *Vases* 209–212.

23 Boardman, *Diffusion* 75, 328.

24 I discuss how this affects the decoration of Greek vases, the most prolific medium for the relevant images, in *Vases* 168–173.

Acknowledgements

The author is much indebted to several scholars for advice, correction, help with illustrations, etc.:

Zosia Archibald, Marie-Louise Buhl-Riis, Nicolas Coldstream, Jim Coulton, Stephanie Dalley, Don Evely, Martine Denoyelle, David Hawkins, George Huxley, Catherine Lesseur, François Lissarrague, John Luce, Marcus Lynch, Arthur MacGregor, Adrienne Mayor, Joan Mertens, Olga Palagia, John Prag, Bodil Bundgaard Rasmussen, Jessica Rawson, Sue Sherratt, Nikolaos Stampolidis, Richard Tomlinson, Michael Vickers, Tim Wilson.

Photographic work is by Bob Wilkins, new drawings and maps by Marion Cox.

The authorities of museums and collections named in captions are warmly thanked for photographs and permissions; the sources of other illustrations are indicated in the notes, with the following:

Peter Clayton – *16*; John Luce – *26, 37, 39*; Adrienne Mayor – *6, 10, 98*; Claire Niggli – *58*; Sara Owen – *73*; Francine Tissot – *93*; Richard Tomlinson – *52*. R.L. Wilkins – *69, 104, 112, 128, 135, 166*; author – *75, 79, 137, 142*. British School at Athens – *41–45, 66, 99, 121*; D.A.I. Athens – *17, 72, 101*; D.A.I. Rome – *119, 134*; Hirmer Verlag – *29, 32, 59, 120, 138*.

General Index

References are to page numbers

The Testimonia are indexed separately, on pp. 234–240

pygmies 155
Pylos 20, 76, 78
Pyrrha 33

rejuvenation 41
Rhea 76, 108, 116
Rhegion 114
Rhodes 27, 91
Rome/Roman 30, 43, 58, 59, 61, 85,
    89, 94, 99–103, 114, 123, 146, 152,
    154, 156, 167, 175, 191

Salamis 24
Samos 36, 37, 42, 64, 78, 102, 111,
    112
Sardinia 26, 27, 76
Sarpedon 94
satyrs 9, 35, 55, 125, 152, 156
sceptres 95
Schliemann 24, 53, 55, 58, 67
Scythia/ians 43, 118, 129, 130, 162,
    183
sea monsters 36–38, 43, 127, 144–147
seats, stone 108
Segesta 114
Semele 76, 105, 112
Septimius Severus 123
Seriphos 114, 115
Sesostris 123
Seth 184
shalgram 196
Shield of Achilles 164, 165, 167–169
Shield of Herakles 167, 168
shields 80, 81, 83, 162–165
ships 85
shoulder-blade 40, 66
Siamese twins 155
Sibyl 105
Sicily 39, 71, 72, 87, 96, 123, 124, 131,
    133, 139, 163, 174, 185
Sikyon 29, 95, 98, 108
Silenos 108, 114, 124, 125, 152, 153
Sipylos 23, 56, 57, 106, 107, 114
Sirens 16, 110, 136, 137
Skylla 110, 146, 147
Smyrna 23
Socrates 8, 9
Sophocles 19, 113, 135

Sounion 65, 66
Spain 85, 126
spars 80, 83
Sparta 24, 25, 34, 57, 65, 66, 67, 74, 76,
    83, 85, 88, 98–100, 112, 200
Sperlonga 154
sphinxes 133–135, 156
springs 113, 114
statues 57, 99–103, 116, 117, 119–123,
    186, 187
Strabo 22, 23, 30, 70, 122
swords 81
Sybaris 116

Talos 154, 155
Tanagra 110, 112, 156
Tantalos 40, 56, 106
Tartaros 39
Tauri 100
Tegea 24, 85
Teiresias 67, 76
Telephos 83
Tempe 111
Tenedos 36
Tennyson 122
Tereus 114
Thasos 104, 105
Thebes 12, 24, 25, 40, 58, 62, 63, 66,
    67, 83–88, 92, 94, 96, 103, 134, 135,
    165, 168
Themistocles 103
Theocritus 112, 113
Thera 12
Therapne 65, 78
Thermopylai 114
Theseus 34, 38, 57, 64, 65, 85, 109, 147,
    150, 161, 189
Thespiae 103
Thessalos 20
Thessaly 64, 94, 117, 147
Thetis 26, 144, 147, 149
Thrace 38, 43, 64, 152
Thucydides 25, 80
thyrsos 175
Tiberius 154
Timotheos 95
Tiryns 46–51
Tisamenos 57

Titans 12, 47, 52, 116, 190
Tithonos 119
Tityos 105
tourism 60, 61, 123, 190, 191
Toynbee 186
'Treasuries' 51, 52, 57–59
trees 44, 56, 111, 112
trident mark 109
Triphylia 105
tripods 69, 70, 86, 87
Triptolemos 76
Triton 156
Troizen 76, 109, 113
Trojan Horse 170
trophies 83, 84
Trophonios 105
Troy 12, 13, 19, 23–27, 36, 37, 43,
    53–55, 64–67, 80, 82, 85–88, 95, 99,
    108, 110–113, 116–119, 126, 166,
    170, 174, 187
tumuli 54–57
Typhon 38, 39, 124, 184

Vajrapani 125
vases: Apulian 145; Athenian 19, 44,
    45, 54, 55, 66, 90, 96, 99, 119, 128,
    129, 133, 135–138, 140, 142, 144, 145,
    149, 150–153, 155, 156, 160–162,
    164, 171, 173, 174, 180, 189;
    Campanian 94, 97, 106; Corinthian
    36, 37, 143, 167, 182; Cretan 61, 181;
    East Greek 92, 129; Etruscan 113,
    150; Euboean 166; Laconian 143,
    153; Mycenaean 130; Paestan 161
Vesuvius 30, 38
Vienna 34
Virgil 21, 113
Vishnu 196
volcanoes 38, 39, 110

Warwick, Guy of 34
wings 152, 154, 157

Xenophon 25, 162

Zethos 66
Zeus 33, 38, 59, 78, 82, 88, 102, 106,
    108–112, 114, 122, 173, 175

TESTIMONIA

I give below brief paraphrases of passages which record the identification of 'heroic' antiquities or locales, whether or not they are referred to in the chapters above (prefixed by T...). A few other passages are included which refer to matters which have seemed to me otherwise relevant. It is not altogether complete but nothing of substance is omitted (so far as I can tell), and only some very late comments of dubious currency in the classical period are routinely ignored. I have concentrated on what was apparently visible to the author or his source. The later references, as in Athenaeus, for older authors, are sometimes preferred since they may be easier to check than compendia and give the quotation in what is often a useful context, but *FGrH* and *FHG* references are given where appropriate. This is very much an *aide-mémoire* for the expected readership, not an exhaustive quarry for scholars, who may turn to Pfister. For several authors (Apollonius, Antigonus, [Aristotle], Myrsilus, Phlegon, Paradoxographus Vaticanus) *Paradoxographorum Graecorum Reliquiae* ed. A. Giannini. Milan, 1965, gives all the relevant texts. Most other major sources are available in Loeb translations, and some in Penguin.

Approximate dates for the authors are given, and some cross-references where data are repeated without significant addition. Pfister has virtually all of this, but not translated and often simply referred to, and he has much more, with indexes. The indexes to Frazer's translation and commentary on Pausanias are also most valuable sources. I append indexes to the names of gods, heroes and places, and to classes of object. The Testimonia are presented alphabetically by author and I here retain the traditional latinized version of their names and titles.

Aelian (2nd/3rd cent. AD). A Roman writer, in Greek, who collected anecdotes and wrote moralizing theses. Also T.9,529.

De natura animalium
1. 16.39 Massive bones and a skull found after a forest fire on Mount Pelinnaion on Chios are attributed to a great dragon that lived there.

2. 17.28 (citing Euphorion, 3rd cent. BC; van Groningen, pp. 226–227) Massive creatures called Neädes in Samos split the ground with their bellowing. Their bones are displayed. [Later sources call them Neïdes. Their din was noted by Euagon, 5th cent. BC: *FGrH* 535 F1. See T.528.]

Variae Historiae
3. 13.21 Marsyas' hide at Kelainai moves to the sound of Phrygian music [pipes], not Apolline [lyre]. [See T.118.]

Aeschylus (5th cent. BC). The earliest Athenian tragedian of whom some works have survived complete. See T.68,552.

Amelesagoras (4th/3rd cent. BC). An Athenian collector of Greek stories about miracles. See T.10.

Ampelius (2nd cent. AD). A Roman writer of a handbook to all knowledge.

Liber Memorialis VIII: 'Miracula quae in terris sunt'
4. 3 At Argos (Amphilochian) is a big columned bridge which Medea had made, to which the rudder of the Argo is fixed [or, less probably, on which it is painted], where the ship put in. At the Temple of Jove Typhon there is a descent to the underworld for reception of oracles.
5. 5 At Sikyon in the Temple of Apollo are:
     Agamemnon's shield and sword;
     Odysseus' chlamys and corselet;
     Teukros' bow and arrows;
     Adrastos' chest – contents unknown;
     the bronze pot in which Medea cooked Pelias;
     Palamedes' *litterae* (kithara?);
     Marsyas' pipes and hide;
     the Argonauts' oars, rudder and yard-arm;
     Athena's pebble vote for Orestes;
     Penelope's loom.
6. 11 At Troy is the squared stone to which Kassandra was fastened, which gives forth milk or blood when rubbed; also the tombs of Achilles and Patroklos.

7. 16 At Bargylos is the ancient house of Herakles, where there is a round iron cage (*cavea*) in which Sibylla was confined.

Anthologia Palatina. A tenth-century collection of Greek epigrams of all periods. See T.50

Antigonus (3rd cent. BC). An Athenian biographer, historian and sculptor.

Historiarum mirabilium collectio
8. 2 Cicadas are silent in Rhegion because Herakles' sleep had been disturbed by them. [Diodorus 4.22.5 says they disappeared completely.]
9. 4 Either Perseus or Herakles was responsible for the silence of frogs on Seriphos. [For Perseus, Aelian, *de natura animalium* 3.37; [Aristotle] *de mirabilibus* 70: the frogs will croak if moved away.]
10. 12 Quotes Amelesagoras (4th/3rd cent. *FGrH* 330, F1): Athena (Pallas) advancing with a rock on Hephaistos, drops it, to become Mount Lykabettos, and she denies crows access to the Acropolis, because one misled her.
11. 163 The rivulet in Crete where Europe washed after intercourse with Zeus is immune from rainfall.

Antoninus Liberalis (2nd cent. AD). Mythographer.

Metamorphoseon synagoge
12. 8 The River Sybaris above Delphi is where the monster Sybaris (or Lamia) cracked her head, having been thrown down by Eurybatos.

Apollodorus (1st/2nd cent. AD). An Athenian mythographer and geographer, a major summarizing source for Greek myth. Also T.139,400,411.

Bibliotheca
13. 1.5.1 At Eleusis Demeter sat and mourned on a rock which has been called the Mirthless Stone (*agelastos petra*).
14. 1.6.2 Athena threw Sicily onto the giant Enkelados.
15. 2.5.2 The immortal head of the Hydra was buried by Herakles under a boulder by the Lerna road.
16. 2.7.3 Athena gave Herakles a lock of the Gorgon's hair in a bronze jar; he gave it to Sterope to help save Tegea. [Otherwise, given directly to Sterope's father Kepheus, T.411.]
17. 3.5.5 Dirke's body was thrown into a spring [at Thebes] which is named after her. [Her ashes thrown into a well:

Euripides, *Antiope* Kambitsis XLVIII.112–116. Cf. T.525.]
18. 3.7.7 The sons of Phegeus intended to dedicate the necklace and *peplos* of Eriphyle at Delphi but were killed by the sons of Alkmaion [Eriphyle's son], who made the dedication. [See T.400,476.]

Apollonius (2nd cent. BC). Collector of anecdotes.

Historiae mirabiles
19. 2.3 The 'shaman' Aristeas' regular reappearance in Sicily many years after his disappearance from Prokonnesos gave rise to his worship there as a hero. A similar history of Hermotimos of Klazomenai.

Apollonius Rhodius (3rd cent. BC). Born in Egypt, an epic poet and biographer. Also T.38,103,520,600.

Argonautica
20. 1.1300–1308 Herakles killed the Boreads and buried them in a mound with two stelai, one of which moves with the north wind.
21. 2.841–845 The tomb mound of Idmon (Argonaut) at Herakleia (Bithynia) bears a leafy olive tree trunk (as used to build ships).

Apollonius of Tyana (1st cent. AD). An ascetic and neo-Pythagorean sage. See T.499.

Appianus (1st/2nd cent. AD). Born in Alexandria but taking Roman citizenship, he moved to Rome and wrote regional studies on the history of the Roman Empire.

Mithridatica
22. 77 On Lemnos is shown the altar of Philoktetes, a bronze snake, arrows and a corselet bound with ribbons, memorials of the hero's sufferings. [He nursed a noisome snake-bite.]

Aristoboulos (4th cent. BC). A Greek historian of Alexander, who had served in his army. See T.48.

Aristotle (4th cent. BC). Born at Stagiros (Chalkidike) but worked in Athens and tutored Alexander. Polymath philosopher and scientist.

23. (Schol. Pindar, *Isthmia* 7.18) In Amyklai is the corselet of Timomachos.

[**Aristotle**] (4th/3rd cent. BC). A compilation by scholars in Aristotle's school. Also T.9.

De mirabilibus auscultationibus

24. 51 In the Athens Pantheion is an olive tree 'of the beautiful crowns' (*kallistephanos*), with unusual pale insides to the leaves, near the Ilissos in a stone enclosure, not to be touched. Herakles took a shoot for Olympia, whence the crowns are made.

25. 52 In Lydian mines near Pergamon workmen were suffocated when taking refuge in war. Much later some vessels and the bones were found petrified.

26. 58 Copper found on the sea bed off Demonesos (island of Chalkedon) was used for the statue in the ancient temple of Apollo at Sikyon and for the statues of mountain-copper (*oreichalkos*) in Pheneus. These were inscribed as the gift of Herakles, having captured Elis.

27. 79 Diomedeia is an island in the Adriatic where the companions of Diomedes were turned into birds who attack non-Greeks. [Strabo 284 – they are very tame]. Diomedes had been killed there by the local king, Daunos.

28. 81 On the Amber islands (Elektrides) in the Adriatic there are ancient statues of tin and bronze, by Daidalos, fleeing Minos.

29. 82 Near Enna in Sicily is the cave through which Pluto carried off Persephone, copious with flowers.

30. 83 There are in Crete no wolves, bears, vipers and similar beasts because Zeus was born there.

31. 85 From Italy to the land of the Celts [and Iberians] is a 'road of Herakles' on which Greek travellers are protected by local tribes.

32. 88 Herakles attacked Iberia for the riches of the inhabitants, so money is now forbidden in the Balearics.

33. 95 At Cumae is the subterranean bedroom of the Sibyl.

34. 97 Near the Iapygian promontory, where Herakles fought the giants, ichor [divine blood] flows making the sea not navigable. Many memorials to Herakles are seen on roads in Italy where he travelled, and near Pandosia are his footprints, in which no one may tread.

35. 98 Near the Iapygian promontory is a wagon-sized rock lifted and placed there by Herakles, moved with one finger.

36. 99 At Orchomenos a dog pursued a fox into a large empty space where the dog barked, setting up a great echoing noise. Hunters followed it in and reported the find to the magistrates.

37. 100 In Sardinia are beautiful buildings in the old Greek style, and circular buildings (*tholoi*) built by Iolaos and the Thespiadai, because Herakles was lord of all the western lands. [Also Diodorus 4.30.1, 5.15.2–4, for Iolaos' buildings.]

38. 105 There are altars set up by Jason by the Danube, deemed to flow into both the Black Sea and the Adriatic, and a temple of Artemis set up by Medea on an Adriatic island. Pebbles on the island of Aithaleia [Elba] are multicoloured from dirt scraped off by the Argonauts after oiling. [The last, also Strabo 224; Apollonius Rhodius 4.655–658, also for their disci and armour; and T.600.]

39. 107 Philoktetes dedicated the bow and arrows of Herakles [which he had taken to Troy] at the temple of Apollo Alaios in Sybaris; taken thence to the temple of Apollo in Kroton. Philoktetes died near Sybaris having helped the Rhodians with Tlepolemos. [Euphorion fr. 45 Powell, the bow; Lycophron, *Alexandra* 919: he is buried by the River Krathis. The arrows were also shown at Thurii, which Philoktetes founded, Justinus 20.1.16]

40. 108 The tools of Epeios [maker of the Wooden Horse at Troy] are in the temple of Athena Heilenia at Lagaria near Metapontion; he was delayed there. [Justinus 20.2.1, *ferramenta*.]

41. 109 The bronze axes and arms of Diomedes and his companions are in the temple of Achaean Athena at Loukeria in Daunia.

42. 110 In the temple of Artemis in Peucetia is a bronze necklace inscribed 'Diomedes to Artemis'. He put it round the neck of a stag, which was then found by King Agathokles of Sicily (who gave it to a sanctuary of Zeus?).

43. 131 When the Athenians were building the temple of Demeter at Eleusis a bronze pillar surrounded by stones was found, inscribed 'this is the tomb (*sema*) of Deiope', wife of Mousaios or mother of Triptolemos.

44. 133 Near Hypate in Thessaly a pillar was found with an archaic inscription on it. They sent it to Athens but en route it was taken to the Ismenion at Thebes, where there were old dedications with similar letter forms. It was deciphered as a verse dedication by Herakles to Aphrodite at Erythos, as he was returning with Geryon's cattle (not from any 'Erytheia' in the west).

Arrianus (1st/2nd cent. AD). Roman philosopher and historian of Alexander, governor of Cappadocia under Hadrian.

Periplus ponti Euxini

45. 9.2 At Phasis (Colchis) is the anchor of the Argo, of iron, and not looking very old though of an odd shape, but there are fragments of a stone anchor which are most likely Jason's. There is no other trace of the Jason story there.

Alexandri anabasis

46. 1.11.7–8 At Troy Alexander dedicated his armour and took in place some of the arms from the Trojan war displayed there, which were carried before him into battle. [Diodorus 17.18 says he wore the armour into battle.]

47. 2.3 The chariot of Gordios [king of Phrygia], with its knotted yoke [cut by Alexander], is seen at Gordion.

Artemidoros (2nd cent. BC). Ephesian geographer. See T.548,550.

Athenaeus (2nd/3rd cent. AD). Of Naucratis in Egypt. His study of dining lore is mainly a compilation of passages from earlier authors.

Deipnosophistae
48. (= Aristoboulos, 4th cent. BC; *FGrH* 139, F60) 43d At Miletos is a spring called the Achilleion which is very sweet, with a salty surface, where the hero purified himself after slaying the Lelegian king.
49. (= Phaenias, 4th cent. BC, fr. 11 Wehrli) 232c At Delphi is the dagger carried by Helikaon at Troy, inscribed; also a tripod staked by Achilles at the Games for Patroklos, and won by Diomedes who dedicated it, also inscribed. [Cf. *Anthologia Palatina* 6.49.]
50. (= Ephorus, 4th cent. BC; *FGrH* 70, F96) 232e At Delphi was the jewellery of Eriphyle, dedicated by Alkmaion, and Helen's necklace dedicated by Menelaos; all stolen.
51. 466e, 489b,c Nestor's cup, of silver with relief letters in gold, was dedicated to Artemis at Capua; 487f–494e, it is discussed, with the description of a reconstruction.
52. (= Polemon, 2nd cent. BC, *FHG* III, 116) 472b,c On the Athens Acropolis are gilt wooden cups (*therikleia*) dedicated by Neoptolemos.
53. (= Charon of Lampsacus, 5th cent. BC; *FGrH* 262, F2) 475b Alkmene's cup (*karchesion*), received from Zeus disguised as Amphitryon, is shown at Sparta.
54. (= Seleucus, 1st cent. AD) 678a,b A wreath twined with myrtle called *hellotis* is carried in the festival of the Hellotia in Crete, containing the bones of Europe.

Callimachus (4th cent. BC). Born in Cyrene, worked in the Alexandria Library; a major poet. Also T.520.

Hymnae
55. 5.35–6 The shield of Diomedes in the temple of Athena at Argos is carried with her statue in procession.

Charon of Lampsacus (5th cent. BC). Historian. See T.53.

Cicero (1st cent. BC). Roman statesman, lawyer, and author of various philosophical works.

56. *de divinatione* 13 A figure like Pan was found in a split stone found in a quarry on Chios.

Clidemus (4th cent. BC). Athenian historian.

57. *FGrH* 323, F6 Agamemnon found cisterns (*phreata*) around Aulis and at many other places in Greece.

Conon (1st cent. BC/AD). Mythographer.

58. *FGrH* 26, F1.45 The head of Orpheus was washed up, still in prime condition and singing, at the mouth of the River Meles (by Smyrna) and buried by women.

Dio Cassius (2nd/3rd cent. AD). Roman governor and consul, writer of a history of Rome to AD 229.

Historiae
59. 36.11 There are two places called Komana in Cappadocia, each claiming to have the relics of Taurian Artemis brought there by Orestes and Iphigeneia, including his hair cut in mourning, and Iphigeneia's sword [the Tauri practised human sacrifice]. [Also Strabo 535 for the hair, whence the name Komana alleged. Dio was probably confused in having two Komanas, swords, etc.]

Diodorus Siculus (1st cent. BC). Of Agyrion, wrote a History of the World. Also T.8,37,46,605.

Bibliotheca historica
60. 1.26.6–7 The Egyptians say that at the time of Isis there were multi-bodied creatures, called Giants by the Greeks, who were defeated by Osiris: a parallel to the Greek Gods fighting Giants.
61. 3.4.5–6 The nymphs made Ortygia (Syracuse) spring forth to please Artemis; it still has sacred fish.
62. 3.73.3 Dionysos killed a monster called Kampe in Libya and buried it under a large mound, visible until recently.
63. 4.18.6–7 Herakles drained Tempe to create the plains along the River Peneios; and by damming a river near Orchomenos he created Lake Copais.
64. 4.19.3–4 Herakles made the highway through the Alps.
65. 4.22.1–2 Herakles cut off Lake Avernus from the sea and constructed the seaside road.

66. 4.23.1 The warm baths at Himera and Egesteia [Segesta] were made by the nymphs for Herakles. [3.4.4, at Himera, at the request of Athena.]

67. 4.24.3–4 Herakles made the lake at Agyrion (Sicily), gave his name to the petrified cattle tracks [fossil impressions] and founded the sanctuaries of Geryon and Iolaos.

68. 4.28.2 The Amazon camp in Athens, Amazoneion. [Probably by the Areiopagos; see Aeschylus, *Eumenides* 685–690.]

69. 4.49.8 The Argonauts dedicated *phialai* on Samothrake, which are still there.

70. 4.56.6 The Argonauts gave Triton, King of Libya, a bronze tripod inscribed in ancient letters, until recently at Euesperides.

71. 4.78.5 Daidalos' engineering works in Sicily are all long vanished.

72. 4.79.2–4 Minos died in Sicily, buried by comrades in a two-storey tomb, part below ground, the open part a shrine to Aphrodite. The bones were sent back to Crete by Theron of Akragas. [The tomb has been likened to the 'Temple Tomb' at Knossos. On the fate of the bones, G.L. Huxley, *Kretologia* 8 (1979) 76–80.]

73. 5.3.3 Pluto took Persephone through a cave near Enna. 5.4.2 - through a cleft he made in the ground near Syracuse, at the fountain Kyane.

74. 5.66.1 The foundations of the house of Rhea and a sacred cypress grove are shown at Knossos.

75. 5.70.4 In Crete Omphalos is where the infant Zeus' umbilical cord fell off; and the Idaean Cave is where he was nursed.

Diogenes Laertius (3rd cent. AD). Biographer of philosophers.

Vitae philosophorum
76. 8.1.5 The shield of Euphorbos was dedicated at Didyma by Menelaos; it is now rotten except for its ivory facing [or mask, *prosopon*]. [Cf. 8.45 (= *Appendix Anthologiae* 5.35), on looking at the *omphalion* of Euphorbos' shield. T.219 for another location for the shield.]

Dionysius of Halicarnassus (1st cent. BC). Worked in Rome, writing a Roman History and various works of literary criticism.

Antiquitates Romanae
77. 1.51.1 Bronze bowls dedicated by Trojans are at Dodona, with old inscriptions. Aineias gave an inscribed bronze cup to the temple of Hera Lakinia at Kroton.

Ephorus (4th cent. BC). Of Kyme, wrote a World History. See T.50.

Euagon (5th cent. BC). A Samian historian. See T.2.

Euphorion (3rd cent. BC). Of Chalcis, studied in Athens, and wrote mainly mythographical poems. See T.21,39,156.

Euripides (later 5th cent. BC). One of the three major Athenian tragedians. Also T.17,427.

Andromache
78. 1139 scholium A spring issued where Achilles leapt ashore at Troy. [Also Lycophron, *Alexandra* 245–248.]

Ion
79. 1141–1162 At the Temple of Apollo at Delphi are the *peploi* of the Amazons, dedicated by Herakles, woven with many scenes, which are described. They are used by Ion as a canopy.

80. 1001–1009, 1029–1030 Two drops of the Gorgon's blood were given by Athena to Erichthonios, later set in jewellery for his grand-daughter Kreousa.

Heracles
81. 408–418 The dress and belt of the Amazon queen are kept at Mycenae [= Argive Heraion]. [See Seneca, *Hercules Furens* 546–547, golden.]

Hippolytus
82. 29–33 Phaidra built a temple of Aphrodite beside the Acropolis at Athens, where Hippolytos was later worshipped.

Eustathius (12th cent. AD). A priest at Constantinople and Thessalonike, who published studies of classical literature.

Commentarii in Homeri Iliadem
83. 2.308.228 The stone on which Palamedes played dice [which he had invented] with the Greek heroes is shown at Troy.

Hegesias (3rd cent. BC). Orator and historian. See T.573.

Herodotus (mid-5th cent. BC). The 'Father of History'; historian of the Persian Wars and their origins, and of eastern empires. Also T.142,147,384,521.

Historiae

84. 1.14 In the Corinthian Treasury at Delphi are offerings by the Lydian kings [8th/7th cent.], gold and silver vessels, and Midas' throne.

85. 1.66 The fetters the Spartans brought to bind the Tegeans, but with which they were themselves bound, are on show in the temple of Athena Alea.

86. 1.67–68 The Spartans were told by Delphi to recover the bones of Orestes. Lichas explains the oracle as indicating that the tomb was under a smithy. They are found at Tegea in a coffin seven cubits long and taken to Sparta. [Their probable source was Oresthasion: G.L. Huxley, *GRBS* 20 (1979) 145–148.]

87. 2.12 He observed shells on the hills in Egypt, indicating that the country was once an inland gulf. [First, Xenophanes (6th cent. BC), also fish fossils in stones; Ovid, *Metamorphoses* 15.259–267, also ancient anchors (probably pierced stones); Pausanias 1.44.9; Plutarch, *Isis* 40; Strabo 50.]

88. 2.91 The footprint of Perseus is often observed at Chemmis in Egypt, two cubits long. The Egyptian origin of Perseus is alleged.

89. 4.34–35 The tomb of the Hyperborean maidens is in the Artemision on Delos, with an olive tree, and their depository (*theke*) for offerings, behind the Artemision.

90. 4.82 In Scythia near the Tyras [River Dniestr] is Herakles' footprint impressed on rock, two cubits long.

91. 5.59–61 He saw Kadmeian letters, like the Ionic, for inscribed verses on tripods in the Temple of Apollo Ismenios at Thebes; one dedicated by Amphitryon; another by Skaios (son of Hippokoon?); another by King Laodamas, son of Eteokles.

92. 5.64 Athens' Acropolis wall is called Pelargikon [= 'Pelasgian'].

93. 5.80–81 The Aeginetans sent the Aiakidai to help the Thebans (who would have preferred men) against the Athenians.

94. 7.26 Marsyas' hide hangs in the market place at Kelainai.

95. 8.55 In the temple of Erechtheus on the Athens Acropolis is the olive tree and sea (*thalassa*), evidence of the struggle between Athena and Poseidon for Attica.

96. 8.64, 83 Aiakos and Aiakidai were sent from Aegina by ship to support the Greeks at the battle of Salamis.

97. 9.116 At Elaious was the tomb of Protesilaos, with treasures in the sanctuary there, carried off by the Persians. [More detail in Philostratus, *Heroicus* 289 (Pfister, 411 quotes); also Pliny, *Historia Naturalis* 16.238; a grove of the Nymphs.]

Hesiod (about 700 BC). Mythographer and agricultural poet. See T.462,568.

Homer (7th cent. BC). Epic poet. Also T.393, 440, 447, 448, 478, 481, 507, 583, 596, 597.

Iliad

98. 2.811–814 The hill at Troy called by men Batieia is called by the gods the tomb of Myrine [probably the Amazon, or a heroine of Lemnos].

99. 7. 86–90 The tomb of a Greek champion killed by Hektor will be pointed out as a landmark by sailors in later days.

Hyginus (2nd cent. AD). Roman mythographer. Also T.115,222.

100. 140 The body of the Python dragon slain by Apollo at Delphi was put by him into a cauldron [his mantic tripod?]. [For the tomb and the Delphic omphalos, Pfister, 328–329.]

Josephus (1st cent. AD). Jewish priest who took Roman citizenship and worked in Rome, writing Roman and Jewish histories.

101. *de Bello Judaico* 3.420 The marks of Andromeda's fetters are shown at Joppa. [Also Pliny, *Historia Naturalis* 5.69.]

102. *Antiquitates Judaicae* 5.2.3 Near Hebron the Israelites destroyed a race of giants whose bones are still shown.

Justinus (2nd/3rd cent. AD), epitome of the work of the Roman historian Trogus (1st cent. BC). See T.39,40.

Lucianus (late 2nd cent. AD). Of Samosata (Commagene). Man of letters and wit.

Adversus indoctum

103. 11–12 The head of Orpheus was buried at the Baccheion in Lesbos, and his lyre in the temple of Apollo. Neanthos, son of Pittakos is said to have acquired the lyre. [Phanocles, 3rd cent. BC (Powell, *Coll.Alex.* 106–108; Stobaeus 64.14): the lyre was buried with the head. Apollonius Rhodius 2.928–9: Orpheus with the Argonauts dedicated his lyre at Lyre in Bithynia.]

104. 13–14 a contemporary bought Epiktetos' clay lamp, and another, Proteus the Cynic's stick; 15 Philoxenos acquired Aeschylus' writing tablet.

105. 14 The Tegeans have the Calydonian boar hide, the Thebans the bones of Geryon, the Memphites the locks of Isis.

106. *de Dea Syria* 13 He saw at Hierapolis (Syria) a temple of Hera and altars made by Deukalion, and the rather small hole for the Flood water to run away, rather than the chasm reported to him.

107. *Verae Historiae* 1.7 On a fantasy voyage to the west, the finding of an inscription stating that thus far Dionysos and Herakles had journeyed, and left their footprints on rock, the former's a *plethron* long (100 feet), the latter's shorter.

108. *Piscator* 42 The tomb of Talos is beside the Athens Acropolis. [Cf. T.135.]

Lycophron (4th/3rd cent. BC). Of Chalcis; poet. Also T.39,78,498,601.

Alexandra

109. 615–618 At Arpi are the stones from Diomedes' ship's ballast [from Troy].

110. 852–855 Menelaos came to Iapygia where he dedicated to Athena [Ageleie] the crater from Tamassos, an ox-hide shield, and his wife's [Helen's] fur-lined shoes.

Myrsilus (3rd cent. BC). Of Methymna (Lesbos), historian.

Historika paradoxa

111. F2 A tumulus containing the head of Orpheus is at Antissa [Lesbos] where the nightingales sing more sweetly than all others.

112. F4 Nessos is buried in Mount Taphios ['burial'] in Locris where the water smells and flows into the sea like pus.

113. F5 Lemnian women are smelly and unapproachable on days on which Medea was said to have arrived with Jason, with her drugs.

Ovidius (1st cent. BC). Roman poet and mythographer. Also T.87,118,156.

Metamorphoses

114. 7.443–447 Skiron's bones were turned to rock, thrown down by Theseus.

115. 9.217–229 Lichas, thrown into the sea by Herakles, changes into a rock still in human shape on the coast of Euboea. [Also Hyginus, *Fabulae* 36.]

Paradoxographus Vaticanus (2nd cent. AD). Anonymous compilation of oddities.

Admiranda

116. 15 Some trees on Mount Olympos, like willows, are said to be virgins who turned into trees to avoid the attention of Boreas. If they are touched a wind arises for three days.

117. 18 Drops of the blood of the Gorgon carried by Perseus fell into the River Perinthos; whence it swells the stomachs of those who drink from it.

118. 19 Marsyas was drowned in the River Marsyas at Kelainai, which is noisy if pipes are played, silent if a kithara. [See T.3. Ovid, *Metamorphoses* 6.382–400, it was formed of the tears of mourners.]

119. 23 The statue of Memnon, son of Dawn, in Egypt sings to the rising sun.

Pausanias, (2nd cent. AD). Of Lydia; traveller and geographer. Also T.16,87,565.

Graeciae descriptio

120. 1.1.2 The bones of Themistokles were brought back to Athens by his kinsmen and buried beside the largest harbour at Piraeus, the Athenians having repented of his banishment.

121. 1.1.4 At Phaleron is the Altar of Androgeus, son of Minos, called the altar of 'the hero', but local experts know it to be of Androgeus.

122. 1.1.5 Between Phaleron and Athens is a temple of Hera without doors or roof, said to be that burned by the Persian Mardonios [in 479 BC], but this cannot be true since the statue is by Alkamenes [after mid-5th cent].

123. 1.2.1 On entering Athens from Phaleron is the tomb of the Amazon queen Antiope [beloved by Theseus]. The tomb of the Amazon Molpadia, said to have killed Antiope and herself killed by Theseus, is also in Athens. [T.536 for Antiope's gravestone; as [Plato], *Axiochos* 364d-365a.]

124. 1.4.5 The anchor found by the Phrygian king Midas still exists in the sanctuary of Zeus at Ankyra ['anchor'].

125. 1.4.5 At Ankyra there is the fountain of Midas, in which he mixed wine and water to catch Silenos.

126. 1.4.5 Attis [Anatolian deity, a young consort of Kybele] is said to be buried at Pessinous under Mt Agdistis.

127. 1.5.3 The tomb of Pandion, king of Megara, son of the Athenian king Kekrops, is by the sea shore near Megara, on the Cliff of the Diver-bird (*aithyuia* = shearwater) Athena. [also Pausanias 1.39.4, 41.6.]

128. 1.13.2–3 Celtic shields were dedicated by the Molossian Pyrrhos to Athena Itonia; inscribed 'for the Aiakids are warriors now as of old'.

129. 1.17.5 The rivers Acheron and Kokytos: Homer

models his picture of hell on them and named rivers of hell after rivers of Thesprotis.

130. 1.17.6 Kimon laid waste Skyros for the murder of Theseus, then brought his bones to Athens.

131. 1.18.4 Near the Athens Sarapeion is the place where Theseus and Peirithoos took their oaths before their expedition to Laconia, then Thesprotis. [Cf. Sophocles, *Oedipus Coloneus* 1592–1594.]

132. 1.18.7–8 In the enclosure of the Temple of Olympian Zeus in Athens the ground is cloven to a cubit width. After the flood in the time of Deukalion the water ran away here. Meal and honey is thrown in each year. Deukalion's 'grave' is near the temple. [Also Strabo 425.]

133. 1.19.5 The place is shown near the Ilissos where the Peloponnesians slew King Kodros.

134. 1.21.3 The rock and cliff on Mount Sipylos, which Pausanias climbed, is believed to be the petrified Niobe, but does not look like a woman bowed with grief except at a distance. [Also 8.2.7.]

135. 1.21.4 The tomb of Kalos is between the Acropolis and the Theseion. [= Talos? see T.108.]

136. 1.22.1–2 A barrow was piled up in memory of Hippolytos in front of the Temple of Themis, between the Asklepieion and the Acropolis at Athens. His tomb is at Troizen [near where he was said to have died through Phaidra's plot]. A myrtle tree at Troizen has perforated leaves, pierced by Phaidra's hairpin, in her distress. [Also T.264.]

137. 1.23.5 On Athens Acropolis, by the statue of Diitrephes, is a stone of no great size but big enough for a little man to sit on, where Silenos rested when Dionysos came to Attica.

138. 1.23.7 At Brauron is the old wooden statue of Taurian Artemis which was brought with Iphigeneia. [But in 1.33.1 he believes it is elsewhere, and at 3.16.7 he prefers the one at Artemis Orthia, at Sparta.]

139. 1.26.5 In the Erechtheion on Athens Acropolis there is a well which emits the sound of waves with the south wind, and beside it a trident mark in the rock: Poseidon's evidence for his claim on Attica.

140. 1.26.6 The old Athena image on Athens Acropolis fell from heaven; Pausanias reserves judgement on the truth of this. [Apollodorus 3.14.6: it was set up by Erichthonios.]

141. 1.27.1 In the Temple of Polias on Athens Acropolis is a wooden Hermes dedicated by King Kekrops, but hidden under myrtle branches; also the folding chair made by Daidalos.

142. 1.27.2 On Athens Acropolis is the sacred olive of Athena, her evidence for control of Attica. It was burned by the Persians but grew again the same day to a height of two cubits. [Also T.95.]

143. 1.28.3 The Athens Acropolis wall was built by Pelasgians who dwelt at the foot of the rock.

144. 1.28.5 On Athens Areiopagos is the altar dedicated by Orestes to Athena Areia.

145. 1.28.5 On the Areiopagos at Athens the unwrought stones where accused and accuser stand are called the stones of Hybris and Shamelessness (Anaideia).

146. 1.28.7 The tomb of Oidipous is near the Areiopagos.

147. 1.28.11 Of lifeless things said to have inflicted punishment of their own accord the most famous is the sword of Cambyses [Persian king, late 6th cent. BC; Herodotus 3.64.].

148. 1.30.2 In Athens Academy is the second olive plant ever to have appeared.

149. 1.31.2 At Prasiai is the tomb of Erysichthon [son of King Kekrops of Athens], having died on the voyage back from a sacred embassy to Delos.

150. 1.31.3 At Lamptrai is the tomb of King Kranaos of Athens, who had fled there, and at Potamoi in Attica is the tomb of Ion [7.1.5; eponym of the Ionians and adopted by Athens as a king].

151. 1.32.6 At Marathon is the spring Makaria, named for the daughter of Herakles who killed herself there to ensure Athenian victory over the Peloponnesians pursuing the Heraklids.

152. 1.32.7 The stone mangers of the Persian general Artaphernes and marks of his tents are to be seen above the lake at Marathon.

153. 1.32.7 Near Marathon is a cave sacred to Pan and rocks that are called Pan's herd of goats since they resemble goats.

154. 1.34.4 At Oropos is the spring of Amphiaraos, where he arose as a god; there is no sacrifice or use of the water, but coins are dropped in to pay for healing.

155. 1.35.3 A stone on Salamis near the harbour is where Telamon sat watching his children sail off to Aulis for the Trojan war.

156. 1.35.4 On Salamis, once Ajax died, a flower appeared, white and red with letters on it as on the hyacinth. [The same told of his grave at Troy: Euphorion (3rd cent. BC) fr. 40 Powell; Ovid, *Metamorphoses* 13.394–398.]

157. 1.35.4 When Odysseus was shipwrecked the arms [of Achilles] were washed ashore at the grave of Ajax.

158. 1.35.5 At Troy the grave of Ajax was washed against and opened by the waves. His kneecaps are as big as the discus used in the boys' pentathlon. Other remarks on the stature of heroic corpses.

159. 1.35.6 Asterios, son of the giant Anax, was buried on an islet opposite Lade. His corpse is not less than ten cubits long.

160. 1.35.7–8 At Temenothyrai in Lydia there were found on a hillside colossal bones of human type, attributed to Geryon, his chair carved on a rocky spur, and a local stream called Okeanos, where cow horns had been found in ploughing [Geryon's herd]. Pausanias pointed out to the locals that

Geryon was at Cadiz, though with no tomb, only a tree that takes diverse forms. The Lydians then admitted that their tomb was of the giant Hyllos, with a river Hyllos (whence Herakles took the name for his son by Omphale in Lydia).

161. 1.36.4 On the road to Eleusis there is a tomb and torrent of Skiros, a seer from Dodona, killed fighting for the Eleusinians in the war with Erechtheus.

162. 1.37.2 On the road from Eleusis is the tomb of Phytalos, where he was given a fig tree by Demeter in return for hospitality. The tomb is inscribed with a verse which is quoted.

163. 1.38.2 The tomb of the Thracian bard Eumolpos, who fought for the Eleusinians, is at Rheitoi on the road to Athens.

164. 1.38.5 At Eleusis is a place called Erineus where Pluto descended with Persephone.

165. 1.38.5 At the Eleusis Kephissos Theseus killed Prokroustes.

166. 1.38.6 At Eleusis is the well Kallichoron where women first danced and sang for Demeter; and the threshing floor of Triptolemos is shown.

167. 1.38.9 Near Eleutherai is the spring and cave where Antiope put her children and the shepherd found and washed them. Ruins of the town wall and houses of Eleutherai still exist.

168. 1.39.1 At Eleusis, on the road to Megara, is the well Anthion where Demeter sat disguised as an old woman after the rape of Persephone.

169. 1.39.2 At Eleusis, on the road to Megara, are the graves of the Seven Argives who marched on Thebes.

170. 1.39.3 On the road to Megara is the tomb of Alope killed by her father Kerkyon for bearing Hippothoon to Poseidon. Near by is a place called the wrestling ground of Kerkyon [defeated by Theseus].

171. 1.39.5 The tomb of Megareus is at Megara [by the second acropolis, 1.42.1] where he fell in battle.

172. 1.41.1 The tomb of Alkmene is near the Olympieion at Megara, where she died. Her children were told by Delphi to bury her there. Her sons by Herakles and by King Amphitryon, are buried at Thebes.

173. 1.41.2 At Megara is the tomb of Hyllos son of Herakles.

174. 1.41.7 At Megara is the tomb of the Amazon Hippolyte, who escaped there and died of grief after the defeat at Athens. Her grave [memorial? – *mnema*] is in the shape of a pelta [Amazonian light shield, crescent-shaped].

175. 1.41.8–9 At Megara is the tomb of Tereus, a suicide, with annual sacrifice using gravel instead of barley. The hoopoe, into which he was turned, first appeared there.

176. 1.42.1–2 At Megara is the hearth of the Prodomeis gods, where Alkathoos first sacrificed before building the walls; also the stone on which Apollo laid his lyre while helping Alkathoos; it sounds like a lyre if struck by a stone.

177. 1.42.3 On the music of the statue Memnon (who marched from Ethiopia to Egypt and then Susa) at Egyptian Thebes. (Also T.118 and Strabo 816.)

178. 1.42.4 The Megarian Council House was once the tomb of Timalkos (not slain by Theseus). [1.43.3 – the Megarians were advised by Delphi that they could thus profit from the counsel of heroes buried there.]

179. 1.42.6 At Megara is the tomb of Kallipolis, son of Alkathoos, killed by his father for impiety.

180. 1.42.6 The body of Ino was washed up on the shore at Megara, and buried; there is a shrine and olive trees.

181. 1.43.2 In the Prytaneion of Megara are the tombs of Euippos, son of Megareus, and Ischepolis, son of Alkathoos.

182. 1.43.2 Near the Prytaneion of Megara is a rock called Anaklethra ('recall'), where Demeter called back her daughter; the story is re-enacted there.

183. 1.43.4 The shrine of Alkathoos at Megara is used as a Record Office, where are the tombs of Pyrgo, wife of Alkathoos, and of Iphinoe, his daughter, which receives libations and cut hair from girls before marriage.

184. 1.43.5 Beside the entrance to the sanctuary of Dionysos at Megara are the tombs of Astykrateia and Manto, daughters of Polyidos, who purified Alkathoos and built the sanctuary, dedicating a wooden statue, now hidden all but the face.

185. 1.43.8 In Megara market place is the tomb of Koroibos, with an elegiac inscription, and a figure of Koroibos murdering Poine (Punishment) – the most ancient images in stone he has seen.

186. 1.44.1 Near the tomb of Koroibos in Megara is the tomb of Orsippos – the first naked runner at Olympia [8th cent. BC], who later annexed nearby territory for the city.

187. 1.44.3 By the sea at Nisaea (Megara) is the tomb of Lelex, who came to reign from Egypt.

188. 1.44.3 By the island Minoa off Megara the Cretan fleet anchored in their war with Nisos (of Megara). [An explanation for the name Minoa.]

189. 1.44.4 On the road from Megara to Pagai is a rock with arrows stuck in it, shot at by the Medes at night. [It is not recorded that the Persians reached so far west.]

190. 1.44.4 At Pagai is the shrine and tomb of Aigaleus, son of Adrastos, a member of the second expedition against Thebes, killed in the first battle, at Glisas.

191. 1.44.5 At Ereneia, a Megarian village, is the tomb of Autonoe, daughter of Kadmos, who went there in grief at the death of Aktaion.

192. 1.44.6 On the Megara-Corinth road is the tomb of Kar, son of Phoroneus, once just a mound of earth, then adorned with *konchites*, a white stone found only in Megara. ['Shell-stone', i.e., with shell fossils in it.]

193. 1.44.7 On the Megara-Corinth road is the Molouris

rock where Ino threw herself into the sea with her son Melikertes.

194. 1.44.8 On the Megara-Corinth road is the rock beside which Skiron the robber dwelt; he cast travellers into the sea, to be eaten by turtles [of which large specimens were perhaps to be found locally].

195. 1.44.10 On the Megara-Corinth road is the tomb of King Eurystheus, killed there by Iolaos fleeing from Attica after the battle with the Heraklids.

196. 2.1.3 Near Corinth at Krommyon the pine tree is still visible by the sea, and the altar of Melikertes, who was landed here by a dolphin, and buried by Sisyphos on the Isthmus (whence the Isthmian Games).

197. 2.1.8 At Gabala [in Palestine] is the *peplos* robe, dedicated to the Nereid Doto, with which Eriphyle was bribed [to persuade her son to lead the second expedition against Thebes].

198. 2.2.1 At the Isthmos is an ancient altar of the Kyklopes.

199. 2.2.2 The graves of Neleus and Sisyphos at Isthmos had to remain unknown. [So, remarkably, not identified locally.]

200. 2.2.3 Opposite Kenchreai is the bath of Helen, a copious stream of tepid salt water flowing from a rock.

201. 2.2.6 Some remains of ancient Corinth are visible [i.e., before the sack of 146 BC] but most are of the period of restoration.

202. 2.2.6–7 At Corinth are wooden images of Dionysos, gilt except for the faces which are painted red, made from the tree from which Pentheus watched the dancing women [on Mount Kithairon, possessed by Dionysos; they killed him].

203. 2.3.2 The spring Peirene at Corinth came from the tears of Peirene mourning her son, killed by Artemis.

204. 2.3.6 At Corinth on the road to Sikyon is the water basin into which Glauke threw herself, to counter Medea's drugs.

205. 2.3.6–7 At Corinth by the Odeion is the tomb of Medea's children, stoned to death by the Corinthians for the gifts they brought to Glauke: an unjust death, punished until the Corinthians set up an image of Deima (Terror), still there (a woman of terrifying aspect). [Perhaps the *aition* explanation for an archaic image; in most versions Medea killed her own children.]

206. 2.5.5 A burnt temple on the Corinth-Sikyon road is said to be that of Apollo burnt by Pyrrhos [son of Achilles = Neoptolemos]; others say a temple to Olympian Zeus, accidentally burned.

207. 2.7.8 A temple of Apollo in the Agora of Sikyon was built by Proitos, because his daughters recovered from madness there.

208. 2.7.9 At Sikyon, temple of Apollo, Meleager dedicated the spear that killed the Calydonian Boar; also there are the pipes of Marsyas, which had been swept into the river Maeander, reappeared in the Asopos, and were then washed up at Sikyon and given to Apollo by a shepherd.

209. 2.10.2 In the temple of Asklepios at Sikyon, in the colonnade, is the huge bone of a sea monster.

210. 2.11.1 At Sikyon, before the temple of Athena altar, is a barrow memorial of Epopeus who made the sanctuary of Apollo and Artemis near by.

211. 2.12.4–5 At Keleai is the tomb of Aras, who founded a city near Phlious, and a successor, Dysaules [also 2.14.4]; and the tombs of Aras' children are on the site of the old city, he believes, with stelai [conspicuous *periphaneis*, or round *periphereis*?].

212. 2.13.7 Behind the Agora at Phlious is the house of divination where Amphiaraos slept and started to prophesy. Nearby is the *omphalos* ('navel') of all the Peloponnese.

213. 2.14.4 At Keleai, on the roof of the Anaktoron, is the chariot of Pelops.

214. 2.15.1 At Kleonai are the tombs of Eurytos and Kteatos, killed by Herakles, having opposed him in his war with Augeias.

215. 2.15.2 From Nemea it is fifteen stadia to the lion's cave, which is still shown.

216. 2.15.3 At Nemea is the tomb of Opheltes, within a stone wall with altars; also the barrow of Lykourgos, his father.

217. 2.15.3 At Nemea is a spring named after Adrastos, perhaps because he found it, 'or for some other reason'.

218. 2.16.5–7 At Mycenae are left the gate surmounted by lions, and parts of the walls, made by the Kyklopes who also made the walls of Tiryns for Proitos. Also a spring called Perseia and the underground buildings (*oikodomemata*) of Atreus and his children, where their treasure was kept; also the tombs of Atreus and of all those murdered with Agamemnon on his return from Troy; also perhaps the tomb of Kassandra, but the Laconians say it is at Amyklai; also the tombs of Agamemnon, Eurymedon the charioteer, Teledamos, Pelops (the last said to be twin children of Kassandra). The tombs of Klytaimnestra and Aigisthos are a little way from the walls.

219. 2.17.3 In the Argive Heraion is the couch of Hera, and the shield taken by Menelaos from Euphorbos at Troy. [A famous duel, but Menelaos was a Spartan not Argive. See T.76.]

220. 2.17.5 The pear-tree image of Hera was dedicated at Tiryns by Peirasos, son of Argos, thence taken to the Heraion: a small seated figure, which he saw.

221. 2.18.1 On the Mycenae-Argos road is the tomb of Thyestes, with a stone ram on it [also 2.18.3, called The Rams].

222. 2.19.3 At Argos is the temple of Apollo Lykios and its original wooden image dedicated by Danaos; in those days all images were of wood, especially the Egyptian. Also

(2.19.5) the throne of Danaos [egyptianizing furniture?]. And before the temple (2.19.7) Danaos dedicated a pedestal with reliefs (a bull and wolf fighting, and a woman throwing stones at the bull) and some pillars. [Most likely an archaic relief with a lion and bull and part of a myth scene. The shield of Danaos, much spoken of (e.g., Hyginus, *Fabulae* 273.2), seems not to have survived.]

223. 2.19.8 At Argos is the tomb of Linos, one of the sons of Apollo, and another of the poet Linos; also an alleged tomb of Prometheus but Pausanias prefers the story of the Opuntians about it.

224. 2.20.3 At Argos is the tomb of Phoroneus [a founder], worshipped as hero.

225. 2.20.3 At Argos is a very old Temple of Tyche (Fortune), if it is true that this is where Palamedes dedicated his dice. [Palamedes invented dice games for the heroes waiting for a wind to Troy.]

226. 2.20.4 At Argos is the tomb of Choreia the Maenad who marched with Dionysos to Argos, and was killed by Perseus. And by the Temple of Hera Antheia (2.22.1) the tombs of the women who followed Dionysos from the islands, whence called Haliai [Sea-women].

227. 2.20.6 At Argos is the tomb of Danaos; and near by the cenotaph of Argives who fell at Troy or on their way home.

228. 2.20.7 At Argos is a head of a stone Medusa made by the Kyklopes. The place is called Kriterion because it was where Hypermestra was brought to judgement by Danaos.

229. 2.21.1 Towards the Argos agora is the tomb of Kerdo, wife of Phoroneus.

230. 2.21.2 At Argos is the tomb of Hypermestra, mother of Amphiaraos, and of Hypermestra, daughter of Danaos, and of Lynkeus; opposite is the grave of Talaos, son of Bias.

231. 2.21.5 In the agora of Argos is a mound containing the head of the Gorgon Medusa; beside it (2.21.7) the tomb of Gorgophone, daughter of Perseus.

232. 2.22.1–3 At Argos is the tomb of Pelasgos who founded the nearby sanctuary of Demeter. Opposite the tomb is a bronze vessel of no great size supporting ancient figures of Artemis, Zeus and Athena, where the Argives swore to continue the war at Troy to the end; others say it holds the bones of Tantalos, son of Thyestes. Pausanias has seen the tomb of the famous Tantalos, son of Zeus, on Mount Sipylos.

233. 2.22.4 At Argos is the place where Hera persuaded Poseidon to send back the flood, a sanctuary of Poseidon Prosklystios.

234. 2.22.5 At Argos is the tomb of Argos, son of Zeus and Niobe, daughter of Phoroneus.

235. 2.22.6 At Argos is the sanctuary of Eileithyia dedicated by Helen when being returned to Laconia [from Attica where she had been held by Theseus] by the Dioskouroi.

236. 2.22.8 At Argos is the tomb of Likymnios, son of Elektryon, killed by Tleptolemos, son of Herakles.

237. 2.23.1 The image in the Temple of Dionysos at Argos had been found in a cave on Euboea by Greeks returning from Troy.

238. 2.23.2 Near the Temple of Dionysos in Argos is the house of Adrastos and sanctuary of Amphiaraos; opposite is the tomb of Eriphyle.

239. 2.23.3 At Argos is the tomb of Hyrnetho, though empty.

240. 2.23.5 Pausanias does not believe that Argos has the tombs of Deianeira or of Helenos, son of Priam, or the Palladion from Troy. The Palladion went to Italy with Aineias; Deianeira's tomb is near Herakleia at the foot of Mount Oita [central Greece], and Helenos went to Epirus with Neoptolemos.

241. 2.23.7 At Argos is the underground structure over which was the bronze chamber made by Akrisios to imprison his daughter [Danae], pulled down by the tyrant Perilaos; beside it the tomb of Krotopos.

242. 2.23.7 The Temple of Cretan Dionysos at Argos is where he buried Ariadne; when the temple was being rebuilt her clay coffin was found, and seen by Lykeas [2nd cent. AD Argive historian].

243. 2.24.2 On the Larisa acropolis at Argos the Temple of Athena Oxyderkes (sharp-sighted) dedicated by Diomedes for her lifting darkness from his eyes at Troy.

244. 2.24.2 On the Larisa acropolis at Argos are the tombs of the sons of Aigyptos, with their heads only (cut off by their wives); their trunks are at Lerna where they were killed.

245. 2.24.3 On the Larisa acropolis at Argos is a wooden image of Zeus with three eyes, from the altar to which Priam fled at Troy, taken by Sthenelos, son of Kapaneus.

246. 2.25.1 On the Argos-Mantinea road are wooden images of Ares and Aphrodite, dedicated by Polyneikes and the Argives.

247. 2.25.2 The tomb of Oineus is at Oinoë, buried by Diomedes.

248. 2.25.7 On the Argos-Epidauria road is a structure like a pyramid with relief shields of Argive shape. Here was the battle between Proitos and Akrisios for the kingdom, the first where generals and common soldiers all had shields. A common tomb was made for all who died.

249. 2.25.8 The walls of Tiryns, all that is left of the town, were built by the Kyklopes.

250. 2.25.9 From Tiryns towards the sea are the chambers (*thalamoi*) of the daughters of Proitos.

251. 2.26.4 A mountain near Epidauros is called Titthion [nipple], where Asklepios was born.

252. 2.27.4 At Epidauros is an ancient stele with an inscription saying that Hippolytos dedicated twenty horses to Asklepios, who brought him back from the dead.

253. 2.28.2 On the road to Mount Koryphon near Epidauros is a twisted olive, wrenched into this shape by Herakles, perhaps as a boundary with Asine.

254. 2.28.3–7 On the road to Epidauros are sacred wild olives at Hyrnethion where Hyrnetho was buried.

255. 2.29.8–9 On Aigina, a low altar is the tomb of Aiakos, in an enclosure with olive trees. Beside it is the tomb of Phokos, a mound surrounded by a base, with a rough stone on top. [Pindar, *Olympia* 13.109, for the grave of the Aiakidai, and *Nemea* 5.53–54 for the enclosure entrance.]

256. 2.30.7 The drowned Saron [eponym of the Saronic Gulf] was buried in the grove of Artemis at Troizen.

257. 2.31.2 At Troizen the temple of Artemis is where Semele was brought up from Hades by Dionysos, and where Herakles pulled up Kerberos.

258. 2.31.3 At Troizen is the tomb of Pittheus with three marble chairs on it.

259. 2.31.4 A sacred stone before the temple of Artemis at Troizen is where nine Troizenians purified Orestes.

260. 2.31.6 Pittheus built the temple of Thearian Apollo at Troizen, 'the oldest temple I know'.

261. 2.31.8 Before the temple of Apollo at Troizen is the booth (*skene*) of Orestes, where he lived until purified; the things used in purification are buried near by where a bay tree is still standing.

262. 2.31.9 The spring Hippokrene at Troizen was where Pegasos stamped his foot.

263. 2.31.10 Herakles lent his club against the image of Hermes Polygios at Troizen; it took root, and still grows.

264. 2.32.1–4 The temple and image of Hippolytos at Troizen were made by Diomedes; locals know Hippolytos' grave but do not show it. A myrtle tree has pierced leaves [T.136], where Phaidra spied on Hippolytos exercising, by the temple of Aphrodite Kataskopia (Peeping). Her tomb is near by; also the house of Hippolytos.

265. 2.32.4 Before the house of Hippolytos at Troizen is the fountain of Herakles, so called because he found the water.

266. 2.32.7 On the Troizen-Hermione road is the rock of Theseus, under which he found the boots and sword of Aigeus (formerly altar of Zeus Sthenios). [Also 2.34.6.]

267. 2.32.9 On the road to Kelenderis near the temple of Ares is a place called Genethlion, where Theseus was born, and the site of one of his victories over Amazons.

268. 2.32.10 On the road to Kelenderis is a twisted olive called *rhachos*, where Hippolytos' chariot reins got caught.

269. 2.33.1 Off Troizen is the island Hiera (once called Sphairia) where there is the tomb of Sphairos, charioteer of Pelops. This is where Poseidon took Aithra [mother of Theseus].

270. 2.34.7 A cape at Hermione is called Skyllaion after the daughter of Niseus, where her body was washed ashore, but there is no grave.

271. 2.34.10 At Hermione are the foundations of the stadion where the Dioskouroi exercised.

272. 2.35.10 Near Hermione, at Klymenos, is the chasm where Herakles dragged up Kerberos.

273. 2.36.3 Between Hermione and Asine are heaps of unhewn stones called Boleoi.

274. 2.36.8 At Lerna are the foundations of the house of Hippomedon who went with Polyneikes to Thebes.

275. 2.37.3 At Lerna are Mysteries founded by Philammon. Stories of Philammon are inscribed on a heart-shaped piece of copper, proved spurious by Arriphon on philological grounds.

276. 2.37.4 At Lerna by the spring of Amymone is the plane tree where the Hydra was bred.

277. 2.37.5 At Lerna is the spring of Amphiaraos where Dionysos fetched up Semele from Hades. [See T.257 for another location.]

278. 2.38.1 On the Lerna-Temenion road is the tomb of Temenos.

279. 2.38.4 Near Lerna, at Genesion, is Apobathmoi where Danaos and his daughters landed.

280. 3.1.3 The tomb of Hyakinthos is under the statue of Apollo at Amyklai. [Also 3.19.3.]

281. 3.3.6 The Spartans were looking for the bones of Orestes. Lichas realized from the oracle that they must be buried in a smithy, where they were found, at Tegea, and taken to Sparta [T.285].

282. 3.3.7 An oracle told the Athenians to bring back the bones of Theseus from Skyros if they wished to conquer the island. Kimon found them and took them to Athens.

283. 3.3.8 Heroic weapons are bronze, as shown by Homer, and because this is the material of the blade and butt-spike of the spear of Achilles at Phaselis, and of the sword of Memnon at the temple of Asklepios at Nikomedeia.

284. 3.10.6 On the road to Karyai is an image of Herakles and the trophy he erected for his victory over Hippokoon and his sons.

285. 3.11.10 Beside the sanctuary of the Fates at Sparta is the grave of Orestes.

286. 3.11.11 The Old Ephoreia at Sparta has the tombs of Epimenides and Aphareus.

287. 3.11.4 By the office of the Bidiaioi at Sparta is the image of Athena set up by Odysseus and called Keleutheia [of the Paths] for his victory in the contest with the suitors, and three sanctuaries for her, at a distance from each other.

288. 3.12.5 The shrines of the hero Iops, and of Amphiaraos at Sparta, were made by the sons of Tyndareus.

289. 3.12.7 At Sparta near the Hellenion is the tomb of Talthybios; also shown in the agora of Aigion in Achaia [T.376].

290. 3.12.8 At Sparta is the tomb of the Iamids, seers from Elis.

291. 3.12.10 In the Skias at Sparta hangs the kithara of

Timotheos of Miletus, who had been condemned for adding four strings to the usual seven.

292. 3.12.11 Spartans allege that the *tholos* with statues of Zeus and Aphrodite was built by Epimenides.

293. 3.13.1 At Sparta are the tombs of Kynortas, Kastor, and, beside the Skias, of Idas and Lynkeus, but he would have expected them to be buried in Messenia.

294. 3.13.2 At Sparta the temple of Kore Soteira is said to have been made by Orpheus, or by Abaris from the Hyperboreans.

295. 3.14.1 In Sparta are the tombs of kings and the bones of Leonidas brought from Thermopylai.

296. 3.14.2 At Sparta is the tomb of Tainaros, eponym of the cape.

297. 3.14.6 At Sparta is the tomb of Eumedes, a son of Hippokoon.

298. 3.14.6 At Sparta is the house of Menelaos, now privately owned.

299. 3.14.7 At Sparta is the trophy erected by Polydeukes for his victory over Lynkeus. So the sons of Aphareus [T.293] were probably not buried at Sparta.

300. 3.15.5 At Sparta is the tomb of Oionos, by the sanctuary of Herakles who punished Hippokoon for his death.

301. 3.16.1–2 In the shrines of Hilaeira and Phoibe is an egg hung by ribbons from the roof, said to be the egg of Leda [containing Helen].

302. 3.16.2 At Sparta is the house of the sons of Tyndareus [Dioskouroi].

303. 3.16.7–8 In the temple of Artemis Orthia the wooden image of Orthia is the one brought by Iphigeneia, not the one at Brauron which was taken to Susa, rescued by Seleukos and given to Laodikeia, where it is still.

304. 3.17.4 At Sparta before the temple of Zeus is the tomb of Tyndareus.

305. 3.19.6 At Amyklai is the reputed tomb of Agamemnon [but T.218, at Mycenae].

306. 3.19.7 On the road to Therapne is the image of Ares brought by the Dioskouroi [with the Argonauts] from Colchis.

307. 3.19.9 At Therapne the tombs of Menelaos and Helen are said to be in the temple of Menelaos.

308. 3.20.2 Near Therapne is a place called Alesiai where Myles, who invented the mill, ground corn.

309. 3.20.9 On the Sparta-Arcadia road is the Horse's Tomb, where Tyndareus swore suitors of Helen on the body of the sacrificed horse.

310. 3.22.1 Near Gythion is the unwrought stone where Orestes was relieved of his madness; the stone is called Zeus Kappotas.

311. 3.22.1 Off Gythion is the island Kranae where Paris first made love to Helen.

312. 3.22.9 Near Asopos (south Peloponnese) in the gymnasium of Asklepios are bones which are human despite their great size.

313. 3.22.10 Near Asopos (south Peloponnese) is a cape called *Onou gnathos* (jaw of ass), and a sanctuary of Athena with no image or roof, said to have been made by Agamemnon; also the tomb of Kinados, Menelaos' pilot.

314. 3.22.12 At Boiai is the myrtle tree (still worshipped) in which a hare took refuge, showing the place for the city.

315. 3.24.2 At Kyphanta near Zarax is a rock with water flowing from it, struck by a thirsty Atalante with her spear.

316. 3.24.4 At Prasiai is the cave where Ino nursed Dionysos.

317. 3.24.7 At Las near Gythion is the temple of Athena Asia, made by the Dioskouroi, returned from Colchis, where there is another.

318. 3.24.10 At Las is the tomb of the founder Las, killed by Patroklos (not Achilles), who also wooed Helen.

319. 3.25.1 A river is called Skyras because Neoptolemos put in here sailing from Skyros to marry Hermione.

320. 3.25.3 At Pyrrichos is a well given by Silenos.

321. 3.25.5 Cape Tainaron is where Herakles dragged up Kerberos from Hades.

322. 3.36.2 The island Pephnos is where the Dioskouroi were born.

323. 3.36.7 Near Kardamyle is a sanctuary of the Nereids, where they came out of the sea to see Neoptolemos arrive.

324. 3.36.9–10 At Gerenia is the tomb of Machaon [also 4.3.2], his bones brought back [from Troy] by Nestor.

325. 4.1.6 An oak grove of Lykos, son of Pandion, where he purified the initiated, is near Messene.

326. 4.15.8 A place called *Kaprou sema* [Boar's grave] at Stenyklaros in Messenia is where Herakles exchanged oaths with the sons of Neleus, over the pieces of a boar.

327. 4.16.7 Aristomenes dedicated the shield he lost in battle at Lebadeia. The blazon is a spread eagle.

328. 4.26.7–8 Aischines, an Argive general, was told in a dream to dig by a yew and myrtle on Mount Ithome, where he found a bronze urn. He took it to Epameinondas who found a tin scroll in it inscribed with the Mysteries of the Great Goddesses, deposited by Aristomenes. It is preserved in the Karnasian grove [T.333], as revealed to Pausanias in a dream.

329. 4.27.6 For the new Messene the citizens summoned their heroes to dwell with them – Messene, Eurytos, Aphareus and children, Kresphontes and Aipytos (Heraklids), and especially Aristomenes.

330. 4.32.3–4,6 At Messene is the tomb of Aristomenes, his bones brought from Rhodes at Delphi's command. The dead Aristomenes was present at the battle of Leuktra, to help the Thebans against the Spartans, and his shield was put on the trophy at Leuktra at the request of Epameinondas. [T.327 and 9.39.14, the shield is at Lebadeia.]

331. 4.33.1 On Ithome is the spring Klepsydra where the infant Zeus was washed.

332. 4.33.3 The stream Balyra is so-called because here Thamyris threw away (*apobalontos*) his lyre when he became blind.

333. 4.33.5 In the Karnasian grove are the bronze urn [T.328] and the bones of Eurytos.

334. 4.34.4 On the Korone road is the place where Ino rose from the sea as the goddess Leukothea.

335. 4.34.5 Digging in the foundations of the wall at Korone revealed a bronze crow (*korone*).

336. 4.34.6 At Korone is the tomb of Epimelides, founder.

337. 4.35.9 Blood-red water is seen near Joppa where Perseus washed off the blood of the sea monster he had killed.

338. 4.36.2 At Pylos is the house of Nestor, containing a painting of him. His tomb is at Pylos, and not far away that of Thrasymedes.

339. 4.36.3 At Pylos is the cave where the cows of Neleus and Nestor were stalled – a present to Neleus from his daughter's suitors.

340. 4.36.7 At Kyparissiai is the spring of Dionysos, struck by his thyrsos wand.

341. 5.1.5 At Elis is the tomb of Endymion, but the people of Herakleia near Miletus say he went to Latmos [T.589]. [6.20.9, the tomb at the end of the Olympia stadium.]

342. 5.4.4 At Elis by the gate to Olympia is the tomb of Aitolos.

343. 5.5.4 The tomb of Lepreos, killed by Herakles, is at Phigaleia, but not pointed out by the locals.

344. 5.5.9–10 The odd smell of the River Anigros was where Cheiron washed his wounds; or where Melampous flung the objects he used to purify the Proitidai; its waters cure leprosy [T.565].

345. 5.12.3 Pausanias has seen an elephant's skull in the temple of Artemis in Campania; he observes on the way the tusks grow.

346. 5.13.4–6 To succeed in the Trojan war the Greeks needed the bow and arrows of Herakles and the shoulder blade of Pelops from Olympia. Pelops' shoulder blade was lost on the way back, off Euboea, but washed up at Eretria. Long after Troy a fisherman netted it, was amazed at its size, and took it to Delphi where it was returned to the Eleians. The bone had mouldered away by Pausanias' day [and Pliny's, T.517.].

347. 5.13.7 In Pausanias' country (Lydia) there is the tomb of Tantalos [T.232] and a lake called after him, a throne of Pelops on Mount Sipylos, and the myrtle-wood image of Aphrodite dedicated by Pelops at Temnos, when he prayed he might wed Hippodameia.

348. 5.20.1 At Olympia are Hippodameia's couch, and the discus of Iphitos inscribed with the Eleian truce in a circle of letters.

349. 5.20.6 At Olympia is a wooden pillar from the house of Oinomaos, struck by lightning, protected in a four-pillar structure; a bronze tablet with verse before it.

350. 5.20.8 At Olympia excavations for a Roman's victory monument, near the pillar of Oinomaos, watched by Pausanias, found fragments of arms, bridles and bits.

351. 6.19.6 In the Treasury of Sikyon at Olympia are the sword of Pelops with a gold hilt, the ivory horn of Amaltheia dedicated by Miltiades, with an inscription on it in old Attic letters.

352. 6.20.7 The Eleians brought back to Olympia the bones of Hippodameia from Midea.

353. 6.20.17 Pelops made an empty barrow at Olympia for Myrtilos, the charioteer of Oinomaos.

354. 6.21.3 Across the Kladeus from Olympia is the tomb of Oinomaos, an earth mound within a stone wall; above it the remains of buildings where his mares were stabled.

355. 6.21.3 Across the Erymanthos river is the tomb of Sauros, killed by Herakles.

356. 6.21.7 Near Olympia is the tomb of the horses of Marmax, the first suitor of Hippodameia.

357. 6.21.9–11 Near Olympia is the tomb of the suitors of Hippodameia, buried by Oinomaos with no mark of honour, but Pelops made a great monument and treated them as heroes.

358. 6.22.1 At Olympia is the temple of Artemis Kordax, where the followers of Pelops celebrated their victory with the *kordax* dance. Nearby is a small building with a bronze box containing the bones of Pelops.

359. 6.23.3 In an Elis gymnasium is a cenotaph for Achilles [and 6.24.1].

360. 6.24.9 In the Elis agora is the tomb of Oxylos, like a low temple without walls, the roof supported by oak pillars.

361. 7.1.8 Tisamenos was buried by the Achaeans in Helike, but his bones were taken to Sparta and his tomb is still seen there at Phiditia [dining place].

362. 7.2.6 At Didyma is the tomb of Neleus, son of Kodros.

363. 7.2.9 At Ephesos is the tomb of Androklos, son of Kodros, who helped Priene against the Carians; a warrior figure upon it.

364. 7.3.3 At Kolophon is the tomb of Promethos, son of Kodros, brought back from Naxos.

365. 7.3.5 On the Kolophon-Lebedos road is the tomb of Andraimon, son of Kodros.

366. 7.4.4 The willow tree beneath which Hera was born still grows in her sanctuary on Samos. [8.23.5: it is the oldest tree alive.]

367. 7.5.5–8 At Erythrai is the rope of tresses of Thracian women, with which they pulled in the raft with the egyptianizing image of Herakles from Tyre, now in his temple there.

368. 7.5.12 At Smyrna there is the grotto where Homer composed his poems, at the springs of the river Meles.

369. 7.5.13 On Chios is the tomb of Oinopion.

370. 7.5.13 On Samos is the tomb of the lovers Rhadine and Leontichos.

371. 7.17.8 At Dyme in Achaia is the tomb of Sostratos, loved by Herakles who offered some of his hair; and a stele with a relief of Herakles.

372. 7.19–20.1 At Patrai between the temple of Laphria and the altar is the tomb of Eurypylos. He took from Troy a chest of spoils containing an image of Dionysos, the work of Hephaistos and gift of Zeus to Dardanos. He opened the chest and went out of his mind. Others say Eurypylos is the son of Dexamenos who went with Herakles to Troy, and that Herakles gave him the chest. The chest is carried out annually for a festival; the god in it is called Aisymnetes. [9.41.2, they say the chest was made by Hephaistos, but do not show it.]

373. 7.20.5 In the Patrai agora before the image of Athena is the tomb of the founder Patreus.

374. 7.20.9 At Patrai before the temple of Athena is the tomb of Preugenes.

375. 7.21.10 At Patrai one of the images of Aphrodite was dragged up a generation ago by fishermen.

376. 7.24.1 In the Aigion agora is the tomb of Talthybios; at Sparta also a barrow; both worshipped as for heroes [T.289].

377. 8.4.9 At Pergamum by the Kaikos is the tomb of Auge, a mound with a stone base, altars and the bronze statue of a naked woman on top.

378. 8.5.3 Laodike sent a *peplos* robe to Athena Alea at Tegea, with a dedication indicating her descent from Agapenor.

379. 8.9.3 At Mantinea is the tomb of Arkas, son of Kallisto, his bones brought from Mainalos at Delphi's instance.

380. 8.9.5 At Mantinea near the theatre is a round tomb called Common Hearth (*Hestia koine*), of Antinoe, daughter of Kepheus.

381. 8.11.1 Outside Mantinea are the tombs of the daughters of Pelias.

382. 8.11.4 At Phoizon is a tomb mound with a base of stone little above ground, the tomb of Areithoos called Korynetes because of his weapon (a club).

383. 8.12.2–4 Near Methydrion is a cave where Alkimedon lived, 'one of the heroes as they are called'. His daughter Phialo was seduced by Herakles. The child was exposed but Herakles heard it crying, like a jay, and the place is called Kissa ('jay').

384. 8.12.5–6 On the road to Orchomenos (Arcadia) is a tall mound, the tomb of Penelope, who had been turned out by Odysseus to die eventually in Mantinea. [Herodotus 2.146 has a different Penelope give birth to Pan in Arcadia.]

385. 8.12.9 The tomb of Anchises is at the foot of Mount Anchisia; buried there by Aineias en route from Troy to the west; no tomb of Anchises is shown at Troy.

386. 8.13.5 On Mount Trachy (Arcadia) is the tomb of Aristokrates who raped the priestess of Hymnia.

387. 8.14.5–7 At Pheneus is a bronze statue of Poseidon Hippios dedicated by Odysseus. Pausanias does not believe this because in those days no one could make a bronze image in a single piece.

388. 8.14.9 At Oineus is the tomb of Iphikles, brother of Herakles, on a hill. He died there wounded by Aktor.

389. 8.14.10 At Pheneus behind the temple of Hermes is the tomb of Myrtilos, charioteer of Oinomaos. [T.353, cenotaph at Olympia.]

390. 8.15.1–2 At Pheneus by the temple of Demeter is the Petroma, two stones fitted together, opened to take out writings recited for the Mysteries.

391. 8.15.5–6 On the road from Pheneus are the tombs of heroes who fought with Herakles against the Eleians: Telamon and Chalkodon (but not the better known heroes of those names).

392. 8.16.1 On Mount Geronteion are three springs where the nymphs washed the newborn Hermes.

393. 8.16.3 On Mount Sepia ia the tomb of Aipytos, mentioned by Homer in his lines on the Arcadians [*Iliad* 2.604], a mound with a stone base.

394. 8.17.6 West of Pheneus at Nonakris a very high cliff with a waterfall is known as the waters of the Styx.

395. 8.18.7 Above Nonakris is the cave where the daughters of Proitos fled in their madness.

396. 8.23.4 At Kaphyai (Arcadia) Menelaos planted a plane tree by a spring, both named after him. [T.514,596: planted by Agamemnon.]

397. 8.24.5 At Cumae in the temple of Apollo are the Erymanthian boar's tusks: quite improbable.

398. 8.24.6 At Psophis (Arcadia) are the ruins of the temple of Aphrodite Erykinia, founded by the sons of Psophis.

399. 8.24.7 At Psophis is the tomb of Alkmaion, son of Amphiaraos, murdered there; a building not large or ornate but with high cypresses around, called Parthenoi.

400. 8.24.10 The sons of Phegeus who killed Alkmaion dedicated the necklace of Eriphyle at Delphi. [But see T.18,476.]

401. 8.25.11 The River Ladon passes the sanctuary of the boy Asklepios where there is the tomb of Trygon, his nurse.

402. 8.29.4 When the River Orontes' bed was being dug out a clay coffin eleven cubits long was found and a giant body proportioned to the coffin. The Klaros oracle said it was of Orontes, an Indian. [Philostratus, *Heroicus* 8.3 has a body recently dug from the banks of the Orontes as a giant Aryades, thirty cubits tall; Strabo 750–751, Typhon, struck by bolts, formed the bed of the Orontes.]

403. 8.32.5 At Megalopolis in the sanctuary of Asklepios are superhuman bones, of one of the giants mustered by Hopladamos to defend Rhea.

404. 8.34.2–3 On the road to Messene is a mound surmounted by a stone finger (*Daktylou mnema*), where Orestes in his madness bit off a finger. Nearby, another place called Ake ('cures'), and another where he cut off his hair.

405. 8.35.8 At Krounoi (Arcadia) is the tomb of Kallisto on a high mound with many trees, on it a sanctuary of Artemis Kalliste [8.3.7].

406. 8.36.6 At Mainalos is the tomb of Oikles, father of Amphiaraos.

407. 8.44.8 Near Tegea is the tomb of Leukone, daughter of Aphidas, and a fountain.

408. 8.46 At Tegea, the image of Athena and Calydonian boar tusks were taken by Augustus after the defeat of Antony. 'He was not the first to carry off dedications and images of the gods from his defeated enemies, but followed a long tradition'. He lists such thefts:

> the Greeks from Troy, Sthenelos taking the wooden Zeus Herkeios; in Sicily Antiphemos, founder of Gela, took an image by Daidalos from the Sicanians; Xerxes in Attica took the Brauron image, and from Miletos the bronze Apollo from Branchidai; the Argives still have the images taken from Tiryns; the Cyzicenes took from Prokonnesos the image of Meter Dindymene (gold, with a face of hippopotamos ivory).

So Augustus practised an ancient custom, of Greeks and barbarians alike.

Of the Tegea tusks: those in charge of the curiosities say one is broken and the other in the imperial gardens in the sanctuary of Dionysos, half a fathom long. [In T.397 the Cumaeans alleged the tusks to be of the Erymanthian boar, not the Calydonian.]

409. 8.47.2–3 In the temple of Athena Alea at Tegea is the hide of the Calydonian boar, rotting and bare of bristles; also the rusty fetters of the Laconian captives who dug the plain of Tegea; also the shield of Marpessa who fought against the Laconians (8.48.5).

410. 8.47.4 North of the temple of Athena Alea is the spring where Auge was raped by Herakles.

411. 8.47.5 Athena gave some hair of Medusa to Kepheus, to guard the city. [Possibly kept: T.16.]

412. 8.48.6 At Tegea are the tombs of Tegeates and his wife Maira.

413. 8.53.10 At Tegea is the house of Aleus, and the tomb of Echemos, whose combat with Hyllos is on a relief slab.

414. 8.54.4 On the Tegea-Thyrea road is the tomb of Orestes, whence the Spartans took his bones.

415. 8.54.6 On Mount Parthenion is a sanctuary of Telephos, where he was exposed and fed by a doe.

416. 9.2.3 On the road from Megara is rock called Aktaion's bed, where he rested before spying on Artemis bathing [resulting in his death].

417. 9.2.4 On Kithairon is the Cleft Way (*Schiste hodos*) where Oidipous killed his father; but we do not know where Pentheus was killed or Oidipous exposed.

418. 9.4.3 At Plataia is the tomb of Leitos, the only Boeotian captain to return from Troy.

419. 9.5.14 At Elaia towards the Kaikos is the tomb of Thersandros slain by Telephos; it is a stone in the market place.

420. 9.8.3 On the Thebes road from Potniai is an enclosure with pillars in it where the earth opened for Amphiaraos; birds will not perch on the pillars nor beasts graze there.

421. 9.8.4 Amphion invented the chord of a lyre called *nete* at the Neistan Gate of Thebes (whence its name).

422. 9.10.1 Near the tomb of those fallen at Leuktra is the place where (believe if you will) Kadmos sowed the teeth of the dragon.

423. 9.10.3 At Thebes is the stone on which Manto, daughter of Teiresias, sat.

424. 9.10.4 At Thebes in the temple of Apollo Ismenios is the old tripod dedicated by Amphitryon for Herakles, who wore the bay at the festival. [See T.91.]

425. 9.10.5 At Thebes by the fountain guarded by a dragon set by Ares, is the tomb of Kaanthos, killed by Apollo.

426. 9.11.1 At Thebes by the Elektran Gate is the house of Amphitryon with Alkmene's bridal chamber in the ruins, labelled with an epigram.

427. 9.11.2 At Thebes is the tomb of the children Herakles had by Megara and killed by him in madness. Also the stone *sophronister* thrown at Herakles by Athena to bring him to his senses. [Cf. Euripides, *Herakles* 1002–1004.]

428. 9.11.5 On Ikaria is a mound where Herakles found the drowned Ikaros and buried him. The flying Ikaros story is not accepted.

429. 9.12.2 At Thebes is the place where Kadmos settled his army – where a marked cow lay down exhausted.

430. 9.12.3 At Thebes the house of Kadmos was in the present agora; also the ruins of the bridal chambers of Harmonia and Semele (no admission), and the place where the Muses sang at the wedding of Harmonia.

431. 9.12.4 The log that fell on the chamber of Semele at Thebes with the thunderbolt was covered with bronze by Polydoros who called it Dionysos Kadmos.

432. 9.16.1 At Thebes near the Ammon sanctuary is the observatory (*oionoskopeion*) of Teiresias [for taking omens]. [Cf. Sophocles, *Antigone* 999.]

433. 9.16.3 There are wooden images of Aphrodite at Thebes so old that they are said to have been dedicated by Harmonia, made from Kadmos' ship's timbers.

434. 9.16.5 The sanctuary of Demeter Thesmophoros at Thebes was once the house of Kadmos and his descendants; here are the bronze shields of the Spartan officers who fell at Leuktra.

435. 9.16.7 At Thebes Proitidian Gate are the ruins of the house of Lykos, and the tomb of Semele. There is no tomb of Alkmene because they say she was turned to stone.

436. 9.16.7 At Thebes are the tombs of the children of Amphion, sons separated from daughters. The ashes of their pyre are still visible half a stadion from the graves (9.17.2).

437. 9.17.1 Androkleia and Alkis are said to be buried in the sanctuary of Artemis Eukleia; they died instead of their father Antipoinos to save the city from Herakles and the Thebans.

438. 9.17.2 In front of the temple of Artemis Eukleia at Thebes is a stone lion dedicated by Herakles after victory over the Orchomenians and Erginos.

439. 9.17.4–7 The joint tomb of Amphion and Zethos is a small mound; its earth is sacred, and people of Tithoreia tried to steal it for their crops, to take to the tomb of Antiope, known as the tomb of Phokos, who shares her grave. The rough-hewn stones at the base of Amphion's tomb are those that followed his playing (like Orpheus and animals).

440. 9.18.1–3 On the Thebes-Chalkis road is the tomb of Melanippos; nearby are three unwrought stones marking the tomb of Tydeus, whose burial there is mentioned in the *Iliad* [14.114, as under heaped earth]. Next to this are the tombs of the children of Oidipous. The flames from sacrifices to them divide in two.

441. 9.18.4 At Pioniai in Mysia the tomb of Pionis sends up smoke before a sacrifice; he has seen it happen.

442. 9.18.4 On the Thebes-Chalkis road is the cenotaph of Teiresias, who died in Haliartia. [Cf. T.466.]

443. 9.18.5–6 At Thebes is the tomb of Hektor, brought from Troy in accord with an oracle; beside it the fountain of Oidipous, where he washed off the blood of his murdered father; and the tomb of Asphodikos, who slew Parthenopaios.

444. 9.19.2 At Glisas is the mound tomb of Promachos, son of Parthenopaios, and of other Argives who marched with Aigialeus, son of Adrastos, against Thebes.

445. 9.19.3 On the Thebes-Glisas road is a place enclosed by unhewn stones called Snakes' Head, where a snake emerged and was beheaded by Teiresias.

446. 9.19.3 At Teumessos is the tomb of Chalkodon, killed by Amphitryon in the battle between Thebans and Euboeans.

447. 9.19.7 At Aulis remains of the plane tree mentioned in the *Iliad* [2.305] are still in the temple of Artemis, also the spring beside which it grew, and on the hill nearby is the bronze threshold of Agamemnon's pavilion.

448. 9.20.3 At Tanagra is the tomb of Orion; Mount Kerykios where Hermes was born; and a place called Polos where Atlas sat and pondered, as described by Homer [*Odyssey* 1.52–54].

449. 9.20.4–5 At Tanagra in the temple of Dionysos is the Triton which attacked cattle and people, headless because

the women votaries of Dionysos cut it off, being threatened by it while they were having a purifying bath; or it was made drunk by Tanagraeans whose flocks were being taken, and decapitated.

450. 9.21 Pausanias saw another Triton in Rome, as big as the one at Tanagra. Tritons are described: head hair which resembles that of marsh frogs in colour and tangle, body scales like a shark's, gills, a humanoid nose, wide mouth and animal teeth, blue eyes (he thinks), hands, fingers and nails like shells, tail like a dolphin. He also saw rhinoceroses, Paionian bulls, Indian camels, elks, tigers, asps, winged snakes, winged scorpions.

451. 9.22.2 At Tanagra in the sanctuary of Hermes Promachos, is the wild strawberry tree under which he was nursed.

452. 9.22.6 At Anthedon are the tombs of the children of Iphimedeia and Aloeus, killed by Apollo.

453. 9.22.6–7 On the Anthedon coast is Glaukos' Leap, a fisherman turned into an oracular sea demon.

454. 9.24.3 At Hyettos the statue of Herakles in his temple is an unwrought stone, which heals.

455. 9.25.1 At Thebes by the Neistan Gate is the tomb of Menoikeus, son of Kreon, who slew himself when the Seven attacked, to save the city; on it a pomegranate tree whose fruit seems full of blood. Thebans say they were the first to grow a vine but have no memorial to show.

456. 9.25.2 At Thebes near the tomb of Menoikeus is the place where the sons of Oidipous [Eteokles and Polyneikes] fought and killed each other, marked by a stone pillar with a shield on it.

457. 9.25.2 At Thebes is shown the place where Hera gave suck to Herakles.

458. 9.25.2 At Thebes is a whole area called the Dragging (*Syrma*) of Antigone, where she dragged the corpse of Polyneikes to the pyre of Eteokles.

459. 9.26.2 Near Orchomenos is the Mountain of the Sphinx.

460. 9.29.8–9 Thebans say that Linos was buried in their land but his bones were taken by Philip to Macedonia, and after dreams returned. The tombstone and marker have disappeared.

461. 9.30.7,9,11 Near Dion is a pillar supporting a stone urn with the bones of Orpheus in it. Otherwise, they are at Libethra on Mount Olympos.

462. 9.31.3 On Helikon the oldest tripod dedicated is that won by Hesiod [*Erga* 654–659]. Higher is the fountain Hippokrene where Pegasos touched ground.

463. 9.31.4 On Helikon is a lead tablet on which is inscribed Hesiod's *Erga* poem.

464. 9.31.7 Near Thespiai is Donakon, the site of Narkissos' spring.

465. 9.32.4 At Tipha is the place where the Argo anchored on the return voyage; their townsman Tiphys was the pilot.

466. 9.33.1 The tomb of Teiresias is at Tilphousa spring where he drank and died.

467. 9.33.7 At Alalkomenai is a river Triton, where Athena was brought up, and not in Libya.

468. 9.34.4 Near Koronea are springs like women's breasts with water like milk, called Libethrias (by Mount Libethria) and Petra.

469. 9.34.5 On Mount Laphystios Herakles dragged up Kerberos.

470. 9.36.4 At Orchomenos is Minyas' stone treasury – described at 9.38.2 – stone, circular, rising to a not too narrow top, with a keystone. 9.38.3 – also the graves of Minyas, and of Hesiod, whose bones were brought back from Naupaktos to Orchomenos.

471. 9.37.7 At Lebadeia is the pit where Trophonios entered. [It becomes an important oracle.]

472. 9.38.1 At Orchomenos in the sanctuary of the Charites the stones that fell to Eteokles from heaven are worshipped.

473. 9.39.3 At Lebadeia is the tomb of Arkesilaos, brought back from Troy by Leitos.

474. 9.40.11–2 At Chaironeia is worshipped the sceptre made by Hephaistos for Zeus, whence to Hermes, Pelops, Atreus, Thyestes and Agamemnon. They call it Spear (*doru*), found on the Boeotian border with Phokis together with gold, brought there by Elektra. The priest keeps it at home, and sacrifices are offered to it daily. [9.41.1 – it is the only genuine work of Hephaistos surviving.]

475. 9.41.1 At Patara in the temple of Apollo is the bronze bowl dedicated by Telephos, said to be made by Hephaistos.

476. 9.41.2 At Amathus [Cyprus] in the sanctuary of Aphrodite and Adonis is the necklace of Eriphyle (once Harmonia's), dedicated at Delphi by the sons of Phegeus but carried off by the Phocian tyrants.

477. 10.4.4 At Panopeus on Parnassos are two stones of clay colour, smelling like flesh, the remains of that used by Prometheus to fashion men.

478. 10.4.5 At Panopeus on Parnassos is the tomb of Tityos, a third of a stadion in circumference. His 'nine *pelethra*' in the *Odyssey* [11.577] refer to the tomb, not him.

479. 10.4.10 At Tronis in Daulis the blood of sacrifice is poured through a hole into the grave of the hero founder (Xanthippos or Phokos).

480. 10.5.3–4 On Parnassos at the Cleft Way are the tombs of Laios and his servant, killed by Oidipous, in the middle of the road junction, with stones heaped on them. [See T.417.]

481. 10.8.8 At the Delphi gymnasium was once the wild wood where Odysseus was wounded by a boar. [*Odyssey* 19.428–466.]

482. 10.11.1 At Delphi no treasures are to be seen in any of the Treasuries.

483. 10.12.1,6,7 At Delphi is the rock of the Sibyl where she gave oracles; but she died in the Troad and her tomb is at the temple of Apollo Smintheus; while at Erythrai is the cave where Herophile (the Sibyl) was born.

484. 10.12.8 At Cumae is a small stone urn in the temple of Apollo with the Sibyl's bones.

485. 10.19.3 At Methymne (Lesbos) fishermen brought up a wooden face of rather foreign appearance; the oracle said it was Dionysos Phallen, and a bronze copy was sent to Delphi.

486. 10.24.3 On Ios they show the tomb of Homer and of his mother Klymene.

487. 10.24.4,6 In the Delphi temple is the hearth where the priest of Apollo slew Neoptolemos, whose tomb is near by. [10.26.4; the Cnidian Lesche painting was to be over the tomb.]

488. 10.24.6 Near the tomb of Neoptolemos is the small stone given to Kronos [by Rhea] instead of the child Zeus.

489. 10.26.5 Pausanias describes the ancient two-piece corselet types in the Lesche painting at Delphi.

490. 10.27.1 In Phrygia is the tomb of Mygdon.

491. 10.31.6–7 On the Hellespont the tomb of Memnon is visited by birds who clean it. He came from Susa and they show his road in Phrygia.

492. 10.35.2 The temples at Haliartos, of Hera at Athens and of Demeter at Phaleron, were burned by the Persians and left in ruins to Pausanias' day.

493. 10.36.10 At Antikyra is the rubble tomb of the sons of Iphitos, one returned from Troy.

494. 10.38.5 At Amphissa are the tombs of Amphissa and Andraimon, with his wife Gorgo.

495. 10.38.5–6 At Amphissa the bronze image of Athena was brought from Troy as spoils by Thoas; Pausanias does not believe in bronze casting before Rhoikos and Theodoros of Samos [mid 6th-century].

Phaenias (4th cent. BC). Of Eresos (Lesbos), pupil of Aristotle. See T.49.

Phanocles (3rd cent. BC). Poet. See T.103.

Pherecydes (5th cent. BC). Athenian historian and genealogist.

496. *FGrH* 3,F38 Niobe prays to be turned into stone, and weeps.

Philostratus (2nd/3rd cent. AD). Of Lemnos, biographer of philosophers and mythographer. Also T.97,402.

Heroicus

497. 7.9 The grave of Ajax near Rhoiteion has a skeleton 16 feet tall, reburied by Hadrian at Troy.

498. 8.13–17 Various massive skeletons worldwide, including those identified as of Hyllos, of the Aloadai in Thessaly, at Phlegra (Pozzuoli) of Alkyoneus and other Giants buried by Vesuvius, at Pallene. Herakles dedicated Geryon's bones at Olympia. [Bones to Olympia, Schol. Lycophron, *Alexandra* 663.]

499. [= Apollonius Tyan. (1st cent. AD) 68K; Pfister, 405] The tomb (*kolonos*) of Achilles in the Troad, with stele.

Phlegon (2nd cent. AD). A freedman of Hadrian, historian.

De mirabilibus [W. Hansen, *Phlegon of Tralles' Book of Marvels* (1996)]

500. 11 In Messene a storage jar broken by a storm was found, labelled Idas, and containing three skulls and two jawbones. They were identified with Homer's Idas, the strongest man on earth, and kept as relics in a new jar. 11–19 the finds of giant bones.

501. 17 An island near Athens [Makronisi?; Mayor, 153, suggests the islet Phaura] was to be fortified. Digging for foundations revealed a coffin 100 cubits long with a withered body in it and an inscription naming it Makroseiris.

502. 34, 35. Description of the *hippokentauroi* sent from Arabia to Caesar in Egypt.

Pindarus (5th cent. BC). Boeotian poet who wrote hymns and victory songs. Also T.255,557,574,586.

503. *Olympia* 1.90–93; 10.24 The tomb of Pelops near the altar at Olympia.

Plato (4th cent. BC). Athenian philosopher, interpreter of Socrates, founder of the Academy in Athens. Also T.123,506.

Phaidon

504. 58A,B The ship sent annually to Delos is said by the Athenians to be Theseus'. [Also Plutarch, *Theseus* 23: preserved until the late 4th cent. but the parts regularly replaced.]

Phaidros

505. 264D Epitaph on the tomb of Midas: 'A maid of bronze I stand on Midas' tomb...'.

506. [Plato], *Axiochos* 371a The Hyperborean maidens brought inscribed bronze tablets to Delos which dealt with the fate of the soul after death.

Pliny (1st cent. AD). Roman polymath and encyclopaedist. Also T.97,101,346,596.

Historia Naturalis

507. 4.53 The rock into which Odysseus' ship was turned [*Odyssey* 13.163] is observed at Cape Drasti opposite Kerkyra.

508. 9.9 A Triton playing a conch shell in a cave was reported to the emperor Tiberius from Lisbon, also a Nereid on the same coast; and to Augustus, dead Nereids on the shore in Gaul.

509. 9.11 The skeleton of the sea-monster to which Andromeda was exposed was brought to Rome from Joppa by M. Scaurus: 40 feet long, ribs bigger than an elephant's, spine 1.5 feet thick.

510. 10.5 A phoinix [mythical bird] flew into Egypt [AD 47] and was shown in Rome, but universally regarded as a fake.

511. 11.111 Ants as big as a wolf at Dardae in north India dig out gold from caves in the winter, which is stolen by the Indians in the summer. Their horns are shown in the temple of Herakles at Erythrai.

512. 12.11 Zeus made love to Europe under a plane tree at Gortyn in Crete. [It never loses its leaves: Theophrastus, *Historia Plantarum* 1.9.5.]

513. 13.88 A letter (*charta*, papyrus) of Sarpedon from Troy, is to be seen in a temple in Lycia.

514. 16.238 Plane trees were planted by Agamemnon at Delphi and Kaphyai (Arcadia). An oak tree is on the tomb of Ilos at Troy [also Theophrastus, *Historia Plantarum* 4.13.2].

515. 16.239 At Argos is the tree to which Argos tethered Io. Two oak trees were planted at Herakleia Pontica for Zeus Stratios. The tumulus of King Bebryx at the Port of Amykos is covered with bay.

516. 16.240 The plane tree on which Marsyas was hung for flaying is at Aulokrene on the road from Apameia. At Olympia the olive is still venerated from which Herakles cut his wreath. Athena's olive lives still in Athens. 16.251 – Pliny lists other venerable trees not associated with persons.

517. 28.34 At Olympia there used to be the shoulder blade of Pelops, of ivory, with healing powers.

518. 33.81 In the temple of Athena at Lindos is an electrum cup given by Helen, the size of her breast (*mammae suae mensura*).

519. 36.14 In Paros a split stone showed the features of Silenos. [36.134–5, in Spain, one with the image of a palm branch.]

520. 36.99 In the Kyzikos Prytaneion is the Argonauts'

anchor, 'runaway stone' (*lapis fugitivus*), which has to be held down with lead. [Apollonius Rhodius, 1.955–960: they left there their small anchor, eventually in the temple of Athena, taking a heavier one; Callimachus, *Aetia* fr. 109.]

521. 37.4 Polykrates' famous ring, recovered in a fish, is a sardonyx, set in a gold horn and displayed in the temple of Concord in Rome, given by Livia. [The story in Herodotus 3.41–42, is of a *smaragdos* (not necessarily emerald) set in a gold ring.]

522. 37.170 The Idaean Dactyls of Crete [miners of iron in myth] are thumb-shaped iron-coloured stones [Mayor, 275 – probably belemnites, fossil cuttlefish.].

Plutarchus (1st/2nd cent. AD). Of Chaironeia, biographer and man of letters. Also T.87,123,504.

de genio Socratis

523. 577e,f, 578e,f The tomb of Alkmene was opened at Haliartos before the remains were taken to Sparta at the command of Agesilaos. It contained only a stone, a bronze bracelet and two pots of compacted earth. Before the tomb was a bronze tablet with a long inscription, like Egyptian. It was sent to Egypt, and read, but the text not revealed.

524. 578f–579a Another document was sent to Egypt and deciphered – orders for a contest for the Muses. It was in a script of the period of King Proteus, learned by Herakles.

525. ibid. The tomb of Dirke at Thebes is known only to the hipparch, who shows it only to his successor. [Cf. T.17.]

Parallela minora

526. 6 Amphiaraos' spear was picked up from a feast by an eagle which dropped it, where it took root, at the place where the hero disappeared.

Quaestiones Graecae

527. 45 Hippolyte's axe was given to Omphale by Herakles, whence it became part of the regalia of Lydian royalty; it was taken by Arselis, ally of Gyges, and dedicated to Zeus at Labraunda (whence Zeus Labraundeus carries an axe).

528. 56 Dionysos fought the Amazons and pursued them from Ephesos to Samos, slaughtering them at Panaima ['all-blood']. The bones of some his elephants were found at Phloion ['crust' of earth?] which they had broken through with great roaring. [The text is faulty; see also T.2.].

Vitae

529. *Alexander* 15 Alexander was offered a view of Paris' lyre at Troy, but said he would prefer Achilles'. [Also Aelian, *Variae Historiae* 9.38.]

530. *Cimon* 8, and *Theseus* 36 Kimon brought the bones of Theseus from Skyros to Athens; a gigantic skeleton found, beside it a bronze spear and sword.

531. *Marcellus* 20 At Engyion in the temple of the Mother are the spear and helmet of Odysseus.

532. *Sertorius* 9 At Tingis (Tangier) is the burial mound of the giant Antaios [killed by Herakles], excavated by Sertorius who found a skeleton 60 cubits long [also Strabo 829, at Lynx/Lixos in Morocco].

533. *Solon* 4 Helen's gold tripod is in the temple of Apollo at Thebes. It had been thrown overboard by Helen and fished up by Milesians.

534. *Theseus* 12 The house of Aigeus was at the temple of Apollo Delphinios in Athens.

535. 26 The house of Hermos, a companion of Theseus, is at Pythopolis in Bithynia.

536. 27 Details are given of the topography of Theseus' battle with the Amazons in Athens, with an Amazoneion camp by the Areiopagos. Hippolyte's tomb is marked by a *stele*. Some say that Antiope moved the wounded to Chalcis where they were buried at the Amazoneion. The *horkomosion* near the Theseion in Athens is where Theseus made a treaty with the Amazons. Megara shows Amazon graves at Rhous; others were said to be buried near Chaironeia on the banks of the Haimon (once called Thermodon; cf. his *Demosthenes* 19). Graves are pointed out in Thessaly near Skotoussa and the hills of Kynoskephalai.

Polemon (2nd cent. BC). Of Troy; he was called a tablet-glutton (*stelokopas*) for his obsession with copying inscriptions (Herakleides in Athenaeus 234d). See T.52.

Pollux (2nd cent. AD). Of Naucratis, philologist.

Onomastikon

537. 5.45 Lists the tombs of dogs: of Hekabe turned into a dog at Kynossema, the dog of Atalante at Kalydon, of Geryon in Spain, of Hippaimon in Thessaly.

Polyaenus (2nd cent. AD). Of Macedon, military historian.

Strategemata

538. 6.53 When the Athenians founded Amphipolis they were told to return the bones of Rhesos from Troy to his home.

Procopius (6th cent. AD). Born in Palestine, a Byzantine historian.

De Bello Gothico

539. 4.22 He finds incredible the size of Aineias' ship displayed in a shipshed in Rome.

540. 5.15.8 The tusks of the Calydonian boar are at Beneventum, three handspans round.

Ptolemaeus Chennus (1st/2nd cent. AD). Of Alexandria, mythographer.

Kaine historia

541. (In Photius, *Bibliotheca* 147a-b) The Nemean Lion bit off one of Herakles' fingers, which he buried in Sparta, beneath a stone lion.

Seleucus (1st cent. AD). Of Alexandria, wrote commentaries on classical works. See T.54.

Sencca (1st cent. AD). Born in Spain, worked in Rome; a man of letters. See T.81.

Servius (4th cent. AD). Roman grammarian and commentator.

in Virgilium commentarius

542. *ad Aen.* 2.116 The statue of Artemis from Tauri is at Aricia in Italy.

543. 8.278 Herakles' wooden cup is preserved in pitch, and used in ritual in the Forum Boarium in Rome.

Solinus (2nd/3rd cent. AD). Compiler of geographical items; introduced the term 'Mediterranean'. Also T.550.

Collectanea rerum memorabilium

544. 1.11 Herakles' club was dedicated by Euander in his temple in the Forum Boarium; dogs run from its smell.

545. 9.6 In Pallene, site of the battle of gods and giants, massive bones are found washed out by streams.

546. 11.17 Homer's tomb (*tumulus*) is in Chios.

Sophocles (5th cent. BC). One of the three great Athenian tragedians. See T.131,432.

Stephanus Byzantius (6th cent. AD). Grammarian and encyclopaedist.

547. 'Suessa'. At the Letoon near Xanthos in Lycia is the hut in which Suessa received Leto.

Stobaeus (5th cent. AD). Anthologist. See T.103.

Strabo (1st cent. BC). Born in Amasos (south shore of Black Sea); historian and geographer. Also T.27, 38, 59, 87, 132, 177, 341, 344, 402, 532.

Geographia

548. 138 [= Artemidorus, 2nd cent. BC] At the westernmost Sacred Cape of Spain are Herakles' 'rocking stones' in groups of three or four.

549. 149–150 In the west (Italy, Sicily, Spain) are many traces of Odysseus and other Greek heroes of the period after the Trojan War; also of Trojans, as Aineias, Diomedes. [He takes them as historical figures.]

550. 157 [= Artemidorus, 2nd cent. BC] At Odysseia in Spain in the temple of Athena are the shield and sternpost of Odysseus. [Solinus 23 seems to place this at Lisbon.]

551. 179–180 The *xoanon* of Artemis was taken to Massilia by the Phocaeans, then copied for Rome.

552. 182–183 A stony plain in Liguria [*la plaine de la Crau*] is covered with the stones supplied to Herakles by Zeus as ammunition against the natives. [The story in Aeschylus, *Prometheus Unbound* fr. 112 Lloyd-Jones.]

553. 215 In the precincts of Diomedes among the Heneti wild animals are tame, deer run with wolves.

554. 232 At Kirkaion near Antium, where there is an altar of Athena, the *phiale* of Odysseus is shown.

555. 245 A mole at Baiae eight stadia long, and of wagon-width, is said to have been built by Herakles, driving Geryon's cattle. The foul exhalations of Phlegra near Cumae [seismic] are from the wounds of giants blitzed by Zeus. [See also T.561.]

556. 247 On a cape at Surrenton [Sorrento] is a temple for Athena built by Odysseus.

557. 248 The eruptions of fire and hot water at Pithekoussai [Ischia] are the buried Typhon, turning his body. Pindar [*Pythia* 1. 15–28, and fr. 240 Bowra] has Typhon beneath earth and sea from Cumae to Sicily and Etna [all volcanic].

558. 252 The temple of Hera on the River Silaris was built by Jason.

559. 256 Hipponion in Sicily abounds in flowers, where Kore was when she was taken by Hades.

560. 264 Herakleia on the River Siris was founded by the Trojans and has the wooden statue of the Trojan Athena, which closed its eyes when the town was taken by Ionian refugees [as the statue was said to have done at Troy, at the rape of Kassandra]. Other Trojan Athenas in Italy are at Rome, Lavinium, Luceria.

561. 281 At Leuka [tip of Iapygia] the giants who survived Phlegra [T.555], called Leuternioi, were covered by earth, whence a stream of foul water from their ichor [divine blood].

562. Fr. VII.1c The sacred oak at Dodona is the oldest of all plants created, and the first to supply men with food.

563. Fr.VII.43 Near Abdera is seen the palace of Diomedes [Thracian].

564. 345 The temple of Samian Poseidon near Pylos is where Telemachos landed.

565. 346 At Triphylia is the seashore cave related to the daughters of Atylas and the birth of Dardanos. In the River Anigros the fish are inedible because here the centaurs washed their wounds, poisoned by the Hydra's blood on Herakles' arrows; or, because here Melampous purified the daughters of Proitos (the water cures leprosy). [Repeated in Pausanias T.344, naming the centaurs Cheiron and Pylenor.]

566. 347 Between the River Anigros and the mountains is the tomb of Iardanos.

567. 348 The River Neda was made by Rhea to bathe infant Zeus.

568. 371 The Danaides found wells for Argos, four of them deemed sacred, and at Lerna. [Hesiod fr. 128 West: they make waterless Argos watered.]

569. 371 Danaos' tomb is in the agora of Argos.

570. 371–3 The Kyklopes built Tiryns for Proitos, coming from Lycia. They also probably made the caves at Nauplia and the works within them (369, 'built *labyrinthoi*').

571. 377 Eurystheus is buried at Gargettos, his head at *Eurystheos kephale* by the spring Makaria.

572. 379 The spring Hippokrene on Helikon was produced by being struck by Pegasos' hoof; and the spring Peirene on Acrocorinth was where Pegasos was caught.

573. 396 [= Hegesias, 3rd cent. BC, *FGrH* 142, F24] The mark of Poseidon's trident on Athens' Acropolis.

574. 421 The tomb of Neoptolemos is at Delphi. [Also Pindar, *Nemea* 7.50–52.]

575. 423 Near Panopeus is the cave of Elara, mother of Tityos by Zeus.

576. 427 The hill Taphiassos in Lokris has the tombs of Nessos and other centaurs, from whose putrified bodies flows a smelly and clotted stream at the base of the hill.

577. 445 The *Boos aule* cave on Euboea is where Io gave birth to Epaphos.

578. 487 Under Mykonos lies the last of the giants killed by Herakles.

579. 489 Poseidon crushed the giant Polybotes with a fragment of the island of Kos, which became then Nisyros; some say the giant lies beneath Kos.

580. 495 By the temple of Aphrodite Apatouros at Phanagoria is the cave where she hid Herakles, leading to him the giants who had attacked her, to be slaughtered.

581. 587 Ganymede was snatched by Zeus at Harpagia in the Troad.

582. 595–6 Ajax's grave and shrine is at Rhoiteion opposite Elaious [where Protesilaos is buried]. Near Sigeion is the shrine and grave of Achilles, and graves of Patroklos and Antilochos, to whom offerings are made, as also to Ajax. At Kebrenia are the graves of Oinone and Alexandros (Paris).

583. 597 In the Trojan plain are the places named by Homer – the figtree [*Iliad* 6.433 etc.], the tomb of Aisyetes [2.793, a landfall], Batieia [2.811–14] and the tomb of Ilos [10.415].

584. 599 No trace of the ancient [Homeric] city of Troy remains today.

585. 613 The tomb mound of Killas, charioteer of Pelops, is at Killa (near Adramyttion).

586. 626–8 He quotes Pindar [see T.557] for the body of Typhon lying beneath Etna in Sicily. In Mysia there is a volcanic area, Katakaumene [upper Hermos valley], also associated with the Typhon story [= Xanthus of Lydia, 5th cent. BC, *FGrH* 765, F13].

587. 630–631 At Termessos are the *charax* [camp?] of Bellerophon and grave of his son Peisandros who fought the Solymoi.

588. 633 At the Posideion (Ionia) the altar built by Neleus is to be seen.

589. 636 Near Latmos is the tomb of Endymion in a cave.

590. 639 At Ortygia near Ephesos is the place where Leto gave birth and the olive tree where she rested.

591. 665 Describes the Chimaera gorge and setting for the Chimaera story.

592. 668 A cave in the Hindu Kush is the alleged alternative setting for Herakles' freeing of Prometheus.

593. 755 On the Makra plain in Phoenicia was a fallen dragon, a plethron (100 feet) long, its jaws big enough to admit a horseman, scales bigger than shields.

Suetonius (1st/2nd cent. AD). Roman biographer, born in Numidia.

de Vita Caesarum

594. *Augustus* 72 Augustus collected bones of land and sea monsters known as Giants' Bones, in Capri, and the weapons of ancient heroes.

Theocritus (4th/3rd cent. BC). Born in Syracuse but worked in Alexandria; pastoral and epic poet.

Idyllia

595. VII.6–7 Chalkon [Chalkodon?] kicks the spring Bourina into action on Kos.

Theophrastus (4th cent. BC). Of Eresos (Lesbos), pupil and successor of Aristotle, scientific philosopher. Also T.512,514.

Historia Plantarum

596. 4.13.2 Mentions various long-lived trees associated with divinity or heroes: the olive at Athens, the palm at Delos, the olive at Olympia, oak trees on the tomb of Ilos at Troy, a plane at Delphi planted by Agamemnon, also at Kaphyai (Arcadia). [For Ilos: *Iliad* 11.371–372; Pliny, *Historia Naturalis* 16.238.]

597. 5.8.3 The tomb of Elpenor, at Kirkaion promontory, grows myrtle. [Cf. *Odyssey* 12.9–15, tomb marked by an oar.]

Thucydides (5th cent. BC). Athenian historian of the Peloponnesian War, in which he had served as general.

Historiae

598. 1.8 Graves on Delos are recognized as Carian by the arms found in them and the mode of burial, still practised.

599. 1.10.2 Comments that if only the temples and ground-plan of Sparta were preserved, later ages would not be willing to believe how powerful the city was; while ruined Athens would give an exaggerated impression of her power.

Timonax (4th/3rd cent. BC). Historian.

600. [Schol. Apollonius Rhodius 4.1217] Argonauts dedicate their disci in Colchis, where there is also Medea's wedding chamber.

Tzetzes (12th cent. AD). Byzantine commentator.

601. [Schol. Lycophron, *Alexandra* 50–51] The springs of Thermopylai are hot because Herakles threw himself into the water to cool off.

Virgil (1st cent. BC). Born near Mantua, Roman epic and pastoral poet.

602. *Georgics* 1.493–497 The time will come when farmers on the Thracian frontier will plough up old rusty spears and helmets, and marvel at the big bones from graves.

Xanthus of Lydia (5th cent. BC). Historian. See T.586.

Xenophanes (6th cent. BC). Of Colophon, lived in Sicily; philosopher. See T.87.

Xenophon (4th cent. BC). Athenian, soldier and historian.

603. *Hellenica* 6.4.7 Before the battle of Leuktra the doors

of the temples of Thebes opened, and the arms of Herakles disappeared from his temple, showing that he had set out for the battle.

604. *Anabasis* 1.2.13 By the road at Thymbrion is the spring of Midas, where he caught Silenos.

Inscriptions

605. *The Lindos Chronicle* (National Museum, Copenhagen). [Chr. Blinkenberg, *Lindos* II. Inscriptions Vol. 1 (Berlin/Copenhagen, 1941) 148–199]. Illustrated in our *Fig. 5*.

Dedications to Athena Polias (and Zeus Polieus)

Myth-historical dedications:

B.1 Lindos [founder] dedicated a phiale of unknown composition.

B.2 The Telchines dedicated a pot (*krosos*) as a tithe.

B.3 Kadmos dedicated a bronze lebes inscribed in Phoenician letters. [Also Diodorus 5.58.3.]

B.4 Minos dedicated a silver cup.

B.5 Herakles dedicated two shields, one covered with leather, one with bronze, of Eurypylos [killed at Kos] and Laomedon of Troy.

B.6 Tlapolemos [Rhodian king killed by Sarpedon at Troy, with a *heroon* on Rhodes] dedicated a phiale.

B.7 Rhesos [Thracian king at Troy] dedicated a gold cup.

B. 8 Telephos dedicated a gold omphalos-phiale, a *hilarion* to Athena.

B.9 The nine crews who sailed with Tlapolemos to Troy dedicated panoplies: shields, daggers, helmets, pairs of greaves; spoils of Troy.

B.10 Menelaos dedicated Alexandros' (Paris') helmet.

B.11 Helen [worshipped in Rhodes as *dendritis*] dedicated a pair of bracelets.

B.12 Kanopos, Menelaos' steersman, dedicated steering oars.

B.13 Meriones dedicated a silver quiver, spoils from Troy.

B.14 Teukros dedicated a quiver.

Historical dedications:

B.15 The original tribes dedicated plaques (*pinakes*) bearing the figure of the *phylarchos* and nine runners, each named, in archaic dress or posture (*schema*).

B.16 Aretakritos [unknown] and his sons dedicated a crater stand.

B.17 The sons of Lindian Pankis who colonized Cyrene

with Battos [about 570 BC] dedicated an Athena and Herakles strangling the lion, as a tithe from spoils.

C. 23 Kleoboulos' [6th cent.] army, from an assault on Lycia, dedicated eight shields and a gold crown for the statue.

C. 24 The men of Phaselis [Lindian colony] dedicated helmets and sabres (*drepana*) from victory over the Solymoi [7th cent.?].

C.25 The men of Gela [Lindian colony] dedicated a large crater, from victory over Araitos [unknown].

C.26 Amphinomos and sons of Sybaris [so pre-510 BC] dedicated a wooden cow [more likely than a bull] and calf, for escape from shipwreck.

C.27 Phalaris, tyrant of Akragas [mid-6th cent.], dedicated a relief crater showing a Titanomachy, and Kronos taking the children of Rhea, a gift of Daidalos to Kokalos [Daidalos was said to have fortified Kamikos for Kokalos].

C.28 Deinomenes, founder of Gela [6th cent.] with Antiphamos, dedicated a cypress-wood Gorgon with a stone face, a tithe from Sicilian spoils.

C.29 Amasis, king of Egypt [around 570 BC], dedicated a linen corselet, each fastener (*harpedon*) having 360 threads [thus Herodotos 2.182, adding two stone statues, and 3.47]. Xenagoras adds the statues and ten phialai, the statues inscribed in both Greek and Egyptian.

C.30 The Akragantines dedicated a palladion with ivory extremities, from spoils of Minoa [about 500 BC].

C.31 Pollis tyrant of Syracuse [6th cent.?] dedicated two 'Daidaleia' [viz., archaic] statues.

C.32 Artaphernes, the Persian general [490 BC] dedicated earrings, collar, headdress (*tiara*), bracelets, a sword and boots.

C.33 Soloi [which had Lindian settlers] dedicated a silver phiale with a gilt gorgon at the centre, spoils from victory.

C.34 The Lindians, as a tithe from spoils from Crete, dedicated a gold wreath, necklace and other jewellery for the statue.

C.35 The demos, from gifts of the Persian king Artaxerxes [4th cent.] dedicated a gold collar, headdress (*tiara*), an inlaid (*lithokollon*) sword, inlaid gold jewellery, weighing 1375 gold coins, and the royal raiment (*stola*).

C.36 The Lindians dedicated as a *charisterion* a gold Nike weighing 1300 staters.

C.37 The demos dedicated a shield for success in war against Ptolemy Philadephos [3rd cent.].

C.38 King Alexander [the Great] dedicated bulls' heads for his success in Asia; and arms.

C.39 King Ptolemy [I?] dedicated bucrania.

C.40 King Pyrrhos [3rd cent.] dedicated bulls' heads, and arms.

C.41 King Hieron [3rd cent.] dedicated arms.

C.42 King Philip [V; late 3rd cent.] dedicated ten peltas, sarissas and helmets, from victory over Dardanians and Maidians.

Apparitions (*epiphaneiai*) of the goddess, promoting gifts:

D.1 In the Persian siege [490 BC] Datis sends his personal gear (*kosmos*), cloak, collar, jewellery, tiara, sword and chariot, all burnt in the temple fire.

Names and Places in the Testimonia

References are to T. numbers. # indicates that the reference is to a burial, and + precedes references to temples or the like, set at the end of each entry

The index to the main text appears before the Testimonia on pp. 205–208

Abaris 294
Abdera 563
Acheron, R. 129
Achilles 6#, 10, 48, 49, 78, 157, 283, 318, 359, 499#, 503, 529, 582#
Adonis + 476
Adrastos 5, 190, 217, 238, 444
Adriatic 27–8, 38
Aeschylus 104
Agamemnon 5, 57, 218#, 305#, 313, 396, 447, 474, 514, 596
Agapenor 378
Agathokles 42
Agdistis, Mt. 126
Agesilaos 523
Agyrion 67
Aiakidai 93, 96, 128, 255#
Aiakos 96, 255#
Aigaleus 190#, 444
Aigeus 266, 534
Aigina 93, 96, 255
Aigion 289, 376
Aigisthos 218#
Aigyptos 244#(sons)
Aineias 240, 385, 539, 549; + 77
Aipytos 329, 393#
Aisyetes 583#
Aithalia 38
Aithra 269
Aitolos 342#
Ajax 156#, 157#, 158#, 497#, 582#
Akrisios 241, 248
Aktaion 191, 416
Aktor 388
Alalkomenai 467
Aleus 413
Alexander the Great 46, 529, 605(38)
Alkathoos 176, 179, 181, 184; + 183
Alkimedon 383
Alkis 437#
Alkmaion 18, 50, 399, 400
Alkmene 53, 172#, 426, 435#, 523#
Alkyoneus 498#
Aloadai 498#
Aloeus 452#(children)
Alope 170#
Alps 64
Amaltheia 351
Amathus 476

Amazons 68, 79, 81, 98#, 123#, 174#, 267, 528, 536#
Amphiaraos 154, 212, 230, 238, 277, 288, 399, 406, 420, 526
Amphion 421, 436#(children), 439#
Amphipolis 538
Amphissa 494#
Amphissa (place) 494–5
Amphitryon 53, 91, 172#, 424, 426, 446
Amyklai 23, 218, 280, 305
Amykos Port 515
Amymone 276
Anax 159
Anchises 385#
Anchisia, Mt. 385
Andraimon 365#, 494#
Androgeus + 121
Androkleia 437#
Androklos 346#
Andromeda 101, 509
Anigros, R. 344, 565–6
Ankyra 124–5
Antaios 532#
Anthedon 452–3
Antigone 458
Antikyra 493
Antilochos 582#
Antinoe 380#
Antiope 123#, 167, 439#, 536
Antipoinos 437
Antium 554
Apameia 516
Aphareus 286#, 299, 329
Aphidas 407
Aphrodite 44, 72, 82, 246, 292, 395, 433; + 264, 398, 476, 580
Apollo 26, 100, 176, 425, 452; + 5, 18, 39, 49, 50, 76, 79, 89, 91, 103, 206–8, 210, 222, 260–1, 280, 397, 424, 475, 484, 533–4; and s.v. Delphi
Aras 211#
Areithoos 382#
Ares 246, 306, 425; + 267
Argive Heraion 81, 219, 220
Argonauts 5, 21, 38, 69, 70, 103, 306, 317, 465, 520, 600
Argos 220, 234#, 515
Argos (place) 4, 55, 221–46, 515, 568–9
Ariadne 242#

Aricia 542
Aristeas 19
Aristokrates 386#
Aristomenes 327–9, 330#
Arkas 379#
Arkesilaos 473#
Arpi 109
Artemis 38, 59, 61, 138, 203, 232, 416, 542, 551; + 42, 51, 89, 210, 256–7, 259, 303, 345, 358, 405, 437–8, 447
Aryades 402#
Asklepios 251–2; + 209, 283, 312, 401, 403
Asopos, R. 312–3
Asphodikos 443#
Asterios 159#
Astykrateia 184#
Atalante 315, 537
Athena 5, 10, 14, 16, 66, 80, 95, 127, 140, 142, 144, 232, 287, 408, 411, 427, 467, 495, 516, 520, 560; + 40–1, 55, 85, 105, 110, 127–8, 141, 210, 243, 313, 317, 373, 378, 409, 518, 520, 550, 554, 556, 605
Athens, Acropolis 10, 52, 82, 92, 95, 106, 137, 139–43, 573
Athens 10, 24, 68, 120, 123, 131–3, 135–6, 144–6, 148, 282, 501, 516, 520, 534, 536, 596, 599
Atlas 448
Atreus 218#, 474
Attis 126#
Atylas 565
Auge 377#, 410
Augeias 214
Aulis 57, 447
Aulokrene 516
Autonoe 191#
Avernus 65

Baiae 555
Balearics 32
Balyra, R. 332
Bargylos 7
Bebryx 515#
Bellerophon 587
Beneventum 540
Bias 230
Boiai 314

Subjects in the Testimonia

References are to T. numbers

animals – 8 (cicadas), 9 (frogs), 10 (crow), 27 (birds), 30, 36 (dog), 42 (stag), 61 (fish), 105 (boar), 111 (nightingales), 127 (shearwater), 176 (hoopoe), 194 (turtle), 196 (dolphin), 309 (horse), 313 (ass), 314 (hare), 326 (boar), 335 (crow), 339 (cows), 383 (jay), 397 (boar), 408–9 (boar), 415 (doe), 420, 429 (cow), 445 (snake), 491 (birds), 511 (ants), 528 (elephants), 537 (dogs), 540 (boar), 553 (wild/tame). *See also* bones

arms and armour – 38, 41, 46, 157, 283, 350, 598, 602–3, 605(9); axe 41, 517; bow 5, 22, 39, 346, 545; club 263, 382, 544; corselet 5, 22–3, 489; helmet 531, 605(10); quiver 605 (13,14); shield 5, 55, 76, 110, 128, 219, 222, 327, 330, 409, 434, 550, 605(5); spear 208, 283, 526, 530–1; sword/dagger 5, 49, 59, 147, 283, 351, 530

bones – monstrous 1, 2, 100, 102, 105, 158–60, 209, 312, 345–6, 402–3, 497–8, 500–1, 509, 517, 528, 530, 532, 545, 593–4; moved 54, 72, 86, 120, 130, 281–2, 295, 324, 330, 346, 352, 361, 364, 379, 414, 443, 460, 470, 473, 530, 538; 'petrified' 25, 114

caves 29, 73, 75, 153, 167, 215, 237, 316, 339, 368, 383, 395, 445, 471, 483, 565, 570, 575, 577, 580, 589, 592

cenotaph 227, 239, 353, 359, 442

chariot 47, 213

coffin 86, 242, 402, 501

dice 83, 225

disci 38, 348, 600

discoloration, smells, putridity – 34 (sea), 38 (pebbles), 112 (river), 113 (women), 117 (river), 337 (sea), 344 (river), 544 (club), 555 (fumes), 557 (sea), 561 (river), 565 (river), 576 (river)

dress 5, 18, 79, 81, 110, 197, 378

earthquakes, faults, volcanoes 1, 132, 557, 586

egg 301

equipment – 5 (loom), 40 (tools), 308 (mill)

fetters 85, 101, 409

flood 106, 132, 233

footprints 34, 67, 88, 90, 107

fountains/springs/wells/lakes 17, 48, 57, 63, 65–7, 78, 125, 151, 154, 166–8, 200, 203, 217–8, 262, 265, 277, 315, 320, 331, 340, 368, 392, 396, 410, 425, 442–3, 447, 464, 466, 468

furniture – 84 (throne), 141 (chair), 219 (couch), 222 (throne), 258 (chairs), 347 (throne), 348 (couch)

hair 16, 59, 184, 367, 371, 404, 411

inscriptions 5, 26, 44, 47, 70, 77, 91, 162, 185, 252, 275, 328, 348–9, 351, 378, 390, 424, 462–3, 506, 513, 523–4

jewellery 18, 42, 50, 80–1, 400, 476, 521, 523, 605(11)

landscape and natural features 10, 31, 87, 114–5, 134, 193–4, 251, 270, 394, 453, 459, 465, 507, 573, 579

mines 25, 511

money 32

monsters 1, 2, 12, 60, 62, 100, 422, 425, 449, 450, 502, 508, 510, 576, 593

music/instruments – 3 (Phrygian), 5 (pipes), 58 (Orpheus' head), 103 (Orpheus' head, lyre), 118 (pipes, kithara), 119 (singing statue), 176 (lyre), 177 (musical statue), 208 (pipes), 291 (kithara), 421 (lyre), 430 (Muses' song), 529 (lyre)

oaths 131, 232, 309, 326, 536

omphalos 75, 100, 212

pots and containers – 5 (chest, AE cauldron), 7 (iron cage), 16 (AE jar), 51 (Nestor's cup), 52 (theriklea), 53 (*karchesion*), 69 (phialai), 77 (AE bowls), 84 (AV,AR cups), 100 (cauldron), 110 (crater), 204 (water basin), 232 (AE pot), 328 (AE), 333 (AE), 358 (AE), 372 (wood?), 475 (AE), 500 (stone), 518 (EL mastos), 543 (wood), 554 (phiale), 605 (1–4,6–8; various)

rivers 11, 12, 38, 61, 63, 118, 129, 161, 319, 332, 467, 567

sceptre 474

ships – 188, 433, 504, 539; anchors 45, 87, 124, 520; Argo 4, 5, 45, 465, 520; ballast 109; oars 5, 597, 605 (12); rudders 4, 5; sternpost 550; yardarm 5

statues/figurines/reliefs – 22, 26, 28, 119, 140–1, 177, 184–5, 202, 205, 220, 222, 228, 232, 237, 245–6, 263–4, 287, 292, 306, 335, 347, 367, 371–2, 375, 387, 408, 431, 433, 454, 485, 495; Artemis from Tauri 138, 303, 542, 551; Palladia 240, 560

stones – 5 (pebble vote), 6 (tether), 10 (missile), 35 (balancing), 38 (pebbles), 83 (table), 145 (*bemata*), 153 (=goats), 176 (musical), 189 (with arrows), 259 (altar?), 266 (deposit), 273 (heap), 310 (seat?), 390 (paired), 416 (lookout), 427 (missile), 439 (mobile), 472 (from heaven), 477 (clay), 488 (Zeus substitute), 522 (thumb-shaped), 523 (in tomb), 548 (rocking), 552 (ammunition); as a seat 13, 137, 155, 183, 423; split (fossil) 56, 87, 519

structures – altars 22, 38, 121, 144, 176, 196, 198, 255, 487, 588; bridge 4; camp 68; cistern 95, 139; houses 7, 74, 212, 238, 264, 274, 298, 302, 338, 349, 413, 426, 430, 434–5, 534–5; mole 555; observatory 432; palace 563; palaistra 170; roads 64–5, 417; stables/mangers 152, 354; stadion 271; temples 38, 67, 82, 122, 184, 206–7, 225, 238, 260, 264, 287–8, 294, 313, 317, 398, 492, 556, 558; tents/huts/chambers 261, 447, 547,

structures (*cont.*)
587, 600; tholoi 37, 292; threshing
floor 166; treasuries 89, 218, 470;
underground chambers 33, 241, 250,
570; walls 92, 143, 176, 218, 249,
510, 122, 196, 227

tombs – mounds 21, 62, 98–9, 111, 136,
192, 210, 216, 231, 255, 354, 376–7,
380, 382, 384, 393, 404–5, 428, 439,
444, 478, 499, 532, 546, 585; with
monuments – 20 (two moving stelai),
43 (AE pillar), 72 (two-storey), 123
(stele), 174 (pelta-shaped), 211
(stelai), 216 (with altars), 221 (with
ram), 255 (altar), 258 (with three
chairs), 360 (building), 363 (with
figure), 377 (with AE woman), 399
(building), 404 (finger), 419 (stone),
440 (three stones), 461 (pillar with
urn), 478 (round), 480 (heaped
stones), 484 (urn), 493 (rubble), 499
(stele), 505 (with AE woman), 536
(stele), 541 (with lion); with trees –
21, 89, 255, 399, 405, 514–5, 597
trees and flowers 160, 202, 256, 431,
481, 515–6, 559, 596; bay 261, 515;
cypress 74, 399; fig 162, 583;

'hyacinth' 156; myrtle 136, 264, 314;
oak 325, 514–5, 562, 596; olive 21,
24, 89, 95, 142, 148, 180, 253–5, 268,
516, 590, 596; palm 596; pine 196;
plane 276, 396, 447, 512, 514, 516,
596; pomegranate 455; strawberry
451; vine 455; willow 116, 366
tripods 49, 70, 91, 100, 424, 462, 533
trophies 248, 284, 299, 438, 456

underworld access 4, 29, 73, 164, 257,
272, 277, 321, 394, 420, 469

wreaths 24, 54, 516